TABLE OF CONTENTS

Chapter 3 – Linux System Forensics

Chapter 4 – Windows-System Forensics

Chapter 5 – System Forensic Tools

Chapter 6 – System-Forensics Legal Policies

Chapter 7 – Security Systems as Forensic Tools

Chapter 8 – Advanced Forensics

Chapter 9 – Network Forensics

About NIIT

NIIT is a Global IT Solutions Corporation with a presence in 38 countries. With its unique business model and technology creation capabilities, NIIT delivers Software and Learning Solutions to more than 1000 clients across the world.

The success of NIIT's training solutions lies in its unique approach to education. NIIT's Knowledge Solutions Business conceives, researches, and develops all the course material. A rigorous instructional design methodology is followed to create engaging and compelling course content. NIIT has one of the largest learning material development facilities in the world with more than 5000 person years of experience.

NIIT trains over 200,000 executives and learners each year in different Information Technology areas using stand-up training, video-aided instruction, computer-based training (CBT) and Internet-based training (IBT). NIIT has featured in the Guinness Book of World Records for the largest number of learners trained in one year!

NIIT has developed over 10,000 hours of instructor-led training (ILT) and over 8,500 hours of Internet-based training and computer-based training. IDC ranked NIIT among the Top 15 IT Training providers globally for the year 2000. Through the innovative use of training methods and its commitment to research and development, NIIT has been in the forefront of computer education and training for the past 20 years.

Quality has been the prime focus at NIIT. Most of the processes are ISO-9001 certified. It was the 12th company in the world to be assessed at Level 5 of SEI-CMM. NIIT's Content (Learning Material) Development facility is the first in the world to be assessed at this highest maturity level. NIIT has strategic partnerships with companies such as Computer Associates, IBM, Microsoft, Oracle, and Sun Microsystems.

About the Book

This book is an advanced course in the information systems security and focuses on the concepts of system forensics investigation and response. The course explores the vast areas of cyber crimes and teaches the students forensic sciences to investigate cyber crimes and recover lost information.

The first section of the book covers the threats to information system networks from the outside world and describes the importance of systems forensics for organizations. The process of investigating cyber crimes and methods to preserve digital evidence are explained in detail.

The second section stresses on the processes, tools, and utilities used to investigate crimes in the Windows and Linux environments. It describes the process of carrying out a forensics analysis to recover lost information and prepare evidence. In addition, this section also discusses the popular forensics tools available and the must haves for any crime investigator.

The penultimate section explores the legal aspects of cyber crimes investigations. It describes the laws prevalent in the US related to cyber crimes investigations and forensics as well as the US government's Electronics Communication Privacy Act. This section ends with a discussion about what constitutes admissible evidence in a court of law.

The last section of the book covers the advance concepts of vulnerability tools used for system protection, such as network forensics, operation system fingerprinting, and encryption. It provides hands-on exercises and procedures to help students get a first-hand feel of the concepts and understand the subject better. The book ends with a discussion about covert channels used to investigate computer network-related crimes.

Conventions Used in the Book

This book contains features, such as notes, tips, warnings, and references, identified by various icons. Each of these icons presents a different type of information. Following is the list of icons that will be used in the book.

 A note provides information about the topic in context. This is additional information related to the topic.

 A tip provides an alternative method for performing a task. It can also contain a simplified, although unconventional, method of doing a task.

 Just-a-Minute presents nice-to-know information or a quick question that checks the learners' understanding of the current topic.

 A warning informs you about the dire effects of an action. Focusing on these warnings reduces the likelihood that learners will make the same errors.

 A reference provides links to Web sites or relevant books and white papers for further study on a particular topic.

 Each topic begins with objectives that inform learners about the learning outcome of a topic.

In addition, you will come across *italicized text* that represents newly introduced terms.

System Forensics

1

This chapter describes system forensics, its methodology, and process involved. It further describes the threats to systems and networks. This chapter also discusses the importance of system forensics to individuals and organizations and provides details on the phases of system forensics. At the end of the chapter, you will be able to:

- Explain the concept of system forensics.
- Determine the threats to systems.
- Describe the system forensics methodology.
- Explain the importance of system forensics.
- Describe the process of system forensics.
- Identify the phases of system forensics.
- Establish the relationship between the phases of system forensics.

1.1 System Forensics and Crime

1.2 System Forensics Process

1.1 System Forensics and Crime

Computer or system crime is prevalent. Some of the common crimes are the misuse of credit cards by duplication cards and transfer of huge amounts from one bank account to another. Initially, an organization used to implement security tools, such as intrusion detection systems and firewalls to protect the data against threats. However, organizations soon realized that it was not enough, and they needed to protect their systems from further attacks. For this, it was necessary to find the source and extent of the crime. This led to the development of *system forensics*. In this chapter, you will learn about system forensics, its importance, the various components, and the link between the components.

System threats can be broadly divided into human and environmental threats. Environmental threats include power outages, fire, and floods. Human threats can be malicious or non-malicious. A threat is considered malicious if the attack or crime is committed with full knowledge and understanding of the action that is about to be committed. A threat is considered non-malicious if the individual does not understand its intent or is ignorant of the action that is about to be committed. Figure 1.1 shows the types of security threats.

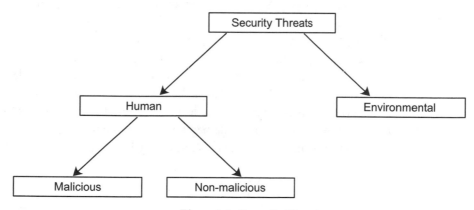

Figure 1.1: Security Threats

System forensics addresses human threats because these threats may lead to crime.

Example 1.1

■ A disgruntled employee in an organization may try to break into the organization's business critical information to damage the information and the business. This is an example of a malicious human threat.

■ An ignorant employee may give out information to a hacker without realizing the consequences. This is an example of non-malicious human threat.

1.1.1 Introduction to System Forensics

 Describe system forensics.

Forensics is one of the oldest practiced arts that make use of science to reach the source of an event, such as theft, crime, and impact of a criminal act. It has existed in forms, such as finger print reading, blood typing, and DNA mapping. All these have been commonly used in proving crimes and prosecuting the accused. Due to the increase in use of computers, they have become an attractive proposition for people with malicious intent. This increased use has also led to the development of new tools and techniques to conduct crime. Misuse can be in the form of data theft, business loss by hacking, or the elimination of competition by damaging a competitors' business to levels that they shut down their business. This can be achieved by blocking the network services of the competitor.

 It is important to note that system forensics provides the ability to determine if a crime has 'possibly been committed'. It is up to 'law enforcement and the judicial system' to determine if crime 'has been' committed. It is also important to note that what may be a crime in one jurisdiction or country is not seen or recognized as a crime in others. This fact alone is a major difficulty in dealing with computer crime.

> **Example 1.2**
>
> You are working as a sales manager for a company that has products in competition with other companies. In such a situation, the managers from the competing company will be interested in the data on your computer. This may lead them to hire someone to steal data from your system or computer. When such services (black hat hacking services) are hired, it is usually referred to as sponsored hacking. There are state sponsored hackers to find and break into a country's national network, to collect sensitive information, such as defense information.

Network-based threats may range from crimes within the network to crimes from outside the network, such as through the Internet.

> **Example 1.3**
>
> One of the commonly witnessed crimes on the Internet is associated with Internet banking, where a huge amount of sum is transferred from one account to another without the knowledge of the account holder. This fraud can be done in two ways:
>
> - Through the use of one of the computers in the banking network.
>
> - By connecting to the banking network through the Internet, and then monitoring people for account numbers and other related details. After the details are captured, the criminals break into the bank account to make transfers.

These activities are on a rise and there has been an increasing demand for information security in the computer industry. As discussed earlier, with time, businesses have realized that it is not enough to protect data, but essential to reach the source of crime and prosecute the criminal, similar to any other criminal activity, such as household theft. This is where system forensics or computer forensics come into play.

Judd Robbins is known for his contribution to system forensics. According to him, *"System forensic or computer forensics is simply the application of computer* *investigation and analysis technique in the interest of determining potential legal evidence.*"

System forensics techniques are not as advanced as mainstream forensics, such as blood typing, DNA mapping, and finger printing. One of the major reasons for this is the constant and fast changing technology landscape. System forensics tools, such as Encase and SafeBack have gained wide acceptance in the industry, and are continually being improved.

System forensics involves the identification, extraction, preservation, and documentation of system evidences.

Evidence is a piece of information that provides an idea or clue that may lead to the source of an event or to another piece of information, which may finally lead to the source of the event.

Systems forensics concepts can be further extended to involve network forensics. Network forensics involves the investigation of events when two or more computers are connected through a network.

> Example 1.4
>
> In an organization network, one of the nodes was used to crack the administrative password and another node was used to log on as administrator and commit a crime. In such a scenario, there will be one computer that will have a set of information and another that will have another set of related information. The nature of the crime can be determined only after both the sets of information are put together and a complete set of events is formed.

1.1.2 Importance of System Forensics

 Identify the importance of system forensics.

System forensics is important to the organization, not only from the perspective of reaching the source of crime and prosecution of the criminal, but also to help organize their security policy and plan future security requirements. System forensics helps the organization in the following ways:

- Identify the reason for the crime: For every organization, it is important to identify the reason for the crime. This helps an organization understand and plan the protection systems that they need to implement. It also helps the organization to rework any human resource or administrative policy.

> **Example 1.5**
>
> Data theft was reported in the organization. It may have been perpetrated by an internal employee or by an external person with malicious intent. If the theft originated internally, it is important to determine if the employee was directly involved and the nature of the involvement. If the employee was not involved, it is important to establish why, how, and to what extent the internal network was compromised from the external threat.

- Validate the security policy: The security policy is one of the most important security guides in an organization. There are different ways to validate a security policy for its effectiveness. System forensics can be used as an effective technique to validate the security policy of an organization.

> **Example 1.6**
>
> One of the organization's employees has sent some important and business critical data to one of the software vendors, without signing a non-disclosure agreement. The data that was sent has been stolen and

sold to the competing organization. This situation may be treated as a crime, and a forensic investigation may be set up. After the forensic investigation is completed, it will be clear if there was a clearly defined security policy for business critical data or whether it was up to an individual employee to make a decision. If there was a policy defining that any business critical data sent out should be backed by a non-disclosure agreement, then the employee should be held responsible. If there was no policy defined, then it indicates a weakness in the organization's security policy.

- Validate the security tools: Computer crimes are also the result of compromises in the system. These compromises may be due to employee ignorance, lack of interest, or carelessness in the execution of jobs. Identifying such a situation is difficult, as the security tools can only tell you that the crime that may have occurred and not the reason for it. In addition, these tools cannot identify if they themselves have been compromised.

Example 1.7

A hacker may have reconfigured the firewall or the intrusion detection system. These reconfigurations are difficult to identify. In such a case, only a forensic investigation can help detect the compromise.

- Prepare for the future: The techniques and tools used in computer crime are constantly evolving. Based on the discovery of a system or a computer crime, it is not possible to specify the possible steps that the criminal must have followed. In an organization, it is important to know the events that occurred before a crime took place. This information helps an organization understand any weak points in its system or practices. In addition, if new techniques and tools have been used, the organization can plan and prepare for any such attacks in the future.

There are services that permit you to perform perimeter vulnerability scanning and penetration testing from a remote location. Anyone can subscribe to such a service, and then locate one of the targeted IPs to scan the perimeter for vulnerabilities. The same can be used for attack. However, identifying such a service is difficult. Only through proper reading and analysis of the logs from perimeter devices, such as firewalls and intrusion detection systems, can the use of such services be identified.

After they are identified, the systems can be configured such that these services are not used in the future to scan perimeter devices. It is important to note that while system administrators and investigators might use these services to test the security holes within the network of the organization, attackers might use the same services to identify the loopholes and the weakness of a particular network, before launching an attack.

Example 1.8

Some of the examples of perimeter vulnerability scanning services are CyberCop ASAP from Network Associates Technology, Inc.

 The majority of organizations use firewalls, vulnerability scanning tools, and intrusion detection systems at their network perimeter to protect the confidentiality, integrity, and availability of their internal network, systems, and information.

1.1.2.1 Application of System Forensics

System forensics is no different from any other forensic science when it comes to application. It can be applied to any activity, where other mainstream traditional forensics such as DNA mapping is used, if there has been an involvement of a system or computer in the event.

Some of the common applications of system forensics are:

- **Financial fraud detection:** Corporates and banks can detect financial frauds with the help of evidence collected from systems. Also, insurance companies can detect possible fraud in accident, arson, and workman's compensation cases with the help of computer evidence.

- **Criminal prosecution:** Prosecutors can use computer evidence to establish crimes such as homicides, drug and false record-keeping, financial fraud, and child pornography in the court of law.

- **Civil litigations:** Personal and business records found on computer systems related to fraud, discrimination, and harassment cases can be used in civil litigations.

■ "Corporate Security Policy and Acceptable Use Violations": A lot of computer forensic work done is to support of management and human resources (HR) investigations of employee abuse.

Besides cyber crimes and system crimes, criminals use computers for other criminal activities. In such cases, besides the traditional forensics, system forensic investigation also plays a vital role.

1.1.2.1.1 Computers as Tools to Commit Crime

Criminals use computers to carry out different criminal activities. The computer, in such scenarios, is usually used to extract information about the victims, and strategically plan and manage criminal activities. According to investigating agencies, some of the crimes other than the financial frauds that use computers are:

■ Extortion of money: This refers to criminal activities, in which ransom is demanded in exchange for valuable information or resources of individuals or organizations. Extortion of money from businesses is a common criminal activity. The valuable information usually held by the criminals could be the company's Web site, client information, and other business critical information. In case a Web site has been hacked by the criminal, system forensics can be used to reach the source of the crime.

■ Terrorism: Computers are being used by terrorist agencies to conduct criminal activities. They usually hack into government security systems to gain critical information. They expose the computer systems to malicious programs or viruses, which cause loss of data. Further, to glorify their cause and influence public opinion, they flash provocative messages.

■ Kidnapping: There are reported gangs that operate through the Internet to kidnap people. These gangs normally operate through online chatting. The criminals visit important chatting sites, search for people through profiles, confirm these people's profiles through chatting, extract important information about them, and then plan a kidnapping. System forensics helps to investigate such kidnappings by assessing the files on the victim's system as well as the system logs of both the victim and the kidnapper. Performing forensics on the victims system yielded clues as to who the victim had been talking to and to where the victim and attacker might be located.

■ Running narcotics trade: Narcotics trading has been reported to use encrypted fax and e-mail to place orders for drugs. System forensics is used to analyze the encrypted messages and help catch criminals.

■ Witness killings in hospitals: Crime profiteers call for a hit of a potential witness staying in a hospital. Under direction of the criminals, the hackers then attempt to kill the witness by cracking into the hospital computer network and changing the dosage of medicines to be given to the potential witness.

With these crimes, the only way to locate the source of crimes is to find all possible information that leads to a source. This information can be located on the systems that may have been used in the crime.

In system or computer crimes, the criminal does not have to be physically present, and therefore is difficult to locate. The only source of information is the systems used for the crime. At times, information from the system may also be misleading, especially if the system has been used after the crime has been committed or if the crime originated from an external network, such as the Internet.

1.1.3 Forensics Methodology

- Describe the approach to forensics.
- Identify the key issues that the investigator must address.

Forensic investigation methodology is basically the approach that an investigator follows to complete the forensic investigation. The approach is dependent on factors, such as the type of crime, the investigator's experience, and their working approach. There may be different approaches towards a forensic investigation, but forensic it should broadly address the following:

- Interview the key concerned people: Interviewing gives an insight into the expectation of the client and helps in understanding the possible form of crime.

- Physically and logically secure the system under investigation: It is important that the system should not have undergone any changes, either physically or logically. Therefore, physical and logical security is an important aspect. The chain of custody of any evidence on the system must be maintained if it is to be upheld in a court of law.

- Data collection should follow the guidelines, "Federal Guidelines For Searching and Seizing Computers."

"Federal Guidelines For Searching and Seizing Computers" can be found on the United States Department of Justice Web site at: http://www.usdoj.gov/criminal/cybercrime/searching.html

Data analyses should adhere to the following guidelines:

- Protect the evidence from being changed.
- Discover all files.
- Recover all deleted files.
- Collect and analyze all information from the hidden files, temporary files, and swap files.

Reconstruction of the crime through the chain of evidence.

Practice Questions

1. _____ is the application of computer investigation and analysis technique in the interest of determining potential legal evidence.

2. List the types of threat to systems.

3. How is system forensics important?

4. Define evidence.

5. Can forensics address natural disaster?

1.2 System Forensics Process

The primary requirement in system forensics is to establish the occurrence of the crime. After the crime is established, well-defined, and organized, there are steps are to be followed to conduct forensics analysis. The steps are:

- Identification of data
- Collection of data
- Analysis of data
- Presentation of data

1.2.1 Identification of Data

Describe the process of identifying data in forensics investigation.

Data identification is the first and most important step in system forensics. After it has been established that a crime has occurred, the next step is to identify the information that is required to evidentially prove its occurrence. Identifying data is basically defining the information that is required and depends on the type of crime committed.

> **Example 1.9**
>
> In a financial fraud investigation, a computer has been used to store information. The information required in such a situation is the plan made to execute the crime. If a computer was used in the crime, then the computer's log files should provide clues on the techniques and applications used to commit the crime.

During the data identification phase, a good technique would be to answer the following questions:

- What is the nature and extent of the damage?
- What are the possible ways of committing the crime?
- Who all may be involved?

Similar questions can be framed based on the crime that has been committed. The answers to these questions will give a snapshot of the possible techniques and methodologies that may have been followed to commit the crime. After the snapshot is formed, it is easier to identify the information that may be needed. This will also help in identifying the places, such as system logs and program registries, to look for the information.

1.2.2 Collection of Data

 Describe the process of data collection.

Data collection is the second step in the process of system forensics. It is one of the most complicated phases of system forensics. In this phase, data is searched after identifying the type of data required. An investigator's knowledge of hardware, software, and experience is useful in this phase. It is the investigator's level of knowledge of systems and software that helps in locating the information and the files to collect data.

In the data collection phase, all possible sources of information are studied, and then the relevant information is collected in a forensically sterile environment. Data that is collected in a forensically sterile environment cannot be changed or modified.

The sources of information in a computer or a system are:

- Log files: Log files are the best source of information. Most of the activities are listed in log files with time and date stamps. However, the log files can be tampered on an independent system. It is very easy to change the date and time on a local system. If this has been changed by the criminal, then the information may lead the forensic investigation in a wrong direction or conclusion.

- System registry and program registry: The system registry is another source of information. Registry keys can provide valuable information like the last login and last application used. It also has a similar problem as the system log files. It can easily be tampered with. Every program has a registry entry. The process-related information is located in the registry and can be useful for the investigation.

In Windows 2000, there is a database repository for information about a computer's configuration. The repository is called the registry. In the registry, the information is organized hierarchically as a tree and is made up of keys and their sub keys, hives, and value entries.

 System hard disk: The study of a system hard disk may give important information about the applications that were possibly used in conducting the crime. However, it is easier to remove applications and application-related data from a hard disk. Therefore, the space created because of the deletion can be overwritten with junk or other information, that may not leave any clues about the data that was previously present in that space. This exercise still can be reverted to collect information. There are tools that can attempt to recover this destroyed data. The criminal can still destroy the hard disk physically (for example, with a hammer) or use a *degausser* (it de-magnetizes the disk. Hard disk is a magnetic storage media, and the demagnetized disks are wiped clean.) to prevent the recovery of data.

A degausser is a tool that looks like a microwave oven and makes any magnetic media completely clear. After a media is put into a degausser and cleaned, no data can be recovered.

 System memory: A system consists of physical and virtual memory. Each section of this memory has certain set of information associated with the last process that has been executed on the system. These memories can provide important information about the events that must have occurred during the crime. The system memory (RAM) is volatile in nature. Therefore, it is not easy to capture the data in the system memory. The moment a crime is reported and the system is turned off, the memory is cleared. This may lead to loss of data important for the investigation.

■ Virtual memory: It is the temporary storage space used by a computer to run programs that need more memory than is physically available. For example, your computer might have only 256 MB RAM while a program needs more memory. In such a situation a portion of the system's hard disk is used as memory. This portion is called the virtual memory.

■ Physical memory: This is the memory that is physically present on the system.

■ Physical data collection: This relates to the collection of information about the devices that may have been attached to the system during the crime. These can only be identified by physically checking the devices that are attached to the system.

Example 1.10

A system may have been fitted with a wireless-based communication device, such as a mobile phone that transmits important information, such as login details to a criminal.

All these sources for collection of information have their own associated problems, based on the type of device and the nature of their functionality in the system. However, there are a set of common problems that exist in data collection. To take care of these common problems, the following guidelines or rules are followed:

■ The investigator should keep a journal of all steps taken for investigative and legal review.

■ No data that may be evidence is damaged.

■ No data that may be treated as evidence is changed or destroyed.

■ No data that may be considered as evidence is compromised.

■ No virus is introduced to a subject system during analysis process.

■ Data extracted and possibly relevant as evidence is properly handled and protected from later mechanical or any other form of damages.

■ A continuing chain of custody is established and maintained.

■ Business operators are affected for a limited amount of time.

■ Any client attorney information that is inadvertently and legally acquired during a forensic exploitation is ethically and legally respected and not divulged.

The above mentioned practices are the recommended practices. A detailed discussion on these will be made while explaining evidence in later chapters.

1.2.3 Analysis of Data

 Explain the importance and the process of data analysis.

Data analysis is the third phase of forensic investigation. All the data identified and collected in the identification and collection phases are analyzed in this phase. It provides information on the sequence of events that may have occurred in the process of committing a crime. In this phase, data from different logs and other sources, such as system registry, are studied in isolation, and each bit of data is interpreted.

Example 1.11

One of the event logs in the Windows 2000 system logs displays the following:

The connection to Connection to 24880000 made by user 24121433 using device COM4 was disconnected.

The relevant information in this is:

- Connection to 24880000
- User 24121433
- Device is on Com4

To interpret the same, you can follow the approach:

- Locate the device connected to Com4. In this example, it is a **dial-up modem** and led to the conclusion that a connection was made using a dial-up modem.
- Check the dial-up connection. In this example, a connection named **Connection to 2488000** existed to connect to the Internet.

> ■ Find the user ID that was used to connect to the Internet. In the example, this is **24121433**.
>
> You can confidently conclude that someone was connected to the Internet using the **dial-up connection**, **Connection to 2488000,** and the user ID **24121433**.

After the data is analyzed in isolation, different pieces of information are analyzed in order to find information that is related to each other.

Example 1.12

Consider a case when a user logs on to the network server using the login identity, user1 from a node, machine1 at 9:30 a.m. on August 28, 2003. During the investigation of the node, these details were available in the logs. A similar set of information should be present in the network server logs.

If the information is not available, then there are only two possibilities, one, that the logs are not activated, and two, that there is some manipulation.

Data analysis is one of the most challenging phases in forensic investigation, as a typical system, running Windows, Linux, or any other operating system (OS), can have a little over 20,000 files. The number of files may vary from 35,000 to 50,000, based on the system configuration. In this phase, based on the hardware and software, there are different types of analysis tools that may be required. Sometimes, customized software may be required for data analysis. An investigator must ensure that the information under analysis does not undergo any changes during the investigation process. This requires very careful handling of data.

Data analysis has its own inherent problems associated with it. As mentioned earlier, one of them is the number of files that may have to be addressed, to analyze a set of information. Data encryption and compression techniques can make the process of data analysis very difficult.

If the crime has been committed using the Internet, then there are other related issues, especially if the criminal has configured the system and is making use of public proxies to commit the crime. In such a situation, it will not be possible to easily trace the source of crime.

- Public anonymous proxies are proxy servers that can be used to surf the Internet. The IP address of the public proxy has to be entered into the web proxy option of your browser software. After the configuration, all the communication is sent to you and from you through the public proxy, which does not log any information regarding its use; therefore, guaranteeing your privacy.

- Public anonymous proxies are generally set up by the people who are strong believers of privacy and the hacker's ethics. They can't be located by using search engines with search text as public proxies.

1.2.4 Presentation of Data

Describe the techniques of data presentation and its importance in the process of forensics investigation.

Data presentation plays an important role in all the phases of forensic investigation. In the final stage of forensics investigation, all the findings are documented and the forensics report is made. The report may be used within the organization to punish an employee or in a court of law for legal prosecution of an attacker.

Presentation of information is very crucial. You should ideally follow certain practices to ensure that the following are visible in the forensics report:

- Assumptions made: After the work on the case starts, there are some sets of assumptions made by the investigators, based on the initial findings and reporting by the organization. Especially, if there is no clarity in the crime that may have occurred, then an investigator has to interview some of the key concerned people in the organization and start working on two or more different lines based on certain assumptions.

- Outline the crime: The documentation must clearly outline the crimes that have been committed. This helps in defining the scope of investigation. In addition, it helps the prosecutors to understand the scope of the crime and the extent of damage. It also helps the investigators identify the nature and scope of investigation. It gives the investigators a clear direction towards which they can work.

- Incremental information document: Any information that was located in the process of forensic investigation and was used to proceed further in the directions of investigation needs to be meticulously documented. Such documentation provides a good source of information in linking the chain of events that were possibly committed in the process of the crime.

- Processing of evidence: Evidence is analyzed to develop forensic investigation and reach the source of crime. Each of these processes used to analyze the evidence must be documented and organized. The documentation must have information, such as the tool used, version of the tool used, and the outcome of the process.

- Method of analysis: After processing of evidence, it is sent as input to the analysis phase. In this phase, the evidence is interpreted to extract meaningful information. The method used to analyze the information must be used and documented. The outcome of the methods must also be documented.

- Observations and conclusions: After analysis, the observations and the conclusion must be documented. The observations must evidentially prove the occurrence of a crime, if it has occurred.

The steps to be taken by a forensic investigator as recommended by Judd Robbins are discussed here.

The computer forensics specialist takes several careful steps to identify and attempt to retrieval of possible evidence that may exist on a subject computer system. The investigator:

- Protects the subject computer system during the forensic examination from any possible alteration, damage, data corruption, or virus introduction.

- Discovers all files on the subject system. This includes existing normal files, deleted yet remaining files, hidden files, password-protected files, and encrypted files.

- Recovers all (or as much as possible) of discovered deleted files.

- Reveals (to the extent possible) the contents of hidden files as well as temporary or swap files used by both the application programs and the OS.

- Accesses (if possible and if legally appropriate) the contents of protected or encrypted files.

- Analyzes all possibly relevant data found in special (and typically inaccessible) areas of a disk.

  - This includes, but is not limited to, what is called unallocated space on a disk (currently unused, but possibly the repository of previous data that is relevant evidence)

  - This includes slack space in a file. Slack space is the remnant area at the end of a file, in the last assigned disk cluster, that is unused by current file data. It might serve as a possible site for previously created and relevant evidence

- Prints out an overall analysis of the subject computer system, as well as a listing of all possibly relevant files and discovered file data. Further, it provides an opinion of the system layout, file structures discovered, any discovered data and authorship information, and any attempts to hide, delete, and protect data.

Practice Questions

1. List the phases of forensics investigation.
2. List four problems associated with data collection.
3. Explain the importance of data analysis.
4. What does data protection refer to in forensic investigation?
5. Why is data protection important?

Summary

- Threats to systems are from humans and the environment.
- The majority of system forensics addresses human threat.
- System forensics is the application of the computer investigation and analysis technique.
- The advancement of system forensics is partially due to the rapid change in technology.
- Forensics investigation involves identification, extraction, preservation, analysis, and documentation of system evidence.
- The approach for forensic evidence is dependent on the investigator and the situation.
- There are four phases of forensic investigation:
  - Data identification
  - Data collection
  - Data analysis
  - Data presentation

References

Web Site References

- http://www.microsoft.com
- http://www.computerforensics.net
- http://www.fbi.gov
- http://www.htcia.org
- http://www.infoforensics.org

Book References

- Hosmer, C. 1998. *Time-Lining Computer Evidence. Information Technology*, Conference, IEEE.
- Casey, Eoghan. 2002. *Handbook of Computer Crime Investigation*: *Forensic Tools and Technology*, Academic Press, San Diego, California.

Homework Exercises

1. What is system forensics?

2. Why is system forensic important to an organization?

3. How important is it to take pictures of the system and the site at which it was located at the time of crime?

4. Is it important to document every step in a forensic investigation? Discuss.

5. What are the key points that should be documented during data presentation?

6. List the steps to follow to collect evidence.

7. Is it important to recover deleted files?

8. Is there a way of justifying the call for a forensics investigation?

9. How can an interview prove important in system forensics?

10. How important is experience across different platforms for an investigator?

Lab Exercises

Exercise 1

Objective

- Prepare a strategy to investigate a crime activity, using the principles of system forensics.
- Prepare a forensic report on the case.

Problem Statement

System forensics not only reveals attacks on computers, it also helps collect evidence for crimes such as terrorist activities and kidnappings.

Two criminals belonging to a terrorist agency have planted a series of time bombs at different locations in South Carolina. Bomb blasts have already occurred at two popular hubs of the city. Police suspect that a number of similar blasts will occur in the subsequent weeks. The terrorist organization behind this act has claimed responsibility. The police raided their hideouts and recovered computers through which information relating to the attack was transmitted. Since the communication amongst terrorists over telephone was being closely monitored watched by the Police, the terrorists used Internet as a mode of communication. The Police discovered a system with the following configuration:

- SVGA
- 200 MHz Intel Pentium (R) W/mmx
- System ROM Date 04/22/2003
- 8 GB RAM
- CD-ROM Drive
- Serial Port A
- Serial Port B
- Parallel port 1
- Keyboard
- Mouse (PS2)
- Power-on Password: Disabled

■ Setup Password Disabled

Also, during network identification they recovered a dial up modem, which could have possibly been used for Internet connection. Assume that you are the system forensic investigator, given the responsibility to identify the locations, which could be the next possible targets.

Lab Setup

Linux 7.1

Procedure

Perform the following:

1. Plan a research strategy, which can help solve the case.
2. List the precautions you would take to recover the data and ensure its integrity.
3. List the files and the possible areas in the OS you would analyze for evidence.
4. Document your strategies and checklists.

Conclusion/Observation

Write a report of your forensic analysis that you performed on the program. The report should essentially consist of:

■ Objective

■ Problem Statement

■ Tools and techniques used

■ Solution

■ Conclusion

Lab Activity Checklist

S.No.	Tasks	Completed	
		Yes	No
1.	Planned a strategy.		
2.	Created a checklist to collect and analyze data.		
3.	Documented the proceedings.		

Investigation

2

This chapter discusses the importance of investigation and digital evidence in computer crimes. It describes the investigation process and its limitations. The chapter also provides information about different tools and techniques used to investigate computer crimes. At the end of the chapter, you will be able to:

- Investigate computer crime.
- Describe the method of evidence collection.
- Explain the process of investigation.
- Identify the types of investigation.
- Create a checklist for investigation.

2.1 Investigation: An Overview

Investigation is the process of collecting, analyzing, and recovering evidence, and presenting a report detailing a crime. Evidence is the key factor that determines a crime and helps prosecute the guilty in the court of law. At the end of an investigation, a forensic report is filed in preparation for a lawsuit or criminal charges, or both.

The investigation process consists of procedures and techniques for finding out what happened, what damage was done, and to what extent, whether the intruder is still a threat, and whether any fixes still have to be implemented. An investigation, to a great extent, depends on the skills of an investigator. It is important for an investigator to make a careful evaluation of the incident before deciding on the investigation process. The same holds for system forensics. In this chapter, you will learn about investigation in system forensics.

2.1.1 Introduction to Investigation

 Explain the concept of investigation.

There is an old saying, "every crime leaves its footprint." This means that every time a crime is committed, the criminal leaves behind a clue. Different questions that might arise from these clues are:

- How is this footprint important to the investigation?
- How can the leads direct you to the criminal?
- What are the possible reasons for the crime?
- What are the tools and techniques that were used in committing the crime?

Each of these questions and more are asked. These questions are answered through the *investigation process*. These questions are important so that you can understand the weakness in your security system and prevent the crime from happening again.

There are different definitions of investigation. One of the most widely accepted definitions of investigation is: "it is the process of tracking, in order to find information."

2.1.2 Importance of Investigation

 Describe the importance of investigation.

As discussed in earlier chapters, with the increase in system and cyber crime and the uses of new tools and techniques, organizations have realized that it is not just enough to prevent these crimes and to protect information, it is also important to trace the source of crime.

 Tracing the footprint of a computer crime is important because:

■ It helps to understand the system's security weaknesses: Investigating a computer crime helps an organization understand if the system were exploited for a weakness in the security system. For example, administrators need to know if an existing flaw helped someone transfer money from one bank account to another, and whether that flaw still exists.

■ It helps to understand security violation techniques: The techniques could range from implanting spy ware in the systems to recruiting internal employees to gain security information to sabotage organizations from within. An investigation might collect information such as each employee's involvement, the level of involvement, and the way the crime was organized.

■ It helps to identify future security needs: These investigations also provide information on new tools that were used or are being developed. The investigations may help companies and even law enforcement agencies discover future trends and design new tools to protect networks and information.

■ It helps to prosecute criminals: If the crime has led to financial and other losses, prosecution may be initiated against the criminals. Investigation becomes extremely important, because without it, there can be no case. Investigation may suggest the future possibility of attacks if evidence shows ongoing activity. This may give the organization the chance to entrap the criminals, especially if they are employees.

2.1.3 Components of Investigation *Test*

Describe the components of an investigation.

An investigation has three important components. They are:

- Evidence: *Evidence* is the information that you collect from a system in a physical or logical form. Almost any type of investigation of a system crime relies on the evidence obtained from the target computer. Just like you would investigate a theft at a site, by collecting fingerprints etc., you can collect evidence for a computer crime, by analyzing digital data such as e-mails, files, and other system information. Evidence provides vital information about the crime in terms of the tools and techniques that were used. For example, information in a computer's Random Access Memory (RAM) can provide clues about the last program executed that may have been used in the computer crime. It is important to understand that such information should be untouched and preserved after a crime has been committed. Compared to paper evidence, electronic evidence is usually of volatile nature and finding the relevant evidence is more difficult. Since data residing on the computer can have different copies and can be altered at various times, the authenticity of the original data evidence becomes crucial. Also, unauthorized copies of original data can easily be made, leaving no trace that any data has been copied at all. This usually involves theft of important data such as client lists, intellectual property, and research materials. Digital evidence may include deleted files or e-mails, computer logs, spreadsheets, and accounting information. Electronic data includes record, file, source code, program, computer manufacturer specifications, and other information on the computer storage device.

Digital evidence can take the following forms:

- Word processing documents
- Personal records
- Customer lists
- Financial information
- E-mail via the local network or Internet
- System and application logs
- Voice mail transcripts
- Electronic scheduling systems

- Linking the chain of evidence: After evidence of a crime has been found, it is vital to figure out the complete sequence of activities that may have taken place during the commission of the crime.

- Documentation: Documenting is the most important factor in investigation of systems crimes. Each piece of evidence must be recorded systematically for the law as well as for a better analysis of the system. Failure to document any part of the crime weakens the investigation, and the result may not be correct.

The three components of investigation must be followed systematically. Most organizations today define policies, guidelines, and procedures relating to computer forensics, which helps in the following way:

- Define the requirements: Defining the policies, guidelines, and procedures for systems forensics helps an organization define the required level of investigation. For example, an organization's system forensic policy may say that in case of loss of data, there will be an internal inquiry held by a team of information technology experts from within the organization. System forensic policy also helps in investigation by defining the scope and clearly identifying its primary goals. The scope of investigation defines the limit to which the investigation will be carried out.

- Evaluate the security policy: Investigating computers is one of the most effective ways to evaluate the security policy within an organization. After an investigation is set up, it can provide an excellent picture of the current status of the security practices within the organization. The same can then be evaluated against the company's security policies, guidelines, and procedures. In other words an investigation of computers will help to assess the security gaps in the computer and networks of the organization.

■ Evaluate the effectiveness of security: One of the benefits of a forensic investigation may be the information that points out security breaches and data theft that helps an organization understand how effective their security implementations are. The weakness in implementation could be at the policy level, as discussed earlier, or at the implementation level, or at the practice level, such as the use of common departmental passwords.

Practice Questions

1. Define investigation.
2. List the components of investigation.
3. Explain how documentation is important in investigation.
4. How is evaluation of security effectiveness and investigation related?

2.2 Investigation Process

The investigation process involves a careful and systematic examination of an activity by following one link to another, as if in a chain. It is important to identify the need and set a goal before you start the investigation. If there isn't a goal, or you do not follow one, you may become sidetracked. However, this does not imply that you should overlook anything that does not appear to be leading to the goals of the investigation. These should be well documented, but possibly not be pursued further.

2.2.1 Steps for Investigation

 Describe the steps in an investigation process.

Every investigation follows a well-defined procedure. The procedure involves the following four steps:

- Collecting evidence: The first and the most important step in an investigation is collection of evidence. As discussed in the earlier chapter, the collection of evidence is difficult. At times the evidence may be misleading. As an investigator, it is important to understand, to know and to choose what is to be treated as evidence from the available information. A mistake at this stage will give undesirable and unsuccessful results. The evidence varies from situation to situation. For example, the evidence from investigating a hard disk may be different from investigating a CD-ROM drive. Investigating a CD-RW disk that has been used in a CD-ROM drive that cannot modify information is different from investigating the same disk if it was used in a CD read-write drive, which can modify disks. CD read-write drives can write information on to the media and make changes to the information, increasing the chance that it may have been used in the crime. Therefore, it is important that an investigator is up-to-date on new technologies, and of what they can and cannot do. As an investigator, you must think like a computer criminal to identify the possible activities that will help you to locate evidence.

You can locate digital evidence at various sources such as:

- Workstations
- Servers
- Network Attached Storage
- Scanners
- Proxy Server and ISP Logs

■ Analyzing evidence: The second step is analyzing the evidence. It requires careful and systematic study to determine the answer to questions such as:

- What damage was done?
- Why was the damage done?
- What information is there about the technique used to inflict damage?
- Why this set of information will serve as good evidence?

Answering these questions will give you a clear picture of the extent and nature of damages, such as the theft of information. It will give a broad idea of the direction in which to proceed to get to the source of the crime.

One of the most important questions to ask and answer, and one of the hardest to discover sometimes, is why was the damage done. The motive is often elusive. If, however, the motive can be found, people behind the crime can often be found with it. This is especially true for inside jobs and with former employees.

There are different tools and techniques that are used to commit computer crime. It is important to identify the tools as well as the techniques. These will provide an important source of information about the footprints of the crime. These footprints can then be evaluated to translate them into meaningful sources of evidence. For example, if someone has used vulnerability assessment software on the organization's systems or over the network, then there will be traces from where the scan was launched. Many vulnerability software manufacturers recognize the fact that their softwares are also effective hacking tools, so they are designed to leave their identity traces along the path they followed. After being discovered, this serves as strong forensics evidence against the acts of computer crimes and criminals.

After all the evidence has been collected, it is important to double-check it. For an investigator, it is important to identify why each piece of evidence is being considered. Ascertain whether the evidence will hold good in court, whether it was obtained in a thoroughly clean manner, or in whatever other way you need to ensure that your methods were flawless. This reduces the chances of error. In addition, if evidence is based upon other evidence, it is vital to ensure that the base evidence is rock solid.

Vulnerability assessment tools attack systems and networks to find out the vulnerabilities such as missing patches and other security holes. Hackers can penetrate into systems using vulnerability assessment tools.

- Recovering evidence: There is certain evidence that is removed by computer criminals for various reasons. At times, there are changes in the evidence simply because the system was rebooted. As an investigator, you must attempt to recover all the data that might have been tampered with, and locate the information that may be of some evidence. For example, if some data has been deleted from the hard disk, it must be recovered to obtain more accurate information about what actually had happened.

- Preserving evidence: After all the evidence has been collected, it is important to preserve it, as it existed during or soon after the crime. The procedure should follow a "well-deviced" technique to avoid any changes in the data. Following is a checklist you can use to ensure that your evidence remains protected and preserved:

    - The evidence is not damaged or altered due to the tools and techniques used for investigation.

    - The evidence is protected from mechanical or electromagnetic damage.

    - The target computer is not infected by any virus during the investigation process.

    - Business operations of the organization are not affected during the investigation.

    - Continuing chain of evidence is maintained.

Documenting the evidence also helps you to organize your findings and to make an effective link based on a chain of evidence. Documentation also helps in preparing for legal action.

2.2.2 Limitation of Investigation

 Identify the limitation of investigation.

The most important fact is that the investigation is not a judgment, and an investigator is not a judge. Any investigator must investigate a crime based on evidence. The investigation may start with an assumption of activities that might have happened during the act of crime. These assumptions must then take a clear direction with goals based on the information in the form of evidence available. This is where the limitation of investigation comes into play.

Limitations of investigating a computer crime can broadly be categorized into:

- Inadequate evidence: Many times you find that a computer criminal has removed all information that could be used as evidence. For example, they can remove some of the important system log files, because these files record data about their activities. In such situations, a different course of action must be developed to recreate the sessions and find out the traces that have been removed. However, recreating sessions require tools that can store most of the information away from the system and the network. In addition, monitoring and storing sessions is very expensive and requires resources such as secure storage space. Therefore, companies that are economically sound and have sufficient resources are likely to invest in backup systems like these.

- Lack of resources: Lack of resources is not the only reason organizations fail to trace and prosecute intruders. Sometimes companies have made proper investments, but haven't yet taken the time to implement or configure the tools correctly. In the meantime, they have researched and bought expensive new equipment, but for want of time to set it up, they have been the victims of various crimes. The lack of human resources is one of the strongest limitations that hinder all computer investigations.

- Organization's IT security team: Sometimes the IT (Information Technology) department is all for a security investigation after a crime has been committed, but sometimes, they are wholeheartedly against it. The IT department might be afraid of who will be named as the culprit for leaving the network vulnerable to begin with. This will cause problems for the investigators, because in most organizations, besides the IT department, very few people understand the complexities of the computer network. Therefore, without the support of the IT department, accessing the systems in the organization becomes difficult.

- Delayed information: It is hard to maintain a system or a network untouched between the time that a crime has been discovered and the time you can call in an investigator. It is difficult unless you want to shut down your business, or you can isolate part of your network. Routine work will usually overwrite any clues that are held in RAM. Also, it usually takes quite awhile for employees to discover that there has been a problem, so they tend to go about with their daily work, only to discover much later that they tampered all over the evidence.

- Disorganized security systems: One of the major problems in limiting investigations is disorganized security system that has no security policies, procedures or guidelines to advice employees how to log information. Often, there is also no documentation for current tools, and also for the current versions of the applications.

Practice Questions

1. Define investigation process.
2. What is the importance of analyzing evidence?
3. What are the limitations of investigation?
4. List some of the resources that may lack investigation perspective.
5. How does delayed information affect investigation?

2.3 Types of Investigation

Investigations are done on different lines under different situations. Although investigation techniques vary, they can be categorized broadly into two types:

- Physical investigation
- Logical investigation

These investigations give information about the system usage patterns including application and resource usage. This information might require application-monitoring tools, such as sniffers. In this section, you will learn about the two types of investigation in detail.

2.3.1 Physical Investigation

 Explain the process of physical investigation.

Physical investigations include identifying or locating physical evidence, such as removal of computer hardware. Certain behavior or incidents could trigger a physical investigation. Some examples are people suddenly working late hours, a change in the pattern of working time, or employees attempting to access the devices in the network physically. In the past, network managers and administrators have noticed this type of behavior before computer crimes were committed.

- Unusual or unauthorized late hours: This could be an indication of malicious intent. It is important to identify the usage pattern of such users and to see the work they are doing. Ignoring such activities might lead to system or network sabotage. There are different techniques to identify the intent of the late-hour usage. These techniques could be used to identify the applications that were not used in accordance with the job allocation and resource requirements. For example, a sales department personnel trying to access the accounts department files.

- Changes in the pattern of system usage: If an employee suddenly requests changes in system usage that requires additional hardware, such as more RAM, or another PC, or a sudden stand-alone system, that should raise doubts. These might be indications of malicious intent. Any such changes must be monitored and watched carefully to locate the activity that is being carried out.

Users might also make perfectly acceptable requests. So as an investigator, you need to make sure that you ask questions and watch, before you say anything that could put your job in jeopardy.

- Changes in the login system: If an employee is continuously changing systems to log in, it is important to identify and to notice the usage. This may be a way to avoid being monitored, and an indication of malicious intent. This activity needs to be watched and analyzed carefully.

- Making physical attempts to reach connected devices: An attempt made to access devices attached to a system or the network is an indication of malicious intent. Any such activity should be monitored. The data of the monitored activity must be used for investigation purposes.

The above are some of the physical forms of malicious intent that needs to be monitored through physical investigation, such as checking the system for changes in hardware. You can also use network monitoring software, or asset management software to keep a close eye on the system's physical assets.

2.3.2 Logical Investigation

Explain the concept of logical investigation.

Logical investigation can also be referred to as digital investigation. Logical investigation takes a look at the log files and tries to locate information that can be used as evidence of who had committed the crime. Logical investigation requires a well-designed security policy that clearly defines the process for logging information. It is important for the logs to be maintained systematically. Some of the logical investigation requirements are:

- No modification: The system logs should not be modified at all. The system should remain in the same state as it was during the crime. Any changes in the system can lead to loss of vital evidence. For example, if a computer criminal removes the program that was used to commit the crime, formats the hard disk, and overwrites the free space it will become difficult to retrieve the evidence.

- Log date and time stamp: It is important to ensure that the date and time stamp of the log has not been changed. Any changes in the date and time stamp of the logs will introduce a difference when connecting evidence to the chain of activity that may have occurred at the time of committing the crime. This may lead to the investigation's failure.

- Logs of systems: The logs of systems that are being investigated must be checked and studied to analyze their integrity.

- System registry: System registry keys must be checked to identify the authenticity of the last logged in users and the integrity of critical files.

- Forensic imaging tools: Forensic imaging tools must be used to make multiple copies of the hard disk that have been taken for investigation. The tool that is used must do a bit-by-bit copy so that no portion of the hard disk, whether filled or empty, is left without being copied. The copy should then be used for investigation purposes. An example of a forensic imaging tool is SafeBack.

Practice Questions

1. List the types of investigation.
2. During a physical investigation, which components of a system are analyzed?
3. During a logical investigation, which components of a system are analyzed?
4. What is the importance of system logs in an investigation?

2.4 Investigation Techniques and Tools

There are different techniques of investigation. One of the common techniques is the evidence-chain model. This model introduces the concept of studying and analyzing the system logs, physical evidence, and network monitoring logs individually, and then together. This is done to identify and recreate the complete chain of activities that may have happened.

2.4.1 Evidence-Chain Model

 Describe the evidence-chain model.

The *evidence-chain model* involves developing or recreating the complete chain of activities that happened during the crime. The technique involves studying individual systems, and then analyzing these to obtain information that suggests involvement of individuals or any other resources within an organization. After, these are analyzed; the links are verified again using the techniques of logical investigation. Based on the logical and physical investigation, the chain of activity is evaluated to assess whether the crime is recreated. If the result is the same as it appears in the crime, it is accepted as an investigation result.

2.4.1.1 Limitation of Evidence-Chain Model

Evidence-chain model works on the evidence. Minor changes in any of the linked systems may lead to failure of the investigation. This model is usually implemented for an intranet. It helps in tracing the source of crimes on an intranet.

2.4.2 Tools and Checklists

 ▪ Describe the tools used in an investigation.

▪ Create a checklist using a standard investigation practice.

There are different tools and checklists that help an investigator to investigate a crime effectively. Different tools and checklists are used in different situations.

2.4.2.1 Tools

There are various tools available for investigations. The tools also help in making images of system configurations without modifying them. The tools can make images of a hard disk bit-by-bit so that no portion of information is left out. In addition, these tools do not require the system to be rebooted to create images. This helps preserve the images without any change. These tools are categorized as forensic imaging tools.

Example 2.1

NIKSUN Net Detector is one of the advanced network security appliance. It has the following features:

▪ Intrusion detection

▪ Network forensic analysis

▪ Policy verification

▪ Continuous traffic recording and archival

There are tools that collect all the logs and other related details from different systems to identify all possible malicious intents. These intents are then analyzed and correlated to create a chain of evidence.

Example 2.2

Safe Suite Decision is a tool provided by Internet Security Systems. It collects different logs such as logs from *IDS* and *firewall*s, and consolidates them. It has built-in analytical tools that analyze the log information. It also gives you a pre-defined format for reporting. You

---

can select from one of the many predefined analytical reporting options. The options available are:

- Executive Report
- Management Report
- Technical Report

This tool also has a complementing tool called the secure log manager, which collects different system logs.

2.4.2.2 Checklist

Checklists are made based on requirements. Most of the investigation practices can be understood by going through the points that have been listed in the checklist below for hard disks and floppy drives. The same also helps in limiting the scope of investigations in case there are access constraints. It further explains briefly the presentation techniques of an investigation.

- Overview: It is generally acknowledged that almost all forensic examinations of computer media are different, and that no one can be conducted in the exact same manner. There are three essential requirements for a competent forensic examination. They are:

  - Forensically sterile examination media must be used.

  - The examination must maintain the integrity of the original media.

  - Printouts, copies of data and exhibits resulting from the examination must be properly marked, controlled and transmitted.

- Hard disk examination: The following are the recommended procedures for conducting a complete examination of computer Hard Disk Drive (HDD) media:

  1. Forensically sterile conditions. All media utilized during the examination process must be freshly prepared, completely wiped of non-essential data, scanned for viruses and verified before use.

  2. Examine the original computer physically. Then make and note the specific description of the hardware. Indicate anything unusual found during the physical examination of the computer through comments, in the presence of the user.

  3. Precautions are taken during copying or access to the original media to prevent the transfer of viruses, destructive programs, or other inadvertent writes to or from the original media. This may not always be possible

because of hardware and operating system (OS) limitations or other circumstances.

4. The contents of the CMOS, as well as the internal clock are checked and the accuracy of the date and time is noted, in the presence of the User. The time and date of the internal clock is frequently very important in establishing file creation or modification dates and times.

5. The original media is not normally used for the examination. A bit stream copy or other image of the original media is made. The bit stream copy or other image is used for the actual examination. A detailed description of the bit stream copy or image process and identification of the hardware, software, and the media is noted.

6. The original PC is then sealed and the user's signature is needed to complete the seal. This machine is now placed in quarantine.

7. The copy or image of the original HDD is logically examined and a description of what was found is noted.

8. The boot record data, and user-defined system configuration and operation command files, such as the CONFIG.SYS and the AUTOEXEC.BAT files are examined and the findings are noted.

9. All recoverable deleted files are restored. When practical or possible, the first character of the restored files are changed from a HEX E5 to "-," or other unique character, for identification purposes.

10. A listing of all the files contained on the examined media, whether they contain potential evidence or not, is normally made.

11. If appropriate, the unallocated space is examined for lost or hidden data.

12. If appropriate, the "slack" area of each file is examined for lost or hidden data.

13. The contents of each user data file in the root directory and each sub-directory (if present) is examined.

14. Password-protected files are unlocked and examined.

15. A printout or copy is made of all apparent evidentiary data. The file or location where any apparent evidentiary data was obtained is noted on each printout. All exhibits are marked, sequentially numbered and properly secured and transmitted.

16. Executable programs of specific interest should be examined. User data files that could not be accessed by other means are examined at this time using the native application.

17. All comments and findings are documented at this time.

■ Floppy disk examination. The following are the recommended procedures for conducting a complete examination of a Floppy Diskette (FD) or similar media:

1. Forensically sterile conditions are established. All media utilized during the examination process is freshly prepared, completely wiped of non-essential data, scanned for viruses and verified before use.

2. All forensic software utilized is licensed to, or authorized for use by the examiner and/or agency/company.

3. The media is physically examined. A specific description of the media is made and noted. The media is marked for identification.

4. Hardware/software precautions are taken during any copying process or access to the original media and examination to prevent the transfer of viruses, destructive programs, or other inadvertent writes to or from the original FD or to or from the examination equipment.

5. The write-protect capability of the floppy disk drive (FDD) on the examining machine is tested.

6. A duplicate image of the original write-protected FD is made to another FD. The duplicate image is used for the actual examination. A detailed description of the process is noted.

7. The copy of the examined FD is logically examined and a description of what was found is indicated. Anything unusual is noted.

8. The boot record data, and user-defined system configuration and operation command files (if present) are examined and the findings are noted.

9. All recoverable deleted files are restored. When practical or possible, the first character of the restored files are changed from a HEX E5 to "-," or other unique character, for identification purposes.

10. The unallocated space is examined for lost or hidden data.

11. The "slack" area of each file is examined for lost or hidden data.

12. The contents of each user data file in the root directory and each sub-directory (if present) are examined.

13. Password-protected files are unlocked and examined.

14. If the FD holds apparent evidentiary data that is to be utilized, a listing of all the files contained on the FD, whether they contain apparent evidentiary data or not, is made. The listing will indicate which files were printed, copied, or otherwise recovered.

15. A printout or copy is made of all apparent evidentiary data. The file or location where any apparent evidentiary data was obtained is noted on each printout. All exhibits are marked, sequentially numbered and properly secured and transmitted.

16. Executable programs of specific interest should be examined. User data files that could not be accessed by other means are examined at this time using the native applications.

17. All comments and findings are documented at this time.

■ Limited examinations: In many instances, a complete examination of all the data on media may not be authorized, possible, necessary, or conducted for a variety of reasons. In those instances, the examiner should document the reason for not conducting a complete examination. Some examples of limited examinations would be:

- The search warrant or the courts limit the scope of examination.

- The equipment must be examined on premises. (This may require the examination of the original media. Extreme caution must be used during this type of examination.)

- The media size is so vast that a complete examination is not possible.

- The weight of the evidence already found is so overwhelming that a further search is not necessary.

- It is just not possible to conduct a complete examination because of hardware, OSs or other conditions beyond the examiner's control.

■ Presentation of the evidence: Documental evidence must be gathered as above and a copy given to Personnel and the user so as to allow the user a chance to provide an explanation. Electronic evidence must be presented as follows:

- The User's machine must be unsealed in front of the User and set up to show the file structures and dates those files were last modified.

- The Ghost machine must be set up to show the same as the User's machine.

- The Chairperson and the User must agree that the Ghost machine truly reflects the User's machine.

- The User's machine must be sealed in the presence of the User and the User must sign the seal.

- The Ghost machine is ONLY to be utilized for presentation of evidence.

The checklists described in this chapter have been sourced from:

http://www.itsecurity.com/papers/halcrow1.htm.

Practice Questions

1. List the limitation of the evidence-chain model.

2. Define forensically sterile conditions.

3. What is the importance of a checklist in an investigation?

4. What do forensic imaging tools do?

Case Study

This case study describes the experience of an organization, MAVS, which provides managed antivirus and vulnerability assessment services. These services include carrying out antivirus and security vulnerability assessments from centralized remote location for clients.

Recently, MAVS discovered that most of the details of its strategically important clients with regard to the vulnerability assessment reports were being modified. This issue was raised by a client who was accessing the latest report and the previous report through the online facility provided by MAVS. The client reported that the documents and the online version of the latest report were correct, but the online version and the documents of the previous report varied. Some parts of the information in the old reports stored in the online database with MAVS were incorrect.

MAVS maintains a database server and an interface machine. The employees of MAVS are allowed to access the server from various machines and the clients access the interface machine. In addition to this, MAVS maintains a network server that administers all the machines, including the database server and the interface machine on the network.

MAVS adopted the following investigation procedure to find the cause of modifications to the database:

MAVS made the following assumptions:

- There was no involvement of the employees and the creation of the erroneous report was accidental.

- There was possibly an error in the configuration of the database server.

- There was possibly a cross linking of some field for two different clients because of configuration issues in the database. One of the possible reasons could have been the indexing key that defines the relation between the two tables.

- There was possibly a virus.

MAVS carried out the investigation in the following manner:

- It checked all the configurations of the report generator program (crystal report).
- It checked all the plain text reports.
- It checked all the configurations of the databases.
- It checked the database server for possible virus.

The virus check was done in the following manner:

First, all the log files on the database server were checked for any possible virus signature or infection.

 Usually, organizations create *customized logs*, which consolidate information from different logs such as system event logs and other similar logs.

One such log that MAVS used is referred to as Loguser. This log was maintained on the database server, on which the vulnerability services such as tools were loaded and the reports were being saved. The Loguser log contained the following information:

```
User id: (of the individual who logged on)
Logon time:
Logon Date:
Duration for logon:
Application used in the logon period:
System id from which the user logged on:
```

Code 2.1: Log Loguser

The log contained the following fields:

```
UID:
TimeL: (Time of the local system)
DateL: (Date on the local system)
TimeS: (Time on the network server)
DateS (Date on the network server)
Duration of the logon:
Application used and related details as modified a record, file
or created file:
System ID:
```

Code 2.2: Log Report Format

The log showed an increased number of accesses from various set of nodes. These nodes were the ones used for online help desk. Further, these nodes had permissions only to view the database and not modify it. But the log showed information that the database had not only been viewed but modified. Till now the investigation was being carried out on the assumption that the configurations were erroneous. But this clue forced MAVS to start investigating on the lines of sabotage.

To investigate sabotage, MAVS made two copies of the Loguser log:

■ The first copy of the log was indexed with UID as the first field, DateL as the second field of index, and TimeL as the third field. After indexing, the printout of the log was taken.

■ The second copy of the log was also indexed. But this time, the log was indexed with UID as the first field, DateS as the second field, and TimeS as the third field. The printout of the same was taken.

The two printouts were then matched to see the details of the logons. Interestingly, it was found that quite a few of the TimeL and DateL entries were not matching with the DateS and TimeS entries. Whenever you access the database server, the date and time stamp from the network server is recorded automatically. It was also found that there were several DateL and TimeL entries for consecutive logons from a particular user as well as the node, which showed the usage duration for the first login to be much more than the difference in the duration of the logins between the two records.

The sample log report is shown below:

Record 1		Record 2	
User Id:	User1	User Id:	User1
TimeL showed:	12:30:00	TimeL showed:	12:40:50
DateL showed:	22-07-2003	DateL showed:	22-07-2003
TimeS showed:	10:40:00	TimeS showed:	10:50:50
DateS showed:	22-07-2003	DateS showed:	22-07-2003
Duration:	20minutes	Duration:	30mintues
System ID:	S1	System ID:	S1

Table 2.1: Records in the Log Loguser

This raised an alarm because MAVS knew that such frequent logons are not required and also that any access to the database spanned to atleast 15-20 minutes.

Note the TimeL entries in both the records. The difference between the login time is 10 minutes and 50 seconds. Also, the usage duration of Record 1 is 20 minutes. So, how was it possible for the second logon to happen within 10 minutes of the previous logon? It is not possible that a user who is already logged on from a system logs on again. Secondly, it would not have been possible even if the systems were different, because the authentication system does not permit two logons with the same user ids.

After the above information was collected, MAVS checked the user logon events details on the network server and the systems (S1) that were being shown on the record. All the logs showed the same set of values in the timestamp except for the database server on which the service and reports resided.

The server log and the system log provided the identity of accounts that were used to log on by checking the account logon events. These individuals identified by the accounts were called and interviewed.

While interviews were going on, the systems engineers worked on the user master file that contained user details. They checked to see who all had accessed the user master file and made any changes in the user password or the profile information. They discovered that one of the senior technology officers had been regularly accessing the user master file. Further, all the log details pertaining to that senior technology officer were very close to the server times showed in the records, such as record1 and record2.

Engineers concluded that the particular officer could have been the manipulator and had the administrative password to control the user master file. Therefore, the officer could easily access the master file, extract information about the users, or change access rights. The senior technology officer manipulated with the system in the following manner:

■ The officer would first locally log on to the database server to change the system time and date.

■ The officer would then log off and go to some other system such as S1 and use the information of one of the users obtained from the user master file. The officer would then access the database server to make the manipulations.

The same was confirmed by monitoring the officer's activity on the network with the help of a tool called Sniffer from Sniffer Technologies. This product captures packets and shows the contents of the packet.

Figure 2.1 shows the investigation process followed by MAVS.

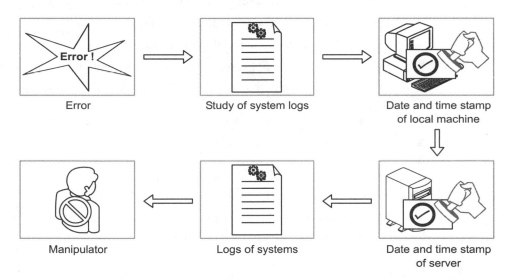

Figure 2.1: Investigation Process

Summary

■ Investigation is the process of collecting, analyzing, recovering and presenting the forensics report.

■ Every crime leaves behind a clue in some form or the other, investigation helps identify these clues.

■ An investigation's success is highly dependent on the investigator's decision.

■ Proper investigation leads to legal prosecution of criminals.

■ Investigation helps an organization identify future security needs and present security practices.

■ Evidences are one of the keys to the success of investigations.

■ It is very important to identify the information that needs to be treated as evidences.

■ Vulnerability assessment tools are good investigation tools.

■ Physical investigation relates to the physical examination of system.

■ Logical investigation relates to the examination of software.

■ Evidence chain model is one of the investigation models for intranet forensics.

■ Forensic imaging tools help create images of the complete system.

■ Protection tools such as IDS and firewall are sources of evidence and information for investigation.

References

Web-site References

- http://www.sans.org
- http://microsoft.com/
- http://securityfocus.net
- http://www.forensic-intl.com

Book References

- Casey, Eoghan. 2001. *Handbook of Computer Crime Investigation: Forensic Tools & Technology*. 1st edition. Academic Press;
- Kruse II, Warren G, and Heiser, Jay G. 2001. *Computer Forensics: Incident Response Essentials*. Addison-Wesley Pub Co.
- Marcella Jr., Albert J. and Greenfield Robert S. 2002. *Cyber Forensics: A Field Manual for Collecting, Examining, and Preserving Evidence of Computer Crimes*. Auerbach Pub.

Home Assignments

1. What is an investigation?
2. What is a system forensic investigation?
3. Explain the importance of an investigation.
4. How does defining policies, guidelines, and procedures relating to computer forensics, help an organization?
5. Prepare a checklist that you would use during hard disk examination.
6. What is physical investigation? Give examples.
7. What is logical investigation? Give examples.
8. Differentiate between physical and logical investigation.
9. What is the evidence-chain model?
10. What is a forensic imaging tool?
11. What is bit-by-bit imaging?
12. What are the benefits of bit-by-bit imaging?
13. How are vulnerability assessment tools used in cyber or system crimes?
14. Is there a way to detect that a vulnerability assessment tools was used in a crime? If yes, describe the way that is used to detect the usage of a vulnerability assessment tool in a cyber crime.

Lab Exercises

Exercise 1

Objective

- Collect information from the security log.
- Interpret the information for investigation.
- Record the evidences obtained through investigation.

Theory

- Logs are source of information of various activities in the system such as the security, the execution of an application, or access to data. To investigate, follow the checklist given below:

    - Check that the log has recorded a minimum of 50 events.

    - Check that the information in the events properties has meaningful information and does not contain junk characters.

    - Check that the system date and time depict the current date and time.

    - If the system does not show the current date and time, do not modify the system date and time. Consider them to be the current date and time.

Problem Statement

- Collect information from the security log in a tabular format. Study the same and interpret the recorded information. Note your observations. These observations should be based on the checklist provided in the theory section.

Lab Setup

A Pentium-based computer with Windows 2000 installed.

Procedure

To collect log information, you need to run the Event Viewer and then check the logs for details on various events. To open the Event Viewer and collect information, perform the following steps given below:

1. Select **Programs** from the Start menu.

2. Select **Event Viewer** from the **Administrative Tools**.

   The Event Viewer window appears, as shown in Figure 2.2.

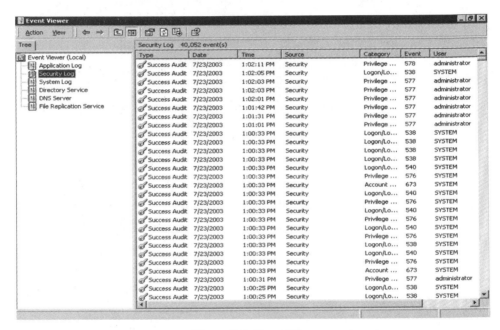

Figure 2.2: Event Viewer

3. In the left panel, double-click **Security Log**. A list of events recorded in the Security Log is displayed in the right panel, as shown in Figure 2.2.

4. Double-click on one of the events.

A window with details on that event appears, as shown in Figure 2.3.

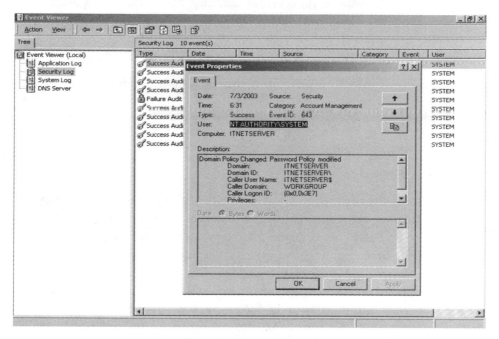

Figure 2.3: Event Properties

The event details include the date and time of the event, the user information, the system id, and the description of the event.

5. Record the information about the event in the following format:

Date	Time	Category	Type	User	Computer	Description	Observation

Table 2.2: Log Observations

Similarly, note your observations in the table for rest of the events from the Security Log. As an investigator, you must be able to interpret the information collected through the logs.

> **Example 2.3**
>
> A sample event description as displayed in the log is given below:
>
> ```
> The user 24121433 successfully established a
> connection to 24880000 using the device COM4.
> ```
>
> Investigating the above, the observation may be noted or interpreted as:
>
> ```
> Dial-up internet was accessed using user name
> 24121433, connection name 24880000 through the modem
> connected to com4 of the system.
> ```

Conclusion/Observation

After you have recorded the information and marked your observations, study it to see if there is a set of information that correlates in the available records. If a correlation exists, study your observations and note the correlating factor. For example, you may come across an event that lists that the account lockout policy has been changed in the security log. When you move up the list, you may come across a lock event listed in the log. These two events are correlated. You can mark your observation by checking the current configuration of the account lockout policy and noting it. You can also note that the user who has been locked out was not aware of the change in the lockout policy.

Lab Activity Checklist

S.No.	Tasks	Completed	
		Yes	No
1.	Checked an event property and made observations.		
2.	Checked events and correlated them.		

Linux System Forensics

3

This chapter explains the different tools and utilities, which an investigator can use to conduct a forensic study on a Linux machine. It further details the investigation procedure including evidence identification and collection of evidence on a Linux machine. At the end of the chapter, you will be able to:

- Describe the basics of Linux internals.
- Describe how Linux can be attacked by a hacker.
- Explain the tools used to gather evidence on a Linux system.
- Explain how Linux can be used by an investigator to carry out analysis of other systems.

3.1 Linux Forensics Essentials

Linux is a powerful open source operating system (OS) that has gained a strong foothold in the network OS market. Linux has many free tools, which have become almost fundamental to any computer forensics investigation. These tools can be used by skilled investigators to extract all sorts of critical forensic evidence from almost any system that they may ever encounter. Knowing how to use these tools well is what separates a casual user from a skilled forensic investigator.

Adding to this fact, Linux runs on many Web servers and is targeted by attackers. Therefore, it is mandatory for the forensics investigator to understand the Linux OS. This section covers these tools along with the details on the different files and programs an investigator needs to assess while conducting a forensic investigation.

3.1.1 Disk Imaging

- Create disk image to conduct a forensic investigation.
- Use common tools that come with Linux to create disk images, which can be used as evidence in a court of law.

Case Study

Consider an environment where a Web server has been hacked and the hacker has modified Web pages that reside on that server. In such a situation, the modified Web pages along with all the server's internal logs and caches are critical evidence and must be preserved in an unmodified state, if they are to be presented in the court. This is where disk imaging plays a vital role.

Disk imaging is the term used to create an exact, bit for bit copy of the contents of any storage device connected to a computer. It is a very crucial step before any further forensic investigation can be carried out on the data stored on the disk. Investigation work is done on the investigator's system, and never on the target computer. It is important to remember that the disk images are connected to the investigator's system as secondary storage devices. Under no circumstances should the investigator allow the OS residing on the disk images to execute. This is important because the OS could easily have been booby-trapped to destroy critical evidence stored on the disks. These disk images will be important in a court of law and their integrity should be preserved. Also, an md5 hash of the disk images and of the original targets disks should be obtained. The md5 hash can be used to prove the integrity of the copy, because even if single bit of the data is modified, the new hash will not match the original one.

3.1.1.1 Mounting

Mounting is the next operation after creating disk images. If the investigators want to carry out any analysis of the disk images, they will need to mount the disk images on their computer system.

Mounting is the process of connecting a storage device with your OS software. Until you mount a device such as a hard disk or a CD-ROM the OS has no idea what data is present on the device, and cannot access the file structure on the disk. Without mounting the devices, it is possible to look at the storage devices byte-by-byte, without the knowledge of the file system that exists on it. However, it will not be an easy task for the investigator to assess the data on the disk, because the file system would not be accessible. You cannot mount a disk device whose file system is not compatible with your OS.

 Disk images should be mounted as read-only devices on the investigator's system so that no program either run intentionally or unintentionally is allowed to modify the disk images.

In certain situations, mounting the disk images is not necessary if the file system of the disk images is not compatible with the OS of the investigator's computer. In such cases, the raw data bytes on the disk images are studied using a disk editor such as Norton Disk Edit or `grep` for Linux.

Linux is a good OS choice for an investigator's computer because it supports a variety of popular file systems, such as EXT2, EXT3, REISERFS, XFS, JFS, VFAT, FAT32/16, and NTFS.

Linux's utilities and tools help to create and assess disk images. They are:

- LSOF tool
- dd utility
- FIND tool
- MOUNT utility

- FILE command
- STRINGS utility

3.1.1.1.1 LSOF Tool

LiSt Open Files (LSOF) is a diagnostic tool that displays information about the files opened by processes. The file can be a normal file, a directory, a special file, a stream, a library, or a network file, which could be an NFS file or a BSD socket. LSOF is used to list the files being used by a specific process, by providing LSOF the PID (Process ID) of the process as an argument on the command line. Without the PID, LSOF will display a list of all the files opened on the system.

NFS or BSD sockets are virtual files used internally by the OS to make connections with remote computers over a network.

In an investigation, LSOF can provide a wealth of information, especially when analyzing already active processes on the system, to find out whether a file is a Trojan horse (bind shell). For example, after running 'ps'command, if you find a process with a regular name such as 'editor' executing, but you don't recall ever starting it, you can execute LSOF on the PID, and see which files are being used by that process. The kind of files that are being used will provide valuable information, such as if the process is writing to a suspicious file. In this case, you can further investigate the specific file to see if the process is a *key logger*, or if the process has a network open, then you will immediately know that something is wrong, because an editor has no reason to open a network socket.

Key loggers are hidden programs that record keystrokes on the victim's computer for later retrieval by the attacker.

The syntax of LSOF command is:

lsof [-p s][-i [i]]

In the above command,

- ◼ -p s: This option selects the listing of files for the processes whose ID numbers are in the comma-separated set s. For example, "123" or "123,456." There should be no spaces in the set.

- ◼ -i [i]: This option selects the listing of files any of whose Internet address matches the address specified in i. If no address is specified, this option selects the listing of all the Internet and network files.

Figure 3.1 shows a sample listing of processes on execution of the LSOF tool.

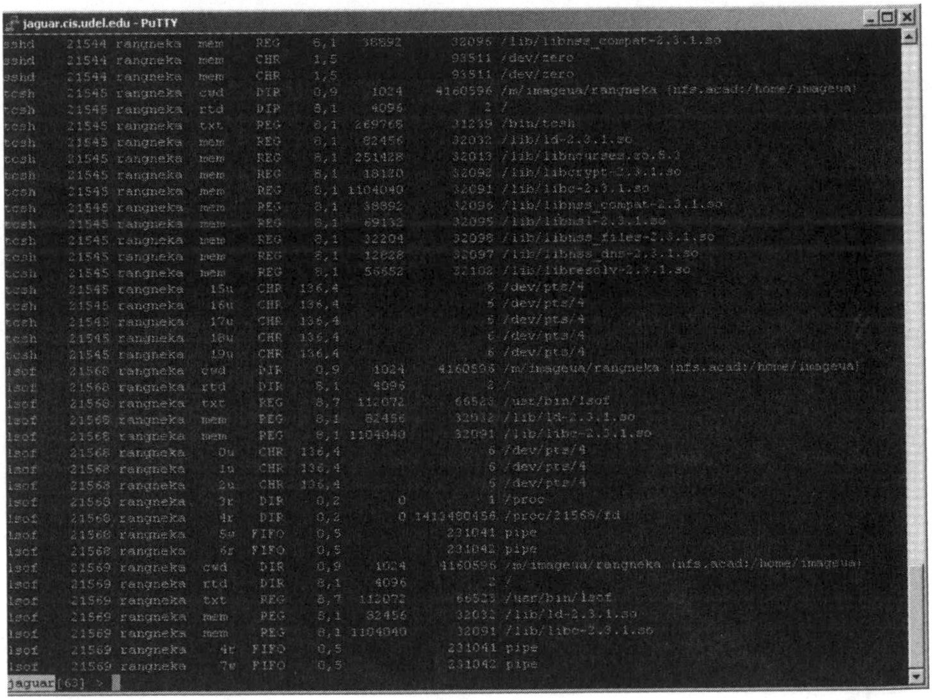

Figure 3.1: LSOF Listing

For example, the command:

```
lsof -p 26774
```

will display the files being used by the process whose ID is: 26774. Code 3.1 shows the listing of these files.

```
COMMAND    PID USER    FD    TYPE DEVICE SIZE/OFF NODE NAME
bash     26774 root   cwd VDIR  136,0     1024      2 /
bash     26774 root   txt VREG  136,0   578964  19473 /usr/bin/bash
bash     26774 root   txt VREG  136,0   866176   2868 /usr/lib/libc.so.1
bash     26774 root   txt VREG  136,0   742696   2911 usr/lib/libnsl.so.1
bash     26774 root   txt VREG  136,0    21676   2908 /usr/lib/libmp.so.2
bash     26774 root   txt VREG  136,0    58504   2932 /usr/lib/libsocket.so.1
bash     26774 root   txt VREG  136,0   237256   2875 /usr/lib/libcurses.so.1
bash     26774 root   txt   VREG 136,0     3984   2881 /usr/lib/libdl.so.1
bash     26774 root   txt   VREG 136,0   184040   1540 /usr/lib/ld.so.1
```

Code 3.1: File Listing of a Process

3.1.1.1.2 dd Utility ~copying any data

dd is a utility used to copy data from the specified input device to the specified output device. The input and output devices can be files or streams. dd copies data from the input stream 512 bytes at a time and writes that data to the output stream. dd is used for a variety of purposes, such as backing up data, overwriting files or devices, and making disk images of entire data storage devices. There are many programs like EnCase, which can do the same but dd is a fast, free, and a popular tool.

The syntax of dd is:

dd if = <input file> of = <output file>

In the above command,

- ▪ 'if' stands for input file
- ▪ 'of' output file
- ▪ 'count' specifies the number of bytes to copy
- ▪ 'skip' specifies the number of bytes to skip over

> **Example 3.1**
>
> The following command:
>
> ```
> dd if=/dev/hda of=/dev/evidence1
> ```
>
> will make an image of the storage device /dev/hda and store that in a file /dev/evidence1; this file can then be written onto a permanent media such as a CD-ROM as evidence.

> **Example 3.2**
>
> The commands given shows how an investigator can make disk images of large storage devices of more than 1 GB by splitting the image into multiple images of 650 MB so that they may be easily written to a CD-ROM.
>
> ```
> dd if=/dev/hda count=650000 of=/dev/evidence1
> dd if=/dev/hda count=650000 skip=650000 of=/dev/evidence2
> dd if=/dev/hda count=650000 skip= 1300000 of=/dev/evidence3
> ```

3.1.1.1.3 FIND Tool

FIND is a complex and powerful tool in the hands of a skilled investigator. Its basic purpose is to search for files stored on the file system. The queries can be based upon a variety of properties that files have in most of the file systems. The different properties that you may need to base your search upon are: filename, size, time/date, inode number, and access permissions. You can also make use of regular expressions in your queries and format the output as you desire.

The syntax of find is:

find <starting directory> -name <name of file to search for>

For a detailed syntax of the find command, you can use the command:

```
man find
```

Example 3.3

When you type the following command at the command prompt, find will search the entire file system starting from / and all the subdirectories under it for a file with the name "shadow" (UNIX shadow password file).

```
find / -name "shadow"
```

Example 3.4

Consider another example. To search for any file with inode number 666, use the following command.

```
find / -inum 666
```

The command will search the file system under / for any file with inode number 666.

Example 3.5

Consider the following command:

```
find / -type f -perm -04000 -ls
```

The above command will display all the files with their SUID and SGID bit set. SUID/SGID files are those files which when executed run with the privileges of root or system administrator. Therefore, these files are targeted by attackers who want to gain root access to your system. Finding files with these bits set does not by itself mean anything, because some programs such as 'passwd' need to run as root, so that they may have access to the password database to change your password.

3.1.1.1.4 MOUNT Utility

The MOUNT utility is used on the investigator's computer to allow the OS to access a storage device, which in this case is usually the device that contains the disk image of the target computer.

The syntax of the mount command is:

mount –o <options> <device to mount> <mount point – where to mount to>

These security options can be appended to the '-o' argument.

ro:	-	read only
noexec	-	do not allow programs to execute
nodev	-	do not interpret character or block devices
noatime	-	prevents inode access time updates

The investigator needs these options to prevent any accidental modifications or damage to the disk image data or the investigator's computer.

 Other options in the `mount` command can easily be looked up using the command:

`man mount`

Example 3.6

In the following example, the system mounts a file system of the VFAT type under the /mnt/C directory structure:

```
mount -t vfat -o noatime,ro,noexec,nodev  /dev/hda5
/mnt/C
```

In simpler terms, the system mounts your Windows drive under Linux so that you have access to the vfat file type. The options ro, noexec, and nodev make the mounted file system read-only and prevent any program stored on the disk image from being run.

3.1.1.1.5 FILE Command

FILE command looks simple but is an indispensable tool to the forensic investigator. During the course of analyzing data on a disk image, the investigator will come across various files, but the type of data stored in these files is not known. In such a case, a tool such as FILE analyzes the data inside any file and displays the file type. FILE performs its analysis based on positions of certain bytes inside a file, which act as the fingerprints of the file. When multiple bytes match, FILE searches its own database and comes up with a file type for that file.

The syntax of file command is:

file <filename>

In the above command,

filename specifies path name of a file to be tested.

Example 3.7

For example, the FILE command given below shows you the type of data inside the file /etc/password. It displays ISO-8859 as the result, which indicates to the investigator that /etc/passwd is a plain text file. This file is the password database on most Linux and other UNIX type OS.

```
file /etc/passwd
Output: /etc/passwd: ISO-8859 text
```

Example 3.8

Consider another example of code:

```
file /boot/boot1
Output: /boot/boot1: x86 boot sector, system
```

The above example shows you FILE analyzed /boot/boot1 as an x86 boot sector file, which means that the file contains information that is normally located in a boot sector on x86 hardware.

3.1.1.1.6 STRINGS Utility

STRINGS is a general purpose utility that is useful for an investigator. The files found on a computer system contain data of different types, most of which is not readable or understandable to humans. What people don't realize is that readable text is also present inside almost all files including executable files. This text can be very interesting to the keen investigator who could use it to form an evidence trail. For example, if the investigators come across a file, named 'cat', which they suspect could be a vicious program of some type, then the investigators can run STRINGS on this file. STRINGS will extract all the readable text strings from the executable file. If the investigators come across any harsh language in that text, it could be a message to the hacker meant to display after his or her program trashed the data on the disk. This will make it clear to the investigator that this program is not what it seems to be.

The syntax of STRINGS utility is:

strings <filename>

In the above syntax:

filename specifies the path name of a regular file to be used as input. If no file operand is specified, the STRINGS utility will read from the standard input.

Example 3.9

On typing the command: `strings /usr/bin/cat`, the following output is displayed:

```
Ha ha all your data is deleted
You have lost your data
```

The above example shows how unusual strings in the executable /usr/bin/cat shows the investigator that this cat is not the usual Unix cat command but some sort of Trojan horse inserted by a clever attacker.

Practice Questions

1. Which command is used to list out the files being used by a process?
2. Which program will you use to list all the text present in a file?
3. Explain the dd command and its uses.

3.2 Evidence Collection in Linux

Evidence collection refers to the assimilation of important data from various files and programs on a target system, which could serve as an evidentiary material. This section describes some of the files in Linux, which can provide important clues to an investigator about a crime. *password, log, history files*

3.2.1 Password Files

 Analyze password files to extract information relating to computer crimes.

Password files are used to store information about users who have accounts on a computer system. Password files are the first files modified by most of the attackers. Therefore, understanding the UNIX password file goes a long way in helping investigators study these files for clues. Also in cases where the suspects have locked their data away, understanding the techniques behind passwords can help a skilled investigator recover that locked information.

Password files on a Linux or UNIX system are similar. They are of a fixed format and readable by any user on the system. On newer Linux systems a feature called *password shadowing* is used where the password field of the file is stored elsewhere in a file, which is protected from all users except the root or Superuser. Even if an attacker on a Linux system were to get his or her hands on a password file, there would be very little information that he or she could gain from it. Passwords are always stored in an encrypted form. This encryption is a one-way encryption, which means that the encrypted passwords cannot be decrypted ever. When the Linux OS asks a user to enter password, it encrypts the entered password in the one-way encryption function and compares the password with the stored encrypted password. If the password matches then the user is given access. This one-way encryption is usually done with a hashing algorithm called md5, which was developed by Professor Ronald L. Rivest of MIT.

Password Cracking programs such as Cracker Jack use large wordlists, which they encrypt with this one-way function and compare with the password file entries until one match. They do not try to decrypt the password, which is impossible, as explained above.

For example, a single entry in a Linux password file, for user 'root' is:

```
root: $1$QxWeYLo1$mraFDKnytJ4vDrXAT:0:0:Sysadmin:/root:/bin/bash
```

Note that elements of an entry are delimited by colon (:). Table 3.1 lists the components of this entry.

Root	User name
1$QxWeYLo1$mraFDKnytJ4vDrXAT	Hashed password
0	User ID
0	Group ID
Sysadmin	GECOS information
/root	User home directory
/bin/bash	User shell program

Table 3.1: Components of an Entry in a Password File

3.2.2 Log Files

Analyze log files to trace a computer crime.

Every Linux system has a variety of log files. These log files log almost all activity on the system. Most of the forensic activities on a Linux system revolves around these log files. There are three primary types of log files. They are listed in Table 3.2.

Type	Name	Description
System Log Files	/var/log/messages	All system messages
	/var/log/dmesg	System initialization information

	/var/log/utmp, /var/log/wtmp	Login and logout information
Process Log Files	/var/log/apache/acces_log	Web server access log
	/var/log/maillog	Mail server logs
User Activity Log Files	.bash_history	Web server access log

Table 3.2: Log Files on Linux

System logs are logs generated by the OS kernel or the heart of the computer system. The system logs cover everything from the hardware detected on the computer to the memory and disk devices initialized. These logs can be used by the investigator to generate a list of devices on the computer and find out the data storage devices connected to the computer so that disk images of these devices can be generated. Besides general system messages, these log files also hold user activity information such as when a certain user logs on or logs out.

Process Log files are log files that hold valuable information about external activity. Process log files store information about the users who used the Web server running on the machine. They also store mail messages delivered to and fro from the computer.

Example 3.10

The following entry is from the Apache log file, which logs the apache Web server process.

```
66.134.157.122 - - [03/Sep/2003:02:18:00 +0200] "GET
/favicon.ico HTTP/1.1" 404 296 "-" "Mozilla/5.0
(Windows NT 5.0)"
```

This entry given above indicates that a user whose IP address was 66.134.157.122 requested the file /favicon.ico out from Web server at 18:00 on Sep 03. This entry also provides other valuable evidence, such as the browser software that the user was using (Mozilla/5.0) and the OS on which the user's system was running (Windows NT 5.0).

> Example 3.11
>
> Following is an e-mail entry from a mail server log file:
>
> ```
> Sep  3 05:00:36 freebsdcluster postfix/smtp[96431]:
> A88C7AC73B: to=<security-officer@freebsd.org>,
> relay=mx1.freebsd.org[216.136.204.125], delay=2,
> status=sent (250 Ok: queued as 8F81744017)
> ```
>
> This line indicates that an e-mail was sent to the e-mail address security-officer@freebsd.org from mail ready mx1.freebsd.org on Sep 3 at 05:00. This information can be further matched to other e-mail records and a chain of evidence or activity can be created.

3.2.3 Hidden Files and History Files

- Search and analyze hidden files to trace a computer crime.
- Assess history files to detect the source of a computer crime.

Besides logs, there are other files, which can help an investigator trace a crime. These files are:

- Hidden files and directories
- History files

3.2.3.1 Hidden Files and Directories

The investigators must scan the disk images of the target system to make sure there are no hidden directories or files. These files are hidden from view and cannot be easily found by a casual scan of the storage device. All directories and files starting with a dot (.) are not listed in a normal directory list operation, like one done with the ls command. The FIND command explained above can be used to find these hidden files and directories.

> **Example 3.12**
>
> Consider the following command:
>
> ```
> find / -name ".*"
> ```
>
> A search will be executed through the entire storage device for all files starting with a dot, which are hidden files. These files could even be directories.

Hidden files are popular with attackers who create hidden directories to hide their tools such as rootkits. On a victim computer where the attacker may not have modified any other file, finding a hidden file can help locate important clues about the attacker.

3.2.3.2 History Files

History files are a type of log file, which hold information on user activity like commands the users entered at the command prompt, and pages the users surfed on their browsers. This information can be helpful in creating activity chains, which can be used as evidence and therefore have to be investigated with care.

> **Example 3.13**
>
> For example, when you type the command:
> ```
> cat .bash_history
> ```
> the following output is displayed:
> ```
> du -h
> mount
> du /
> chmod 777 public_html/class/*
> ls *.tar.gz
> rm -rf *.tar.gz
> ls
> ls *.zip
> rm -rf *.zip
> ls
> ```

```
rm -rf url*
rm -rf resin-3.0.0-beta/
rm -rf 1.txt
rm -rf 2.html
rm -rf *.lic
```

The above command lists out the history information stored by the user shell program (bash). The user shell program stores every command, which is entered at the prompt in a file called .bash_history. Again, if you noticed, this was a hidden file. Also, it is not necessary that the user uses only the shell program (bash). The user could use any shell program, many of which might not even maintain the history information as shown above. It is therefore crucial that the investigator study the hidden files manually.

Practice Questions

1. What is the importance of history files?
2. Explain the importance of process log files.
3. How are passwords stored in the password file?
4. Can password stored in the password file be decrypted? If not, why not?
5. Can Web server logs be used to find out the IP addresses of people visiting the Web server?

3.3 Investigation on Linux

The process of investigation on a Linux system can be complex. Therefore, it is important for the investigators to follow certain guidelines, and use specific tools and skills, which enable them to conduct a successful forensics study. This section describes the investigation process on a Linux system, and details the steps an investigator needs to take to productively perform an investigative study.

3.3.1 Investigation Process

 Explain the steps involved in carrying out an analysis operation on a Linux system.

The initial investigation process begins with the process of imaging and mounting of the storage device, from the target system to the investigator's system. The precautions that must be taken, while mounting the disk images are as follows:

- Mounting disk images on Linux is relatively easy, but care must be taken that images are mounted with certain options enabled, which will prevent accidental deletion or modification of disk images, which would make them void in a court of law.

- Maintaining the integrity of the disk images is essential to the forensic investigator. This can be done by comparing the md5 hash of the disk images with the md5 hash of the original data on the target computer.

- While mounting disk images, the MOUNT command is used. The three options that must be used with the mount command are, 'ro', which makes the mounted image read only and therefore, no data can be written onto the disk image, and the 'nodev' and 'noexec' commands prevent programs on the disk images from being executed. It is necessary to use these options because the disk images taken from the target computer could contain dangerous programs, which, if executed could cause damage to the investigator's computer.

- After the investigators have finished working with the disk images, they should remember to unmount the disk images with the UNMOUNT command so that the media on which the disk image was stored, can be detached from the investigators' computer. If the investigators forget to unmount, the OS on the investigators' computer will not be informed that the disk image data is inaccessible and therefore could cause an error.

- Most disk images are stored on CD-ROMs or on special tape devices. These disks should be marked clearly. Even the hard drive's serial number of the target computer must be noted down if the disk images are made from the hard disks on the target computer.

Example 3.14

Consider the following example. An investigator has three disk images of three Windows drives stored on CD-ROMs. To mount these disk images, the investigator will insert the CD-ROMs into his or her computer and execute the following command. (It is assumed that the investigator has three or more CD-ROM drives.)

```
mount -o noatime, ro, nodev, noexec -t vfat /dev/hda5
/mnt/disk1
mount -o noatime, ro, nodev, noexec -t vfat /dev/hda6
/mnt/disk2
mount -o noatime, ro, nodev, noexec -t vfat /dev/hda7
/mnt/disk3
```

The investigator can change directory into the respective directory where the disk image was mounted (for example, cd /mnt/disk1) and use the forensic investigation tools to analyze the data.

When dealing with a large disk image split over several CD-ROMs, Tapes, or DVDs, you will need a large hard disk to save the combined disk images before it can be mounted. The generated hash of the disk image should also be stored.

To combine these images, you can use the command cat. The cat command is used on Linux to output any text in a file on the screen. The '>' sign can be used to redirect that output into another file.

> **Example 3.15**
>
> For example, the command
>
> ```
> cat img1 img2 im3 > img
> ```
>
> will combine the three disk images, img1, img2, and img3 to a file named img.

If investigators want low-level access to the data on the disk image without mounting the disk image, they should directly access the device containing the disk image.

> **Example 3.16**
>
> In the following command, the investigator uses grep command to access the device, hda5, which contains the required disk image.
>
> ```
> grep "hacker" /dev/hda5
> ```

3.3.1.1 Data Integrity Through md5sum Program

md5sum is a program that uses the md5 algorithm to generate 128-bit hash of the data fed to the md5sum program. The program gets its input from the standard input stream, such as your kcyboard, and instantly outputs the generated hash. Even if one bit changes in this input information, the second time it is passed through the md5sum program, a totally different hash will be generated. It is this property of the algorithm, which is used to guarantee the integrity of data.

During investigation, the hashes of disk images and hashes of the target computer's storage devices are generated. If these hashes match it can be proved that the data has not been tampered with in any way.

md5sum can also be used to make hash of single file of any type. Therefore, if the investigators want to check the authenticity of common system files, they can match the hash generated with online hash databases. If the hash of a common file does not match with online hash databases, the file could be a Trojan horse or a back door program.

> **Example 3.17**
>
> If you want to create an md5 hash of the device /dev/hda1, you will type the command:
>
> ```
> cat /dev/hda1 | md5sum
> ```
>
> The output would be something like:
>
> ```
> b1ad573b37d50f304a43471d5d80e154 -
> ```
>
> This is the md5 hash of the device.

> **Example 3.18**
>
> If you want to create an md5 hash of the /etc/passwd file, you will type the command:
>
> ```
> cat /etc/passwd | md5sum
> ```
>
> The output would be something like:
>
> ```
> 11fa00f7170afecc45baab5c228080c156 -
> ```
>
> This is the md5 hash of the /etc/passwd file.

3.3.2 Analysis of File System

 Analyze the file system of a Linux system.

A file system analysis is a very crucial aspect of any system forensic study. The information relating to various processes and activities on a computer are stored in files. Therefore, a keen investigator must have sound knowledge of the structure and components of the file system of an OS. All files including the memory files can provide critical data pertaining to system crime. The native file system used by Linux is EXT2, which is updated to EXT3.

3.3.2.1 Inode Forensics

 Inode numbers can be used with various programs to give us information on the files to which the programs are connected. Inodes hold valuable information about files, such as file type, access rights, owners, timestamps, size, and pointers to data blocks. This inode information can be used for recovering deleted files or for searching for specific files. If a process which has been executed in memory has its binary deleted by an attacker, a skilled investigator can get access to the binary of the file from the memory by using the /proc/<pid>/exe and cat and recover the file.

Two tools can be found in The Coroner's Toolkit (developed by Dan Farmer), which directly uses inode information.

They are:

- ils: Lists inode information. By default, ils only lists inodes of removed or unallocated files. ils also gets the state information of the inode and outputs other information such as inode number, allocation status, user, group, MACtimes, permission, file size, and disk blocks for each inode. This helps reduce the amount of information an investigator would need to analyze, and helps target the correct data more accurately.

- Icat: This tool lists the contents of files for a given inode. It works similar to the popular cat found on all UNIX systems, but in forensics it is usually used to read deleted files. When files are deleted under Linux the inode number corresponding to the filename is changed to zero, but the inode entry along with its data is still preserved on the storage media, until it is overwritten by other data.

Besides ils and icat there are other utilities in TCT, which are explained in detail in Chapter 5, System Forensic Tools.

3.3.2.2 SUID/GUID Files

SUID and GUID are two bits on the array of security attribute bits that each file on a Linux file system has. A file, with its SUID or GUID bits set, executes with the UID or GID of the owner rather than of the person executing it. This means that such a file will have access to the files, processes, and resources that were available to the owner. This was a security feature to allow processes such as a password changer program to access the password database, when executed by a lower privilege user. Many programs on a default Linux installation have their SUID bit set. This is a potentially deadly situation, since if the attackers manage to make such a program crash, they will be able to execute their own code with elevated rights and, thus, even manage a full system compromise and get super user access to the computer system. SUID and GUID files don't help a forensic investigator directly in any way. They only help them narrow down their search on a compromised system. There are many other ways through which an attacker can take over a Linux system, but understanding SUID and GUID files properly adds to the investigator's knowledge of ways that attackers use to enter a computer system.

3.3.2.3 Modified, Access, Created (MAC) Time

In Linux and other UNIX variants, file times and dates are stored as three separate fields which are: creation time, last access time, and last write/modification time. This information is stored in the inode of the file. These three fields are used to detect changes on a target system, which is suspected of being possibly compromised.

Investigators can narrow their scope of analysis by looking for recently modified files, which can done with the find command.

Example 3.19

To view the files that have been modified in the last 24 hours, type the following command:

```
./find —mtime —1 —print
```

The list of files appears, as shown in Figure 3.2.

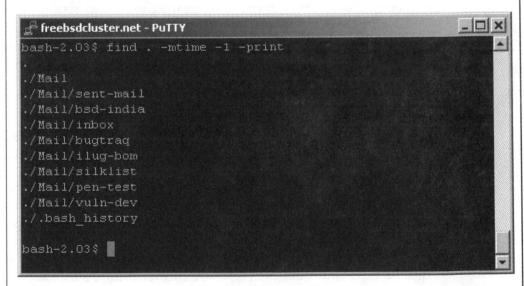

Figure 3.2: MACtimes Analysis

To do more granular searches, you can use the –newer switch. All time switches use 24-hour periods, while the –newer switch compares file access and modification times down to a minute.

MAC_DADDY is another tool that can be used for MACtimes forensic analysis. It is written entirely in Perl and requires the perl interpreter to be loaded on the investigator's system.

Perl is a programming language popular in the Linux software developing community. It is mostly used to process data. It is an interpreted language and so you need the perl software whenever a program written in Perl is executed.

The investigator should keep in mind that the target computer system might be set to another time zone and that should be taken into account when matching file access times.

3.3.2.4 String Searching

String searching in files is not a new concept. This section describes a new way of applying string search for a forensics investigation. When dealing with disk images, search for information can be done on the disk image itself. Disk images are nothing but large files, which contain exact images of the target's data. Therefore, an investigator can simply run `grep` or `STRINGS` directly on the disk images, without mounting the disk image. You must keep in mind that the disk image is nothing but a file until it is mounted. Therefore, you can search through it like you would with any file and even search through deleted data that still resides on the disk image. If you mount the disk image and run a search on its file system, you will be searching through data that exists on the file system and not the deleted data.

> Example 3.20
>
> Consider the statement:
>
> ```
> grep "virus program" /mnt/cdrom/img1 -before-
> context=10 -after-context=10
> ```
>
> This statement uses the grep command to search through the entire disk image file. When the grep command comes across the defined string, it displays ten lines before it and ten lines after it, thus giving the investigator a clear picture of the context in which this text was used.

3.3.2.5 Unallocated Space and SlackSpace

In any computer system, unallocated space exists on the storage device, and this is the part of the disk drive that does not have any data on it. The deleted data existing on a section of a disk is also considered unallocated space. This is because if any new data is to be stored, the OS will overwrite the deleted data first. Unallocated space on a computer contains a wealth of valuable information from old deleted e-mails to old image files and even music or video data. This data can be salvaged by the investigator and can be used as evidence. Most users don't know that deleting data does not mean that it cannot be retrieved and therefore, indiscriminately delete the data that they wish to destroy. Information on how you can recover this deleted data will be covered further.

The OS of computers with less RAM save unused parts of the RAM on the hard disk in the swap partition. Data, which was on that part, is requested from the OS by a process, and the data saved in the swap space is swapped with the data in the RAM. Using this technique, the OS can simulate almost endless RAM space. So programs can use more RAM than the computer physically has installed on it. Since data is constantly read and written on the swap space it is cluttered with sometimes valuable information like passwords and username, which unintentionally may be stored in RAM by some processes. People have known to get valuable data such as Private keys off the swap space.

Data on the unallocated space on the disk devices is automatically copied when a disk image is taken of the drive.

Data on the swapspace needs to be copied off the swap space using dd, as mentioned above. Just like the other disk devices, the swap space has its own file system.

Therefore, it can be mounted and studied using the usual forensic tools or a hex editor, which can be very useful when studying raw or non-text data on disk images.

A hex editor is a utility, which displays the file in hexadecimal format and allows the use to edit any byte or bytes in the file.

3.3.2.6 File Recovery

File recovery is the art of getting back files that have already been deleted. This is a tricky process and it is necessary for the investigator to understand it completely because one of the most common activities in data analysis by a forensic investigator is recovering old deleted data.

There are some steps that the investigators must keep in mind when attempting to recover deleted files. They must be prepared to change inode information manually, find the deleted inodes, obtain the details of those inodes (details like file size, attributes, flags, and disk blocks used to store the file), recover data blocks, and modify inodes directly.

You have to recover some deleted files in a mounted file system named /office which could be done on a disk image that the investigator has back at his or her lab or on the target computer. You will first need to unmount /office so that no more file read or write activity takes place on that partition, which could potentially overwrite your deleted files, destroying the data completely. In case the files you deleted were in a root partition, then make a disk image of the root partition, and mount that on another computer where you can carry out the same operation.

You can use the debugfs program used in Linux and UNIX to examine your file system. Debugfs is a file system debugger used to perform maintenance operation on the file system.

To recover a deleted file with the help of debugfs program, perform the following steps:

1. Start debugfs on the same device, which contains your partition.

    ```
    # debugfs /dev/hda1
    ```

2. If you wish to modify the inodes, add a -w option to enable writing to the file system:

    ```
    # debugfs -w /dev/hda1
    ```

3. Use the debugfs command, lsdel, to find the deleted inodes.

    ```
    debugfs:  lsdel
    ```

    Debugfs will output its result after some time. If you can pipe this output to a file and obtain a printout of that file, it will make referencing inode information much

---

simpler. For example, you can use the following command to transfer data to a text file:

```
Echo "lsdel" | debugfs /dev/hda1 > lsdel.txt
```

4. Use the stat command, which comes with debugfs, to get detailed information about an inode. For example, if you want information about inode no 383, type the following command:

```
debugfs:  stat <383>
```

The output of the stat command is shown in Code 3.2.

```
Inode: 383    Type: regular    Mode:  0644    Flags: 0x0
Version: 1
User:   503    Group:   100    Size: 6065
File ACL: 0    Directory ACL: 0
Links: 0    Blockcount: 12
Fragment:  Address: 0    Number: 0    Size: 0
ctime: 0x31a9a574 -- Mon May 27 13:52:04 1996
atime: 0x31a21dd1 -- Tue May 21 20:47:29 1996
mtime: 0x313bf4d7 -- Tue Mar  5 08:01:27 1996
dtime: 0x31a9a574 -- Mon May 27 13:52:04 1996
BLOCKS:
594810 594811 594814 594815 594816 594817
TOTAL: 6
```

Code 3.2: Output of stat Command

From the above output, you know that the file you want to recover had six blocks, which is less than the limit of twelve, so you can now go ahead and recover the file.

5. Use the dump command to recover the file.

```
dump <383> /mnt/recovered001
```

A copy of your deleted file is in /mnt/recovered001.

Practice Questions

1. Explain unallocated space.
2. Explain Linux swap file.
3. State steps to recover a delete file on the /dev/hda1 device.
4. Explain the lsdel command of the debugfs program.
5. Explain what dump command does.

Case Study

Crime

An attacker, Jack, after an `nmap` scanning of a network, discovers an old Linux computer running sendmail. After some banner grabbing or connecting to an open port to check which program advertises itself on the port, he realizes that the port is using a vulnerable version of sendmail, which has a huge remote buffer overflow bug in its SMTP handling code. The attacker, who is only a script kiddie, was looking for a machine to joy ride on or to use as his zombie for DDOS attacks on other machines. He is thrilled with his discovery. He goes on to his familiar IRC channels and begins to ask around for the exploit code for this particular bug. He soon trades sendmail exploits with another hacker.

After obtaining the exploit, the attacker comes back to the same victim computer the next day and after probing around a bit to see if his victim is still the way he had left it, directs the exploit code to the IP address of the server.

After a couple of seconds the exploit code terminates and he's left at a blank terminal window. After running `uname` and a few other utilities, the attacker knows he's inside the Linux computer. He quickly types `whoami` and the computer replies "root". Now, the hacker uses `wget` to download his favorite rootkit and bind shell. After connecting the bind shell to a port he exits from his terminal and telnets into the port on which the bind shell is running. Being a script kiddie, he has trouble compiling the rootkit on the server because some of the libraries are missing. After some failed attempts, the attacker gets frustrated and leaves for the time being.

A system administrator, Lisa, looking casually at the NIDS (Network Intruder detection Service, Snort) logs realizes that a sendmail exploit has been tried against one of her Linux computers and because it wasn't tried at random against any of her other computers, she gets even more suspicious.

Investigation

The system administrator calls on the services of a computer forensics investigator, Jon. The investigator is in a tough situation because if he starts to work on the computer, the attacker, if he's still on, might figure out something is wrong, and destroy all the data on the computer. So as a precaution, the investigator pulls out the network cable from the network card to isolate the computer from the network and starts his work.

The danger is not completely eliminated because the computer could be booby-trapped. Therefore, the investigator turns off the computer and extracts the hard disk, which he takes back to his lab. Here, he first makes disk images of the drives and mounting them gets to work. The system administrator has provided the investigator with the IP address of the attacker and information that the detected was over the network and directed to the sendmail server. With this data, the investigator starts to look at the sendmail logs and sees funny entries, which could have been the result of the exploit trying to gain access to the system. Recording this as evidence along with the other information, he uses find to search for files that have been created or modified in the last 24 hours, and comes across the downloads done by the attacker. He also finds the bind shell that was compiled by the attacker. After recording the MACtimes for these files as evidence, the investigator looks at the .bash_history file, which gives him every single command typed by the attacker, and the time the last command was typed. Gathering all this information, the investigator creates an evidence chain, which can then be submitted to a law enforcement agency such as the FBI, who can prosecute the culprit.

Summary

- Linux has many free tools that enable effective computer forensics investigation.
- Disk imaging is the term used to create an exact (bit-for-bit) copy of the contents of any storage device connected to a computer.
- Mounting is the process of connecting a storage device with your OS software.
- Linux includes various utilities and tools, which help to create and assess disk images. They are:
  - LSOF tool
  - dd utility
  - FIND tool
  - MOUNT utility
  - FILE command
  - STRINGS utility
- Password files can provide crucial clues to the investigator during a forensic study.
- Password files store user information about users who have accounts on a computer system.
- Most of the forensic activity on a Linux system revolves around these log files:
  - System Log Files
  - Process Log Files
  - User Activity Log Files
- Besides logs, there are other files, which can help an investigator trace a crime. These files are:
  - Hidden files and directories
  - History files
- md5sum is a program that uses the md5 algorithm to generate 128-bit hash of the data fed to the md5sum program. md5sum program is used to maintain the integrity of data.
- Inode numbers can be used with various programs to give us information on the files the programs are connected to.

- The Coroner's Toolkit, developed by Dan Farmer, contains the tools which directly use inode information:
  - ils
  - icat
- In Linux and other UNIX variants, file times and dates are stored as three separate fields: creation time, last access time, and last write/modification time.
- MACtimes are used to detect changes on a target system, which is suspected of being possibly compromised.
- MAC_DADDY is a tool, which can be used for MACtimes forensic analysis.
- Unallocated space and swap space on a computer contain valuable information, from old deleted e-mails to old image files and also music or video data.
- File recovery is the art of getting back files that have already been deleted.

References

- www.opensourceforensics.com
- www.freshmeat.net
- http://e2fsprogs.sourceforge.net/ext2.html
- http://security.ucdavis.edu/unixlinux_deskserv_secure.cfm

Homework Exercises

1. Explain how dd can be used to create disk image of large disks so that the image can fit on one 650MB CD-ROM.

2. Explain the importance of guaranteeing the integrity of the disk images and how this guarantee can be made.

3. Explain LSOF and give examples of its use.

4. Write a note on inodes and inode forensics.

5. Explain step-by-step file recovery in the Linux ext2 file system.

6. Write a note on how you would have carried out forensic investigation if you had been called upon for investigating the hacking incident (Case Study) mentioned above.

7. Write a brief note on buffer overflow attacks.

8. Write a note on debugfs.

9. Explain Web server logs and their use in detail.

10. Explain Mail server logs and their use in detail.

11. Explain the stat command found in debugfs.

12. Explain MACtimes.

13. What are GUID/SUID files?

14. Explain the structure of password files in Linux.

15. Write a note on the STRINGS program.

Lab Exercises

Exercise 1

Objective

- Find a suspicious process running in memory.
- Analyze the suspicious process using Linux tools.

Problem Statement

Code 3.3, shows a process, bad.c, being executed in memory.

```
------- bad.c cut here -------
int main()
{
     char *text = "bad hacker program";
     for(;;);
}
-----------------------------

gcc -o bad bad.c

./bad &

rm -rf bad
```

Code 3.3: Execution of bad.c

As a forensic investigator you need to:

- Recover the program from memory and save it using cat.
- Use STRINGS, FILE, lsof, and grep to investigate this suspicious file.
- Gather other forensic information about the process.

                                                                    Linux System Forensics 3.37

■ Use lsof to analyze what files have been opened by the process.

■ Prepare a report to detail your procedure and findings.

Lab Setup

Computer with Linux installed.

The GCC Compile should be installed.

Procedure

To run the program, bad.c, follow the steps:

1. Type the program in Code 3.3 into a file, named bad.c.

2. Compile it using GCC.

```
gcc -o bad bad.c
```

3. Execute the above program at the command line with the & switch:

```
./bad &
```

4. Delete the program executable from the file system.

```
rm -rf <program name>
```

5. Use the cat command and, with the knowledge that has been gained from the chapter, recover the program executable from the system memory. Once you recover the program executable:

- Use the explanation given above to check if the executable contains any suspicious text.

- Analyze the suspicious executable using Linux tools such as lsof, file, and the /proc file system.

You can use the following methods to conduct your study:

■ Use the ps command to find the process id of the executable.

■ Use the cat command to extract the program from memory

cat /proc/<pid>/exe > program

Then use lsof –p <pid> to see the listing of files being used by the program.

■ Finally, use the /proc/<pid> file system to analyze various information that Linux holds about the executing process.

■ By making copies of the data in /proc/<pid> the investigator can capture volatile information about the process. Don't forget to use md5sum to finally generate md5 signatures of all the captured data. This data could be used as evidence, and therefore md5 signatures are required to prove the integrity of the data.

For example:

    cat <filename> | md5sum

Conclusion/Observation

Write a report of your forensic analysis that you performed on the program. The report should essentially consist of:

- Objective
- Problem Statement
- Tools and techniques used
- Solution
- Conclusion

Lab Activity Checklist

S.No.	Tasks	Completed	
		Yes	No
1.	Compiled, executed, and deleted the executable		
2.	Recovered the executable from memory		
3.	Analyzed the recovered file for suspicious text		

Windows-System Forensics

4

Windows, currently the most popular desktop operating system (OS), comes under the magnifying glass of forensic investigators almost daily. However, Windows, being a commercial OS, does not come with built-in forensic tools as Linux does. This chapter describes how investigators analyze a Windows computer for clues and evidence. At the end of the chapter, you will be able to:

- Describe the tools required for a Windows forensic investigation.
- Explain how to carry out disk imaging in Windows.
- Explain how to use Linux tools to carry out a Windows forensic analysis.
- Explain the internal Windows operating-system components, which can be a source of crucial evidential material.

4.1 Windows-System Examination

Windows is one of the most popular operating systems. Different organizations and corporations run their servers and store databases with critical information on Windows systems. Hacking a Windows machine or storing malicious programs on it could be lucrative for an attacker. Given this wide usage and utility of Windows, system-forensic expertise for Windows machines is essential.

This section covers the basic preparation required for investigators before they go on site to inspect a computer running Windows. Unlike Linux, Windows does not come with any built-in utilities. The investigator needs to create a Windows toolkit to carry out the investigation.

4.1.1 Prerequisites for Windows Examination

 Identify the tools and components of a Windows system essential for a forensic investigation.

Before conducting a forensic study on a Windows machine, you must be aware of the basic tools and types of files. This will help you know how and where to look for and collect forensic data.

Remember that each step in the investigation must be documented. The information needs to include date and time, must pinpoint responsibility for computers and hard drives, and list unique information such as device serial numbers.

4.1.1.1 Data-Acquisition Utilities

Windows, a commercial software, does not provide built-in tools for investigation. However, there are different Windows versions of the forensic utilities available for Linux. These utilities enable you to make disk images of the Windows drives and generate md5 hashes of the acquired disk images to ensure their integrity.

You should not try to mount a disk for forensic analysis on a Windows machine. This can enable write operations to take place on the attached hard disk that, if modified even by mistake, will immediately lose its evidential value. It is preferable to do the analysis on a Linux computer because under Windows you cannot control the methods used by the OS to mount the disk.

The different tools and utilities that you can use to build your own toolkit for a forensic study of a Windows machine are:

- dd: Used in Linux and also in Windows to create a disk image of the evidence computer. The latest version of dd for Windows contains a new feature not available in the Linux version of dd. This feature, in addition to making disk images, can make memory images. These are a replica of the entire RAM of the victim computer. This RAM content can provide a wealth of information that would otherwise have been wiped out on the next reboot. It contains information such as the last Web site visited and passwords.

 When using the Windows dd command, you should create the image via a hardware write-blocking device. Use of dd on an unprotected hard drive WILL destroy evidence.

- Hex editor: Used to edit nontext files, such as program files, or to view these files. It is known as hex editor because it displays the contents of the file in hexadecimal notation. Many hex editors are available on the Internet. One of the commonly used hex editors for Windows is HexEdit by Expert Commercial Software.

- Galleta: Analyzes cookies from Web sites that have been stored on the computer. It can extract valuable information from the cookies and output it in a field-delimited manner. The presentation makes it easy for the investigator to decipher the information. This is a tool developed by Foundstone, Inc.

- md5deep: Used to recursively go through every file in the file system and generate md5 hashes of the files. This hash database can be very useful in a court of law because the investigator can prove whether certain files have been modified or not. This is a utility developed by the US Air Force Office of Special Investigations (AFOSI).

- Pasco: Parses the information in an index.dat found in Microsoft Internet Explorer's cache directory and outputs the results in a field-delimited manner so that the evidence can be imported into a spreadsheet program for analysis. An investigator will find a lot of valuable data in the IE cache files of a computer that has been used to surf the Internet. IE uses these cache files to store recently accessed Web pages so that the next time the Web page is required it can be retrieved from your hard disk itself. This makes surfing appear faster.

- wipe.exe: A utility that allows secure wiping of data before forensic duplication.

Some of the utilities listed above are similar to their Linux counterparts, except that these are designed to run only on Windows.

- EnCase: Provides a vast amount of information bout such things as deleted files, file clusters, and swap files. It is a complete forensic package popularly used for disk imaging and disk-image analysis in the computer forensic community. There are versions of this software for Windows 95/98, W2K, XP, and NT.

Figure 4.1 shows a sample of the output generated by EnCase. In the figure, EnCase has found a text fragment in the slack space of a computer, and the message displayed is a live message regarding the search for explosives. The ability to find this kind of information and to catalog it in a presentable form makes EnCase popular.

Evidentiary Text Fragments

Case: **Mad_Bomber**	Page 1

Evidentiary Text Fragments
___

Full Path   Quantum\C\America Online 4.0\csl\mdmgen.csl

File Created   08/12/00 06:30:48PM
Last Written   05/25/99 05:06:56PM
Last Accessed 08/12/00

Comment: Note that this message is in slack space.

```
Just a quick note to say hi - I know you are in a hurry, but I have to look and find the file you want.
You have to be careful when you make these things, or you may find yourself laying in a field that used
to be your house.

I will get back to you when I find it. Also, make sure you get the money, cause I am not sending anythi
ng to you without payment.

Boomer
```

Figure 4.1: Encase Output

Other commercial software packages used by professionals for forensic investigation are SMART, Forensics Toolkit, and Ilook.

4.1.1.2 Hardware Identification

Hardware identification can be done manually by opening the computer case and visually identifying devices inside. The hardware must be located and recorded along with information on manufacturer and serial numbers of devices. The exact hardware configuration is identified by:

▪ Type and speed of processor

▪ Memory (size and how much of each slot is filled)

▪ Network and other cards that are installed

- Removable media devices (floppy, ZIP, tape, CD, and DVD)
- Hard drives by make, model, and serial number

This exercise, however, should be conducted carefully because computers are electronic devices, and if you shut down the power, you will lose a lot of volatile data that could have been used as evidence.

You can use the Window OS's internal utilities to get a list of hardware devices. To access the list, run Start Menu → Control Panel → System → **Properties**.

Click the **Hardware** tab, and double-click the **Device Manger** tab. The screen, as shown in Figure 4.2 appears.

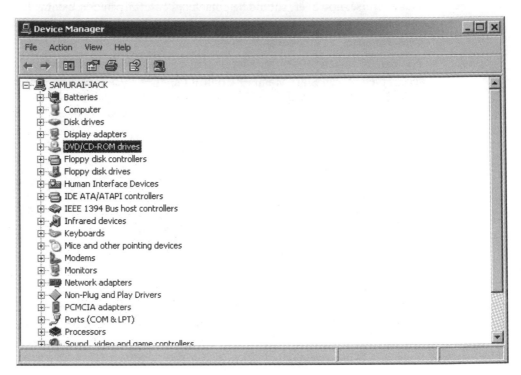

Figure 4.2: Device Manager

In forensic cases, hardware identification lies in opening the box and actually seeing what is inside. You should not completely rely on what is listed in the currently loaded OS as the installed hardware. For example, in various cases, investigators have opened a computer case and found an old hard drive that was installed, but not connected to power or data cables. These drives should also be examined as they could contain valuable information.

Another vital part of hardware identification is noting the computer's current clock/calendar settings and documenting these values in relation to the correct date/time. This is usually done, after the evidence on the hard drive has been removed for imaging, by starting the computer and checking the BIOS settings.

4.1.2 Clues in Windows System

 Identify the areas in a Windows machine that can provide key evidence.

You can assess numerous places for clues when dealing with a Windows system. The clues that you look for are related to the crime being investigated. For example, if you analyze a hacker computer, then you will look for IP address or clues that the attacker left behind in the system logs. On the other hand, if it is a case of a suspicious program, then you will be searching for deleted files or newly created files.

Some of the specific areas where you can find traces of crime on a Windows machine are:

- Windows registry: This is clearly the most important place, after the file system, where important material can be found. The Windows registry is a database of Windows settings and options, not only of the file system, but also of the various software packages installed on the computer. The registry contains everything from product serial number to the Internet settings of the user.

- System files: The entire Windows OS is under a sub-directory called WINDOWS that contains other sub-directories such as SYSTEM and SYSTEM32. The sub-directories under the WINDOWS directory contain dynamic-link libraries. These directories can help the investigator locate hidden spyware or key loggers installed on the system.

- Web browser caches: Most browsers like Internet Explorer save copies of previously surfed pages so that repetitive access to them will be faster. Looking at these caches can help the investigator understand the surfing history of the target machine.

- Program logs: Many programs, such as instant messengers (MSN, ICQ, AIM, and YAHOO), ftp, and IRC clients (MIRC), store entire logs of chats. For example, it is a well documented fact that many times hackers use these tools to coordinate their attacks, and in the investigation of a hacker's computer, these conversation logs can give away the hacker's entire history of crime.

- Recycle Bin: Here, there is the possibility that you will find useful data that can be used as evidence. Therefore, an investigator must never neglect to look at the Recycle Bin.

■ Deleted files: Listing and looking at deleted files in Windows requires extra tools such as Norton Utilities that can neatly list all the deleted files on the drive. Windows deletes the first letter of a deleted file as a way of marking the file as deleted. Therefore, you need to make a calculated guess at the whole filename.

4.1.3 Methods for Assessing Damage

■ Describe the methods for assessing the extent of the damage to a Windows system.

■ Explain the importance of damage assessment in narrowing the scope of investigation.

Assessing the damage to a computer is carried out only if the computer was the target of an attack. If the computer itself was used for an attack or was used to hide information that you are looking for, there would be no point in assessing damage to it. The word *damage* is used not for physical damage to the computer, but for the damage to the integrity of the software. This damage could involve the installation of a Trojan horse such as Netbus, modification of system files so as to add a *backdoor*, or simply deletion of critical files as an act of vandalism.

A backdoor is a hidden program that allows the attacker to easily access a computer system.

You can detect modified system files by first installing the same version of Windows on a different machine and then running md5deep on it so as to get a list of md5 signatures for all the system files that come with the Windows installation. This database of signatures can then be written onto a CD-ROM and used by the investigator for comparison with the md5root database of the target computer. This comparison can be done on the target computer, but is not recommended. It should usually be done on a Linux computer because an investigator has better control of the OS in Linux than in Windows. You also need to make sure that modification of data doesn't take place on the investigator's computer. Once the two md5 databases are created, you should compare them using the Linux diff command or any other file-text comparison tool.

The syntax of the diff command is:

diff <database1> <database 2>

The files that show up with different md5 signatures are the files modified by the attacker. These files can then be quarantined and examined at a later date.

Trojan horses and *rootkits* are much harder to detect, and there is no fixed way to detect them. Some rootkits are designed so that as long as they are resident in the memory, they will not allow themselves to be seen by any Windows tools. The only way to detect them is to search for their executables on the file system. You can also detect rootkits through the previously deleted files list because attackers tend to delete the original executable after installing the rootkit or Trojan horse. These programs are also supposed to auto-load themselves into the memory if the system is ever rebooted. To do this, they register themselves and make changes to the system registry, fooling Windows into loading them on the next restart. This makes the registry a useful place to look for traces of these programs. The registry path to start from is:

HKEY_LOCAL_MACHINE\SOFTWARE\Microsoft\Windows\CurrentVersion\Run

Programs that are supposed to be started by Windows on booting up are always located here.

 Rootkits are programs installed by hackers on attacked systems to help hide their own presence.

Example 4.1

Figure 4.3 shows the registry of a computer infected with the MSBLAST Internet worm.

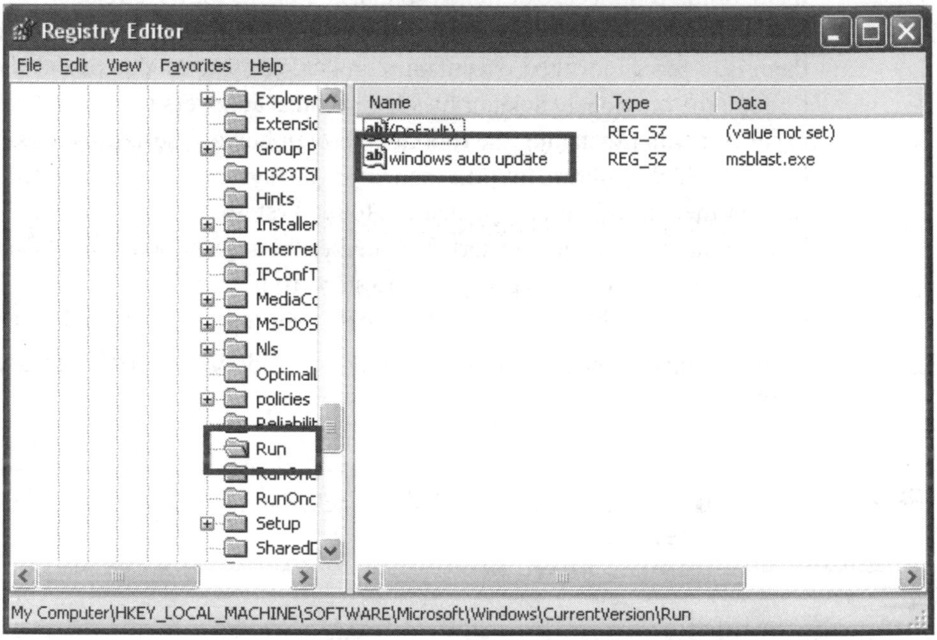

Figure 4.3: Registry Entry for Msblast

Practice Questions

1. List some of the tools that you would need to build your own forensics toolkit for Windows.

2. Name one of the most popular of the commercial software used for Windows forensic study.

3. During hardware identification, what are the components of the computer that you would assess?

4. List some specific files or areas of a Windows system that can provide useful clues to a crime.

5. What is the function of md5deep?

4.2 Disk Imaging in Windows

Today many computers are *dual-boot* computers, which means that they can have both Windows and Linux installed on a single hard disk. A disk image created on such a dual-boot machine will not only create a disk image of the Windows part, but also of the Linux part. This section describes the different imaging tools used by Windows.

4.2.1 Imaging Principals

Explain the disk imaging principles in the Windows OS.

The principal of examination that an investigator follows while imaging a Windows disk is exactly the same as the one followed for imaging a Linux disk. The examination of data is carried out on the investigators' computer and not on the target computer. If the investigator ran Windows on the computer, the tools used for disk examination would be a bit different. These tools are described below.

Forensically sound images can be taken of a system that has been started using a system disk or CD. In such cases, the startup files must be specially modified to ensure that compressed volumes are not automatically mounted from drive C, as this will change file-access dates.

The investigator running Windows will need to use a disk editor such as the commercial Acronis Disk Editor. This is a powerful editor that enables the investigator to search through or examine a disk sector by sector, regardless of the file system used.

Example 4.2

Figure 4.4 shows Acronis Disk Editor displaying the partition table of a hard disk.

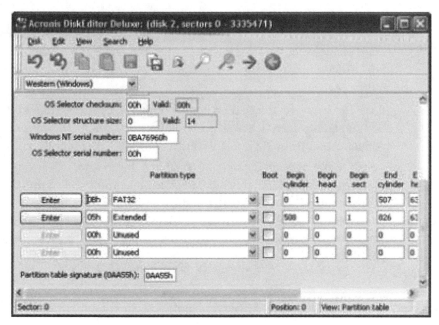

Figure 4.4: Acronis DiskEditor

Such a disk editor is invaluable to an investigator because it enables performing important tasks quickly. The investigator may need to view important disk sectors clearly, search for keywords through the entire hard disk, and save important sectors elsewhere for closer examination.

Disk editors clearly show deleted files because they look at the byte information on the storage device regardless of file system. A keyword search executed on a drive will search through all the data that is deleted, undeleted, or stored in unallocated spaces.

4.2.2 Obtaining Raw Images

 Use dd to create disk or raw images of the data on the target computer.

A raw image is for the same as a disk image. It is very important for investigators to know exactly how to create raw images of the Windows file system so as to examine it on their own computer.

dd, as you have previously seen in the Chapter 3, Linux System Forensics, is a very powerful and feature-rich utility. Developers have modified this open-source utility to add interesting features. You will find a number of dd binaries on the Internet.

Even though the Windows version of dd and the creation of disk images on Windows has been explained here, it is recommended that you use a startup disk with Linux on it. Disks such as FIRE work similar to dd. These tools use Linux as the OS, and the tools on it are the same tools as covered in Chapter 3. The computer must be started using such a disk, and then the Linux environment that comes up should be used to create the boot disks.

 You can download FIRE from http://fire.dmzs.com/.

Creating an image of a logical drive, such as drive C will miss any data outside that partition. You should always image a physical drive. The use of DOS dd is acceptable only if you use a write-block device to keep the evidence on the hard drive safe or if you boot the system from a known startup disk that has been specially modified as described above. Making an image of a network is not practical in most cases because it takes too long. In most cases, the hard drive used for evidence is mounted in an analysis computer that has enough hard-drive space to accept the image, or the machine containing evidence is started in a safe manner as described above with an analysis hard drive added to the system to accept the image files.

Example 4.3

Suppose an investigator, John, wants to create a disk image of a Windows file system so that he can later examine it on a Linux computer. John, however, does not have enough space to store these images before he transfers them to the Linux computer. In such a case, John can use a network connection between the two computers to transfer the disk image as it is generated directly onto the Linux computer:

```
dd.exe if = \\.\c: |nc.exe <investigators machine IP>
<port>
```

The above command looks very different from the way dd is used to make disk images on Linux because the example shows you a real-life situation in which the investigator will not have any space on the target computer to store disk images. Therefore, the investigator pipes the disk images over the network to his own system, which is equipped with enough space to store these disk images. The <port> mentioned in the above command can be any number over 1024. The utility used to pipe data over the network is nc (Netcat), which is provided a port number to listen on. dd.exe pipes the disk-image data over the network to the Linux machine of the investigator when the Windows machine starts to create the disk images.

John then runs the following command on the Linux machine whose port number he had specified while executing dd.exe as above:

```
nc -l -p <port> |dd of=/home/user/ntfs.dd
```

The Netcat running on the Linux machine pipes the data it is receiving into a local file using dd again on its end. This shows you how disk images can be created over the network when space is a concern.

An alternative method is to make disk images on a different drive connected to the target computer.

Example 4.4

Consider the following command:

```
dd if=\\.\c: of=\\.\f:
```

The above example shows you the normal use of dd for making a disk image of the target computer (C drive) and for storing it on (F drive) a device attached to the target computer by the investigator to store disk images.

Investigators usually retain an image-file set as a precautionary measure. They create images in 640MB-sized chunks and archive them to CDs (or DVDs). It is vital that an evidence image be maintained in a safe and unalterable form.

4.2.3 Collecting Information from System Memory

■ Describe the method for collecting and assessing the information in the computer memory.

■ Describe the importance of information stored in the computer memory in a forensic investigation.

The physical memory of a computer is its RAM, which is volatile memory. Therefore, it is important to first take an image of the entire RAM of the system before proceeding on to any other step. This memory can hold information of many types, such as Web sites previously surfed or passwords entered.

Example 4.5

Consider the following command:

```
dd.exe if=\\.\PhysicalMemory
of=d:\images\PhysicalMemory.img bs=4096 --md5sum --
verifymd5 --md5out=d:\images\PhysicalMemory.img.md5
```

This command will create an image of the RAM of a system and store it in d:\images\PhysicalMemory.img. It will also make an md5 signature of the same and store the signature in d:\images\PhysicalMemory.img.md5. The extra option, –verifymd5, will take the md5 signatures of the source and the destination data and compare the two so that integrity of the copied data can be checked.

Example 4.5 uses a different version of dd than the one used for Linux machines. This version of dd has many features used only for forensic purposes, such as a built-in md5 feature.

The version of dd described in this section can be accessed at the following address: http://users.erols.com/gmgarner/forensics/forensic%20acquisition%20utilities-bin-1.0.0.1032%20(beta1).zip.

Access to the file system, bypassing the OS and logical volumes, requires you to have administrative privileges on Microsoft Windows 2000 and Windows XP. If you attempt to image a physical drive using dd and are not logged on as an administrator, dd will present you with a secondary logon dialog. If you enter the appropriate name and password this time, the secondary logon will succeed.

You also need to know the page size being used so as to properly interpret the memory image taken of the system memory.

Figure 4.5 shows the Forensic version of dd making an image of physical memory of a Windows XP machine. The dark lines show that it is RAM being copied and that the md5 of the copy and the original match perfectly. The program internally matches the hashes immediately after it finishes creating the image.

```
C:\WINDOWS\System32\cmd.exe                                          _ □ ×

C:\FORENS~1\bin\UNICOD~2>dd if=\\.\PhysicalMemory of=mem1.img bs=4096 --md5sum -
-verifymd5
Forensic Acquisition Utilities, 1, 0, 0, 1032
dd, 3, 16, 2, 1032
Copyright (C) 2002, 2003 George M. Garner Jr.

Command Line: dd if=\\.\PhysicalMemory of=mem1.img bs=4096 --md5sum --verifymd5
Based on original version developed by Paul Rubin, David MacKenzie, and Stuart K
emp
Microsoft Windows: Version 5.1 (Build 2600.Professional)

07/09/2003  19:39:27 (UTC)
07/09/2003  15:39:27 (local time)

Current User: SAMURAI-JACK\vicky

Total physical memory reported: 261560 KB
Copying physical memory...
C:\FORENS~1\bin\UNICOD~2\dd.exe:
        Stopped reading physical memory:

Attempt to access invalid address.
\43924e006df61c5ccd21026957c05921 [\\\\.\\PhysicalMemory] *C:\\FORENS~1\\bin\\UN
ICOD~2\\mem1.img
\43924e006df61c5ccd21026957c05921 [\\\\.\\PhysicalMemory] *C:\\FORENS~1\\bin\\UN
ICOD~2\\mem1.img

Verifying output file...
\43924e006df61c5ccd21026957c05921 [C:\\FORENS~1\\bin\\UNICOD~2\\mem1.img] *C:\\F
ORENS~1\\bin\\UNICOD~2\\mem1.img
The checksums do match.
Attempt to access invalid address.

Output C:\FORENS~1\bin\UNICOD~2\mem1.img (40960 bytes)
10+0 records in
10+0 records out
```

Figure 4.5: Execution of dd Command

Remember, you can come across cases in which forensic examinations are done on machines that had an inappropriate activity take place days, weeks, or sometimes even years earlier. Running a process like this on an active evidence machine runs a great risk of destroying valuable evidence on the hard drive. Therefore, the assessment of the system memory should be done relative to the situation and risks involved.

Practice Questions

1. What is disk imaging?
2. Which DOS command is used for imaging? Write the syntax.
3. What are disk editors?
4. What is the means of collecting information from system memory?
5. What is the main risk that you would face in collecting data from the system memory?

4.3 Information Analysis in Windows

Analyzing the information that has been gathered is important, because a thorough analysis can generate an information overload, and the investigator must extract only the vital evidence from that information.

4.3.1 Analyzing Logs

 Describe the methods of analyzing different logs files found on a Windows computer.

As explained in the above sections, log information is crucial to any forensic investigation. This topic explains the methods of studying logs maintained by the OS on a Windows computer. In addition to the system logs, a windows computer acting as a Web server or FTP server may have other logs for the respective servers. These logs are in plain text and can be read directly. Also, the format of these log files is similar to their Linux counterparts. The formats of these logs have been explained in the Linux forensics chapter.

Windows keeps its system logs in a binary format, so to read them, you need to use a Windows utility such as Event Viewer, which comes with most Windows installations. Windows logs a lot of information that can be categorized as:

- Application Error Records: Records an error or loggable event in an application.

- System Audit Records: Records a security event such as a wrong password event.

- System Error Records: Records general and critical system errors such as errors at the kernel level.

If you wish to convert all this log information into text files to grep (using the Windows version of the grep utility) through it for information later, you will need to use a freeware utility called dumpel.exe.

The syntax of `dumpel` is given below:

dumpel -f file [-s \\server] [-l log [-m source]] [-e n1 n2 n3...] [-r] [-t] [-d x]

Where:

- -f file: Specifies the file name for the output file. There is no default for –f, so you must specify the file.

- -s server: Specifies the server for which you want to dump the event log. Leading backslashes on the server name are optional.

- -l log: Specifies which log (system, application, or security) to dump. If an invalid log name is specified, the application log will be dumped.

- -m source: Specifies in which source (such as rdr or serial) to dump records. Only one source can be supplied. If this switch is not used, all events are dumped. If a source is used that is not in the registry, the application log will be searched for records of this type.

- -e n_1 n_2 n_3 ...: Filters for event ID n_n (up to ten can be specified). If the -r switch is not used, only records of this type are dumped, but if -r is used, all records except records of this type are dumped. If this switch is not used, all events from the specified source name are selected. You cannot use this switch without the -m switch.

- -r: Specifies whether to filter for specific sources or records or to filter them out.

- -t: Specifies that individual strings are separated by tabs. If -t is not used, strings are separated by spaces.

- -d x: Dumps events for the past x days.

Consider the following examples:

- To dump the system-event log on server \\EVENTSVR to a file named Event.out, use:

  ```
  dumpel -f event.out -s eventsvr -l system
  ```

- To dump the local system-event log to a file named Event.out, but only get RDR events, 2013 use:

  ```
  dumpel -f event.out -l system -m rdr -e 2013
  ```

- To dump the local-application log to a file named Event.out and get all events except ones from the Garbage source, use:

  ```
  dumpel -f event.out -l application -m garbase -r
  ```

Figure 4.6 shows an Event Viewer showing the application-error log.

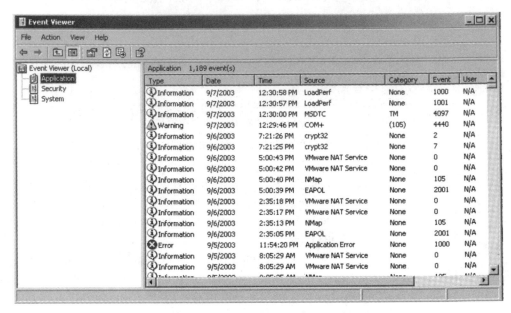

Figure 4.6: Application-Error Log

To view the details of an event, right-click on the event, and choose the **Properties** option. For example, Figure 4.7 shows the properties of an error that occurred during a system process.

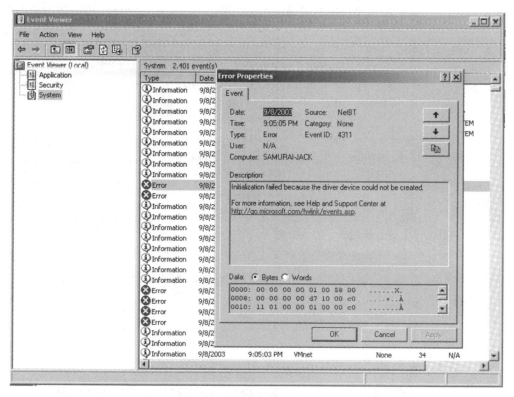

Figure 4.7: Error Properties

4.3.2 Keyword Searches

Use a keyword search to extract valuable information from the vast amounts of data collected by the investigator.

Keywords have to be picked very carefully by the investigator and should be relevant to the investigation being carried out. For example, if an investigator is looking for a spamming backdoor installed by an attacker on a Windows computer, the investigator would not use "e-mail" or "spam" as keywords, but would use "RCPT TO:"or "MAIL FROM:" because these words are part of the Simple Mail Transfer Protocol (SMTP) protocol, which would be used by the spamming Trojan to send spam to other hosts. If a file that should not ordinarily contain these words, such as explorer.exe (Windows shell), contains these words, then it could be understood that the Windows executable has a Trojan horse inserted by the attacker.

Keyword searches can be carried out on the physical disk by means of tools such as the Acronis Disk Editor explained above. For more complex keywords like the ones that contain regular expressions (REGEX), you need to do the queries at the file-system level using tools such as grep for Windows.

grep for Windows can be obtained from http://gnuwin32.sourceforge.net/packages/grep.htm.

Example 4.6

Consider the following command, which will make a grep search through every file on the computer and recursively go through every directory searching for the word "RCPT":

```
grep -r "RCPT" c:\.
```

4.3.3 Finding Evidence from E-mails

Analyze e-mails to piece together an understanding of the incident.

E-mail evidence is crucial to any investigation. E-mails are commonly used as evidence in cases related to computer crime and in cases in which a computer is used. But the latter are not computer crimes as such, but physical-world crimes.

E-mails on a Windows machine can be found in the Microsoft Outlook Explorer application or any of the other e-mail client applications such as Eudora or Lotus Notes.

Today, Web-based e-mail is very popular, and a skilled investigator will be able to locate cached e-mails in the browser caches stored on the system.

Most e-mail clients do not show you most of the mail. They show you only the data and basic header information such as the sender name. Besides this, e-mails contain other headers that can be used to trace the source computer or the server through which they came. In Outlook, to see the entire e-mail, right-click on the e-mail, and choose Properties, as shown in Figure 4.8.

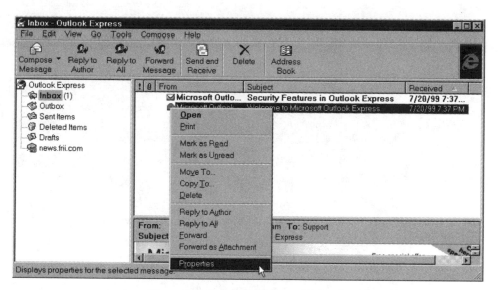

Figure 4.8: E-mail Properties Dialog Box

The screen, as shown in Figure 4.9 appears.

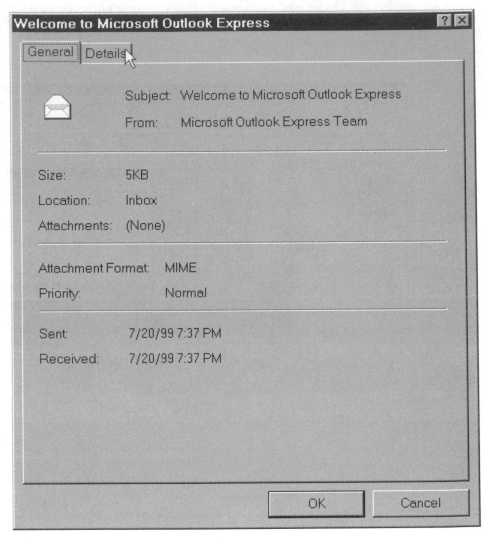

Figure 4.9: E-mail General Properties

Click the **Details** tab to display the e-mail header, as shown in Figure 4.10.

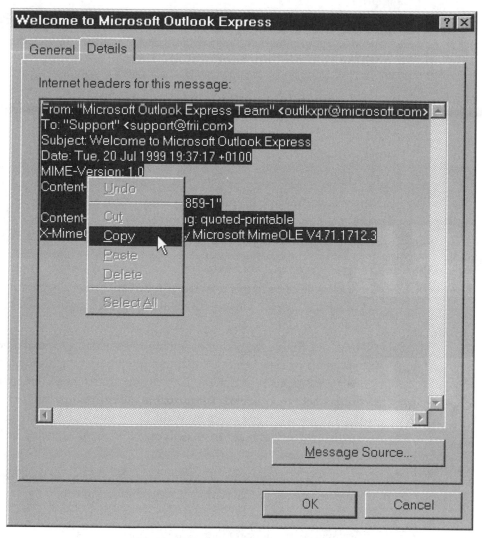

Figure 4.10: Internet Header for the E-mail

Example 4.7

Suppose the e-mail opened by the investigator has the following header:

Received: from unwilling.intermediary.com (unwilling.intermediary.com [98.134.11.32]) by mail.bieberdorf.edu (8.8.5) id 004B32 for <rth@bieberdorf.edu>; Wed, Jul 30 1997 16:39:50 -0800 (PST)

Received: from turmeric.com ([104.128.23.115]) by unwilling.intermediary.com (8.6.5/8.5.8) with SMTP id LAA12741; Wed, Jul 30 1997 19:36:28 -0500 (EST)

From: Anonymous Spammer <junkmail@turmeric.com>

To: victim@bieberdorf.edu

Message-Id: <w45qxz23-34ls5@unwilling.intermediary.com>

X-Mailer: Massive Annoyance

Subject: WANT TO MAKE A LOT OF MONEY???

The various headers in this e-mail are Received, From, To, Message-Id, X-Mailer and Subject. Other mails could have a few more fields such as Priority, X-Sender, and Cc.

- Received: Shows the path the mail took and which servers it came through. You can even find important IP addresses in this header. The above message shows that the e-mail came from tumeric.com, but that is not where it originated. It was sent to the above host by unwilling.intermediary.com on Wednesday, Jul 30, and then received by mail.bieberdorf.edu, which delivered it to victim@bieberdorf.com's e-mail account.

- From: Specifies the account where the message originated. This can very easily be spoofed, so do not rely on it very much.

- Message-Id: A unique identifier assigned to each e-mail, usually by the first mail server it encounters. Conventionally, it is of the form "ABC42IFGH@bieberdorf.edu" where the part before the @ could be anything, and the second part is the name of the machine that assigned the ID. Sometimes, but not often, the Message-Id includes the sender's username. Any e-mail in which the message ID is malformed (for example, an empty string or no @ sign), or in which the site in the message ID is not the real site of origin is probably a forgery.

> ■ X-Mailer (also X-mailer): Software used by the sender to identify itself (as advertising). Most junk e-mail is sent with mailers invented for this purpose. Therefore, this field can provide information for filters.
>
> ■ Subject: Describes the subject of the message.

4.3.4 Evidence from Web Cache, Recycle Bin, and Password File

 Describe the areas to look in for critical clues in a Windows system.

Besides the log files and e-mails, evidential material can also be found in:

■ Web caches and history: Web caches are Web pages saved by the browser software to the local hard disk so that any future access to these pages can be faster. History is a list of previously surfed Web sites and is usually linked to Web cache information so that in the future offline users may go back and see the Web pages they had previously saved.

Web caches have helped investigators uncover even physical crimes. After investigators discovered Web pages about undetectable poisons in a suspect's computer, the police decided to extract and analyze the data further. On analysis, the police concluded that the target had been researching information on a poison called ricen. This made them examine the case and carry out specific tests on the victim. The digital evidence that surfaced led to the arrest of the suspect.

■ Recycle Bin: This is a hidden directory where files deleted in Windows are stored. If a user uses the Shift and Delete key combination to delete a file, then the file will not be saved in the Recycle Bin, but will be instantly deleted. The Recycle Bin is a safety system that prevents accidental deletion of important data. If you delete a file and later realize that you need it, you can simply go to the Recycle Bin and restore the file. Many times deleted files still remain in the Recycle Bin and can be retrieved by an investigator for forensic purposes. As mentioned in the Windows clues section, this utility should not be overlooked during a forensic analysis of a Windows computer system.

Figure 4.11 shows deleted files in the Windows Recycle Bin.

Figure 4.11: Windows Recycle Bin

■ Password files: Windows stores all its password information in special password files. These files can be distinguished with their .PWD extensions. It is important for investigators to know how to extract password information from these files for forensic reasons. For example, if you are called in to investigate a computer that the police seized in a case and you find that the Windows OS running was password protected, then these skills will prove useful. To crack the .PWD files and extract passwords, you will need specific software, for example, l0pht crack commercial software.

This and other hacking and cracking programs (both commercial and underground) do have a place in forensic analysis. They are tools that can be used to harm or amend.

Any unauthorized person using software to crack passwords is subject to legal prosecution.

Figure 4.12 shows l0pht crack breaking Windows password files.

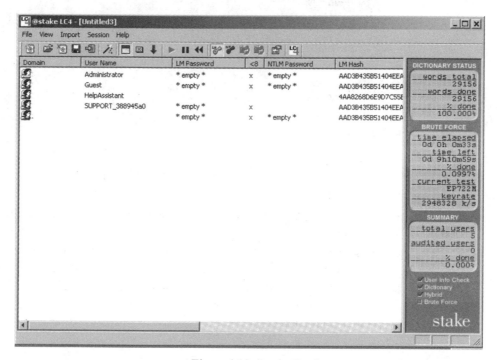

Figure 4.12: Lopht Crack

Besides crack .PWD files provided to it, l0pht crack can even sniff and crack passwords in a network traffic. 10pht crack is useful for dealing with Windows passwords because Windows uses a proprietary encryption algorithm to keep its password secure, and l0pht crack can analyze that algorithm and decrypt the encrypted password.

▨ New Technology File System (NTFS): In NTFS recovering files can be slightly harder because it uses a database to store information about each file. There are also no freeware utilities that can undelete files. Therefore, you can undelete files in NTFS by using a disk editor and searching the entire disk content for keywords that you know existed in the file. You may then find the sector on which the file was stored, and you can save this sector to another disk and recover the deleted file.

Practice Questions

1. List the different types of logs used in Windows.
2. Write the syntax of dumpel.
3. What is the role of keyword searches in an investigation?
4. List the field of e-mail headers.

4.4 Registry Forensics

The registry is a database system in the Windows OS having a tree-like structure. The nodes of the tree structure hold data in a key-value pair format. These key-value pairs can provide you important clues about a crime.

4.4.1 Analyzing System Registry

 Describe how to work through the complexities of the Windows registry to extract clues.

The Windows registry has five top nodes, two of which are the most important to an investigator:

- HKEY_CLASSES_ROOT
- HKEY_CURRENT_USER
- HKEY_LOCAL_MACHINE
- HKEY_USERS
- HKEY_CURRENT_CONFIG

The two important branches for an investigator are HKEY_LOCAL_MACHINE, which stores information local to the target computer such as Windows setting and installed software settings, and HKEY_USERS, which stores important information about users of the Windows system.

The REGEDIT utility can be used in Windows for analyzing the registry. If the investigator's computer is a Linux machine, the KREGEDIT utility can be used. The same team developed KREGEDIT and the Linux KDE GUI. KREGEDIT is used to view the Windows registry on the mounted Windows drive.

Both utilities provide a FIND function that can be used to run keyword searches on the registry. Remember, not all information is stored as text. There is a lot of binary information stored in the system registry. Therefore, keyword searches will not help in looking through values, but will help in searching through keys.

Figure 4.13 shows the interface of the KREGEDIT utility running on a Linux machine analyzing a Windows registry.

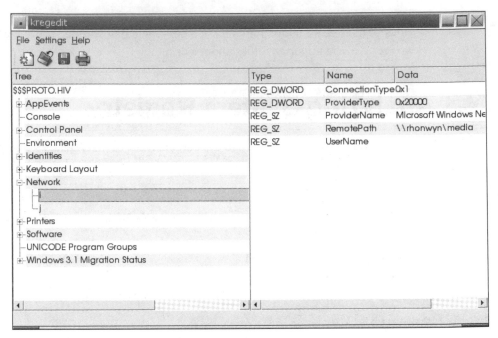

Figure 4.13: KRGEDIT Utility

This utility looks and feels very similar to the Windows REGEDIT utility. Therefore, investigators can familiarize themselves with either. For those who are not familiar with REGEDIT, the left section under the header Tree shows the entire Windows registry tree, and the right section shows the data (key-value pairs) under the Network branch of the registry tree.

Right-click on an entry in the REGEDIT window, and choose modify to display the key (Value name) and its value (Value data), at the top and bottom respectively. Figure 4.14 shows sample Value name and Value data entries.

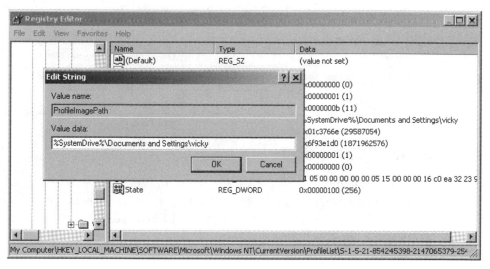

Figure 4.14: Value Name and Data

4.4.1.1 Recently Used Data

Windows records recently accessed programs and files in its recently used setting. Investigators can use these settings to find out the programs recently run on the target machine. This information can be procured from the system registry.

Explorer remembers your most recent entries in many dialog boxes. These lists are called MRUs. An intelligent hacker could have deleted the MRU to avoid detection. The MRUs for Explorer can be found in keys under:
HKEY_CURRENT_USER\Software\Microsoft\Windows\CurrentVersion\Explorer

Table 4.1 lists some sample MRUs.

MRU Key	Value
RunMRU	Start/Run Dialog
RecentDocs	Start/Documents menu
OtherFolder	OtherFolder PowerToys dialog
FindComputerMRU	Find Computer dialog
PrnPortsMRU	Recently used printers

Table 4.1: MRU Description

4.4.1.2 User Information

User information is stored at various places in Windows. Some information is stored in the Windows registry while other information, such as passwords, is stored in the .PWD file explained above. In the registry, you will find user information under HKEY_CURRENT_USER.

Practice Questions

1. What is a registry?
2. What are the two main branches of the Windows registry that can provide valuable information to an investigator?
3. Name two utilities that can be used to view the registry in an interactive manner. What is the difference between these two utilities?
4. What are MRUs?

4.5 Identifying Malicious Programs

There are programs capable of infecting your computer so as to damage data, monitor your computer activity, or invade your privacy. A target computer that you analyze can have any of these malicious programs installed on it. This section describes the methods that you can use to track and analyze such programs and detect the damage caused by them.

4.5.1 Abnormal Processes

 Describe how an investigator can find and analyze abnormal programs.

To check the processes running on the Windows system, you can simultaneously press the Ctl, Alt, and Delete keys and then choose the **Task Manager** option. Click the Process tab in **Task Manager**.

The screen, as shown in Figure 4.15 appears.

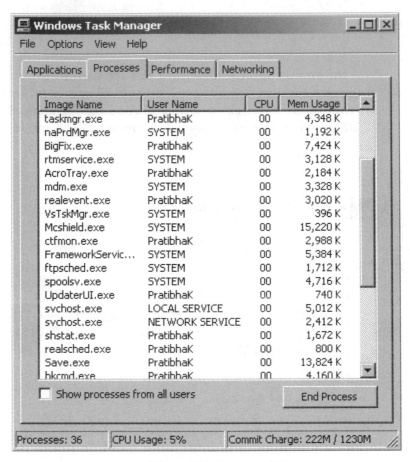

Figure 4.15: Processes Tab

You should carefully scan for unusual programs that have suspicious names or are involved in network activity.

Example 4.8

Figure 4.16 shows the Task Manager Processes window of a system running a suspicious process named Msblast.exe, which has taken 92 percent of the CPU and more than 24 hours of CPU time. This definitely shows it to be a suspicious process that warrants further investigation. This process is a widespread Internet worm, but it could just as well have been a Trojan horse monitoring computer activity and sending it back to a remote listener. In a home PC situation, the Trojan might not cause serious damage, but when it comes to corporate secrets, billions of dollars could be at stake because of this one program stealing or causing damage to corporate secrets.

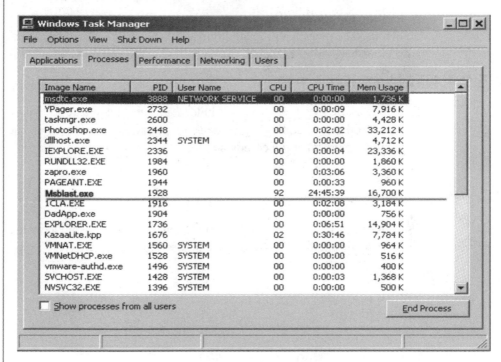

Figure 4.16: Msblast Process

Before you conduct any forensic activity, such as creating an image of the hard drive(s), you should decide whether threat risk is worth the potential value of what might be learned from the forensic activity. The smallest of errors may destroy important material that could have served as valuable evidence.

4.5.2 Reviewing Files

Describe the types of files in Windows that an investigator should analyze.

In addition to the processes, an investigator needs to look out for files that could be malicious. The investigator should find and assess hidden files that appear to be suspicious because of filename, file size, file location, and mac time.

4.5.2.1 Hidden Files

Hidden files are files that have their hidden attribute set to true so that they do not show up in any directory list. Finding hidden files is a simple process. You can type the following command at the command prompt to view the hidden files in your system:

```
dir /ah /s
```

The /ah switch makes dir list all the hidden files, and the /s switch makes dir run recursively through all the directories on the computer.

Figure 4.17 shows a sample listing of hidden files in drive C of a Windows machine.

```
Select C:\WINDOWS\System32\command.com                         _ □ ✕
C:\DOCUME~1\PRATIB~1>dir/ah/s/p
 Volume in drive C has no label
 Volume Serial Number is 24B5-9736

 Directory of C:\DOCUME~1\PRATIB~1

09/01/2003  02:32 PM    <DIR>          Application Data
01/18/2003  01:54 AM    <DIR>          Local Settings
09/05/2003  05:50 PM    <DIR>          NetHood
09/08/2003  09:00 PM         3,932,160 NTUSER.DAT
09/09/2003  11:31 AM             1,024 NTUSER.DAT.LOG
09/08/2003  09:00 PM               280 ntuser.ini
01/18/2003  01:54 AM    <DIR>          PrintHood
09/09/2003  11:13 AM    <DIR>          Recent
05/26/2003  04:30 PM    <DIR>          SendTo
01/17/2003  08:34 PM    <DIR>          Templates
               3 File(s)      3,933,464 bytes

 Directory of C:\DOCUME~1\PRATIB~1\Application Data

08/01/2003  02:32 PM    <DIR>          .
08/01/2003  02:32 PM    <DIR>          ..
01/18/2003  01:54 AM                62 desktop.ini
               1 File(s)             62 bytes
```

Figure 4.17: Viewing Hidden Files

Directories can also be easily hidden, and the above command locates such hidden directories. To make a file or directory hidden, you have to right-click on the file or directory and choose Properties. Inside Properties, you will find the hidden flag, which you need to set to on.

Novice attacks could use the hidden flag to hide executables of rootkits. Most attackers, however, use other techniques to hide their rogue programs. They could give their file an alphanumeric name like MSNT34.EXE and save it to the Windows/System folder. A person who comes across this file would then dismiss it as a Windows-system program.

Another command that can be used to view hidden files is the `attrib` command. It lists all the files with their attributes.

Example 4.9

The attrib command can be executed at the Windows command prompt as:

```
attrib
```

The following output is displayed:

```
A  H   C:\Documents and Settings\vicky\NTUSER.DAT
```

```
   A   H    C:\Documents and Settings\vicky\ntuser.dat.LOG
       SH    C:\Documents and Settings\vicky\ntuser.ini
   A           C:\Documents and Settings\vicky\PUTTY.RND
   A           C:\Documents and Settings\vicky\lwm3.cfg
   A           C:\Documents and Settings\vicky\lw3.cfg
   A           C:\Documents and Settings\vicky\lwext3.cfg
   A           C:\Documents and Settings\vicky\LWHUB.CFG
```

The attrib command can also be used to list hidden files, but this command lists all the files in the directory and their attributes. The files with the H-attribute set are the hidden files.

For example, to view files that do not have their attribute set as hidden, you will use the following command:

```
attrib -H <filename>
```

To view files with the attribute set as hidden, you will use the command:

```
attrib +H <filename>
```

In addition to allowing the viewing file attributes, the attrib command can also be used to hide / unhide (+ = hide, - = unhide) hidden programs.

4.5.3 Trust Relationships and Security Identifiers

 Explain trust relationships and security Identifiers, which are a core part of the Windows security model.

In a Windows network, computers are linked together in what is called a *domain*. When multiple domains need to communicate together, forming a larger network, trust relationships come into play. *Trust relationships* allow single-domain models to be interconnected, which means that they can now share user accounts and other resources across domains. A trust relationship is an administrative and communication link between two Windows server domains. You can create trust relationships using the NT User Manager program.

- A trust relationship between two domains will allow one domain to trust user accounts that already exist in the other domain. This simplifies administration because only one user account for both domains is enough. The benefits of using trust relationships are:

  - All domains can be centrally administered.
  - Users can log on from a domain where they do not have an account.
  - Users can access another domain even when they do not have a user account in that domain.
  - An organization can grow and expand in a managed way.

When two domains trust each other a *two- way trust* exists.

4.5.3.1 Security Identifiers

A security identifier (SID) is a unique value of variable length used to identify a trustee (the user account or group account). Each account has a unique SID issued by an authority such as a Windows domain controller and is stored in a security database. Each time a user logs on to the computer, the OS retrieves the user's SID from the database and places it in the user's access token. The OS uses the SID in the user's access token to identify the user in all subsequent interactions with Windows security.

A user's access token contains the security information for a logon session. Windows creates an access token when a user logs on, and every process executed on behalf of the user has a copy of the token. The token identifies the user, the user's groups, and the user's privileges.

The uses of an SID to a forensic investigator are:

- A SID can be used to identify the perpetrator.
- SIDs are used within Windows to identify a user.
- Windows user logs check SIDs to identify users.

Where to look for SIDs:
HKEY_LOCAL_MACHINE\SOFTWARE\Microsoft\Windows NT\CurrentVersion\ProfileList

Figure 4.18 shows a sample SID in the registry.

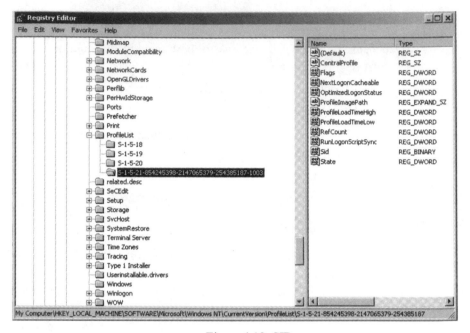

Figure 4.18: SID

When a user logs on, the logon credentials (username/password) are sent from the Windows workstations to the Windows server. The server returns the user's SID, which is then placed in the workstation's registry. Remember, SIDs are never shared between workstations.

The structure of SIDs involves the following:

- Domain Identifier: All values in the series excluding the last value.
- Relative Identifier: The last value identifying the account or group.

Example 4.10

Example of an SID:

S-1-5-21-838281932-1837309565-1144153901-1000

Domain Identifier: S-1-5-21-838281932-1837309565-1144153901
Relative Identifier: 1000

Practice Questions

1. Write the DOS command for viewing hidden files on a computer.

2. What is the function of the attrib command?

3. List the uses of SIDs to an investigator.

4. Identify the domain identifier and relative identifier in:

    S-1-5-21-838281922-1836309564-1144153901-1100

4.6 Basic Forensics Analysis

Analyzing a computer on a Windows system requires a careful study of the file system. NTFS, FAT32, and FAT16 are the native file systems of the Windows OS. Before the file system of the victim computer is accessed, the disk image is created and mounted on a Linux machine, and then different tools are used to study the system on the investigator's computer.

4.6.1 Mounting NTFS/FAT32/FAT16 on Linux

 Describe how to mount Windows' disk images on a Linux computer for analysis.

Mounting the NTFS/FAT32/FAT16 file system on Linux is a simple process that can be easily done with one single command. Here, you need to keep in mind that since you are only mounting the partition, which is most likely a disk image for forensic purposes, you do not want to accidentally modify the data. Therefore, you mount the disk with read-only along with the execution-protection attribute.

For example:

```
mount -t ntfs -o ro, nodev, noexec, loop /root/img1 /mnt/ntfs
```

This command will mount the NTFS file system located in the file /root/img1 on /mnt/ntfs. Now, if you cd into /mnt/ntfs, you will see the NTFS file system.

The word ntfs after the –t command-line switch should be vfat for FAT32 and FAT16 types of Windows file systems.

4.6.2 Analyzing NTFS

Describe how an investigator can analyze an NTFS file system.

You can use the The Sleuth Kit (TASK) to view all aspects of the NTFS file system. If you want to list all the attributes of files, you can use the istat command. Code 4.1 shows the execution of the istat command.

```
# istat -f ntfs ntfs.dd 49
     MFT Entry: 49
     Sequence: 2
     Allocated
     UID: 0
     DOS Mode: File
     Size: 15
     Links: 1
     Name: multiple.txt

     $STANDARD_INFORMATION Times:
     File Modified: Mon Nov 5 19:58:27 2001
     MFT Modified: Mon Nov 5 19:58:27 2001
     Accessed: Mon Nov 5 19:58:27 2001

     $FILE_NAME Times:
     Created: Mon Nov 5 19:57:29 2001
     File Modified: Mon Nov 5 19:57:29 2001
     MFT Modified: Mon Nov 5 19:57:29 2001
     Accessed: Mon Nov 5 19:57:29 2001

     Attributes:
     Type: $STANDARD_INFORMATION (16-0) Name: N/A Resident size:
72
```

```
Type: $FILE_NAME (48-2) Name: N/A Resident size: 90
Type: $OBJECT_ID (64-3) Name: N/A Resident size: 16
Type: $DATA (128-1) Name: $Data Resident size: 15
Type: $DATA (128-5) Name: overhere Resident size: 26
```

Code 4.1: Istat **Command**

The fls command allows you to identify streams in the file system.

```
# fls -f ntfs ntfs.dd
<...>
r/r 48-128-1: test-1.txt
r/r 49-128-1: multiple.txt
r/r 49-128-5: multiple.txt: NEW
r/r 50-128-1: test-2.txt
<...>
```

Code 4.2: fls **Command**

The TASK toolkit cannot analyze security descriptors. It supports only ASCI filenames, and UNICODE compressed and encrypted files are not supported.

Practice Questions

1. Write the syntax of the mount command.
2. What is the command used in TASK to view the attributes of a file?
3. What is the function of fls command?

Summary

- Some of the utilities for data acquisition from a Windows system are:
  - dd command
  - Hex editor
  - Galleta
  - md5deep
  - EnCase
  - FIRE
- Some of the areas in Windows that need to be assessed during an investigation are:
  - Windows registry
  - System files
  - Web-browser caches
  - Program logs
  - Recycle Bin
  - Deleted files
  - File meta-data (a file system's internal information about files)
- Disk editors look at the byte information on the storage device regardless of the file system.
- Information analysis of information on a Windows machine requires examination of:
  - Log files
  - E-mails
  - Web caches
  - Password files
  - Recycle Bin
  - Memory
  - Swap file
  - Slack space
  - NTFS streams

- Network-activity logs
- Application-installed traces

■ Keyword searches on files also provide important clues to a crime.

■ The REGEDIT and KREGEDIT utilities both provide a FIND function, which can be used to run keyword searches on the registry.

- HKEY_LOCAL_MACHINE stores information local to the target computer such as the Windows setting and installed software settings.
- HKEY_USERS stores user information.

■ The dumpel.exe utility converts log information into text files.

■ Trust relationships and security Identifiers are a core part of the Windows security model. Therefore, an investigator needs to have a thorough knowledge of these.

■ Windows forensics involves:

- Mounting Windows disk images on a Linux computer for analysis
- Using the Task toolkit to view all aspects of the NTFS file system

References

Web-Site References

- http://www.opensourceforensics.org/tools/windows.html
- http://www.acronis.de/download/diskeditor/
- http:// http://www.guidancesoftware.com/
  http://www.sysinternals.com/ntw2k/source/regmon.shtml
- http://www.sysinternals.com/ntw2k/source/filemon.shtml

Case Studies

- http://www.securityfocus.com/infocus/1653
- http://www.computercops.biz/article2209.html

Homework Exercises

1. Write a brief explanation of security identifiers and their importance in forensics.

2. Which Windows file stores the password information about users?

3. How would you find out which server an e-mail has passed through?

4. Which Windows files hold registry information?

5. Explain the Windows registry and its uses in forensics.

6. Write a note on Windows trust relationships.

7. Explain what abnormal processes on Windows are?

8. Write a note on the Windows swap file and where is it found.

9. Write brief descriptions at least three Windows forensic tools.

10. Explain Web-browser (Netscape and IE) caches and their importance in a forensic investigation.

11. Explain how you would create a disk image over a network.

12. Explain hidden files in Windows and how you can find them.

13. What is recently used data in Windows?

14. Where is user information stored on a Windows system?

15. Where are SIDs stored in the registry? Give the full path.

Lab Exercises

Exercise 1

Objective

■ Find an e-mail hidden somewhere on a target Windows computer.

■ Analyze the e-mail, and extract the originating server name.

Theory

Many times e-mails hidden inside a computer system can provide valuable clues to the investigator. The investigator needs to:

■ Search for the hidden e-mail in the computer hard disk.

■ Interpret the information in the e-mail header

Problem Statement

Many times an investigator will come upon a computer that was used extensively for e-mailing. Therefore, the investigator knows that a wealth of clues will be found if the e-mails that were present on this computer can be located. Most of the e-mails could have been deleted by the suspect, and some others could have been hidden elsewhere in the hard disk. It is the investigator's responsibility to find an e-mail hidden in this hard disk, locate the e-mail, and analyze the path the e-mail took in reaching its destination. You can assess all this on the basis of information in the e-mail header. The information found in the e-mail headers is useful, because it can be used to obtain log records from the respective servers mentioned in the e-mail headers, through which the e-mail may have passed before reaching its designation.

Lab Setup

A computer with Windows installed and an e-mail, such as below, hidden somewhere on the computer.

```
Received: from unwilling.intermediary.com
(unwilling.intermediary.com [98.134.11.32]) by
mail.bieberdorf.edu (8.8.5) id 004B32 for <rth@bieberdorf.edu>;
Wed, Jul 30 1997 16:39:50 -0800 (PST)
Received: from turmeric.com ([104.128.23.115]) by
unwilling.intermediary.com (8.6.5/8.5.8) with SMTP id LAA12741;
Wed, Jul 30 1997 19:36:28 -0500 (EST)
From: Anonymous Spammer <junkmail@turmeric.com>
To: victim@bieberdorf.edu
Message-Id: <w45qxz23-341s5@unwilling.intermediary.com>
X-Mailer: Massive Annoyance
Subject: WANT TO MAKE ALOT OF MONEY???
```

Code 4.3: E-mail Header

Procedure

Use the different tools for forensic study on a Windows machine. The major challenges in this lab are to:

■ Identify a tool from the ones you learned about in Chapters 3 and 4 that will best serve your purpose and assess whether the chosen tool requires a keyword to locate the e-mail hidden on the system.

■ Use your knowledge about e-mails and headers to come up with a keyword.

■ After locating the hidden e-mail, use your knowledge about e-mail headers to trace the path the e-mail took before reaching its destination.

The report should clearly show the e-mail, the location where it was found, and the severs it passed through.

Conclusion/Observation

Write a report for the forensic analysis that you performed on the program.

You can use the guidelines provided in Chapter 1, Topic: 1.2.4, "Presentation of Data."

Lab Activity Checklist

S. No.	Tasks	Completed	
		Yes	No
1.	Found the hidden e-mail.		
2.	Analyzed the different sections of the e-mail.		

System Forensic Tools

5

The chapter describes the important tools used in a forensic investigation and details the hardware and software that must be included in an investigator's toolkit. The chapter also describes the forensic tools available in The Coroner's Toolkit (TCT) and The @Stack Sleuth Kit (TASK). At the end of the chapter, you will be able to:

- Describe the importance of using different tools in a system forensic study.
- Identify the basic tools required for a system forensic investigation.
- Describe the components of TCT.
- Use the TCT tools in a forensic investigation.
- Describe the components of TASK.
- Use the TASK tools to conduct a system forensic investigation.

5.1 Basic System Forensic Tools

An investigator needs to carry a handy toolkit during the first visit to the site of the crime. This makes the investigation more efficient and quick. The toolkit should include the hardware, software, and other items necessary for a system forensic investigation.

5.1.1 Investigator's Toolkit

 Identify the necessary basic tools for a system forensic investigator.

Some of the important tools that forensic investigators must remember to carry for a system investigation are:

▪ Storage devices: Investigators must have various types of storage devices for storing disk images that they create of the victim's data. For example, a large capacity hard disk or a large number of blank CD-ROMs can be used for storing these disk images. These storage devices can serve as useful assets in the field. CD-ROMs are usually the most convenient and secure way of storing disk images because after a CD-ROM is created, it cannot be altered, and thus the integrity of the data is preserved. Other than these two commonly available tools, investigators may carry a more expensive commercial product such as Image Master. Image Master is a storage device that can be directly connected to the target computer to create the disk images.

Figure 5.1 shows a commercial disk-imaging solution.

Figure 5.1: Commercial Disk-Imaging Solution

Commercial solutions have their advantages and disadvantages. The main advantage is that most of the commercial solutions for disk imaging are hardware solutions and do not require any extra software to be executed on the target computer. In addition, most of these hardware tools are high-speed and large-capacity devices that enable the investigator to generate disk images with minimum trouble. The disadvantage is that commercial solutions tend to be very expensive, and being proprietary products, they are not very flexible. In addition, you need to ensure compatibility with different types of hard disks.

▩ Screwdriver set: This may sound too basic, but many investigators tend to overlook this. A screwdriver set is important because in many situations, an investigator may need to open the computer's casing or attach some device to the computer. In such cases, a simple screwdriver set is handy.

▩ Boot disk for popular operating systems such as Windows 95/98/2000/XP, Linux, Solaris, and Mac: Boot disks are required in case the OS is already in the power-off state, and the investigator suspects that switching on the computer may cause some cleverly hidden program to execute and destroy evidence on the computer. Besides this, some operating systems such as Linux and Solaris have a username/password authentication mechanism that can cause the investigator to waste precious time trying to guess through. A boot disk can usually bypass the password mechanism and give the investigator direct access to the data stored on the computer.

- Required software: Software can be of various types, from simple utilities such as dd for disk imaging to disk editors to a variety of forensic toolkits. The two most popular computer forensics toolkits are TCT and TASK, which will be discussed later in the chapter.

Practice Questions

1. List the components of a toolkit.
2. Besides the components listed in the chapter, what are some other tools that could be beneficial for an investigator?
3. Which of the following media would be a better option for a storage device for investigation purposes? State the reason for your answer.
   a. Large capacity Hard Disk
   b. Blank CDs

5.2 The Coroner's Toolkit

The Coroner's Toolkit (TCT) is a small collection of tools designed to help in the forensic analysis of a computer. It is primarily designed for UNIX systems and was developed by Dan Farmer and Wietse Venema, two independent computer-security specialists. This section covers the relevance and implementation of the tools available in TCT for forensics analysis.

5.2.1 Tools in TCT

- Identify the tools included in TCT.
- Use the TCT tools to conduct a system forensic study.

The tools included in TCT are primarily useful for reconstructing the events that occurred prior to a crime. These tools help determine the course of events with a single static snapshot of a system. Most of these tools are oriented toward data collection and analysis.

The tools that come in TCT are:

- File: Attempts to determine the content type of a file.
- Grave-robber: Main data-gathering program.
- icat: Copies (cat(1)) a file by inode number.
- ils: Lists the file-system inode information.
- Lastcomm: A portable lastcomm command.
- Mactime: The M, A, and C time file-system reporter.
- major_minor: Used internally by the TCT and emits PERL code.
- md5: RSA md5 digital signature tool.
- Pcat: Copies the address space of a running process.
- strip_tct_home: Used internally by the TCT and strips out a variable from various files.
- unrm: Uncovers unallocated blocks from a raw UNIX file system.

5.2.1.1 Installing TCT

The mandatory requirements for using the TCT toolkit are:

- A computer with the Linux operating system
- PERL compiler
- C compiler

 The toolkit can be downloaded from Dan Farmers Web site: http://www.fish.com/tct.

The toolkit comes in a source-code form and can be downloaded as a single compressed file. To install TCT, perform the following steps:

1. Decompress the toolkit with the command:

```
./tar -zxvf <toolkit filename>
```

The above command decompresses the toolkit into the specified directory. After cd'ing into the directory, you will now have to compile the toolkit so that it can be used.

2. Make the directory in which the toolkit has been decompressed your current directory. Then, compile the toolkit with the command:

```
./make
```

The compiled binary versions of the programs are now available. The compiled versions are stored in the /bin directory.

You can now access the tools available in TCT. All the TCT tools are designed based on the fact that to analyze a system, you should be able to examine, fairly extensively, the contents of at least its:

- Disk
- Memory
- Network

5.2.1.2 Grave-Robber

Grave-robber is considered the core component of TCT. It is an intelligent data-capturing tool that understands the structure of a Linux system. After performing automated analysis of the system, this tool proceeds to save only those files that contain important system information from the forensic point of view.

The grave-robber tool captures data and generates two main log files, coroner.log and error.log. The first file logs all the commands as they are executed, and the second file logs the output of the grave-robber program. TCT needs to be run from an account with super-user privileges. Before grave-robber exits, it generates an md5 hash of the output created and stores the hash in the file data/hostname/MD5_all.

Example 5.1

The contents of a sample coroner.log file are given below.

```
2003/09/13 05:22:22 -0400 PIPEFROM_CMD /bin/hostname
2003/09/13 05:22:22 -0400 PIPEFROM_CMD /bin/df /proc
2003/09/13 05:22:23 -0400 PIPEFROM_CMD /bin/uname -s
2003/09/13 05:22:23 -0400 PIPEFROM_CMD /bin/uname -r
2003/09/13 05:22:23 -0400 PIPEFROM_CMD
/export/home/root/tct- 1.12/bin/md5 /bin/acctcom
2003/09/13 05:22:23 -0400 PIPEFROM_CMD
/export/home/root/tct-1.12/bin/md5 /usr/sbin/arp
2003/09/13 05:22:23 -0400 PIPEFROM_CMD
/export/home/root/tct-1.12/bin/md5 /bin/at
2003/09/13 05:22:23 -0400 PIPEFROM_CMD
/export/home/root/tct-1.12/bin/md5 /bin/cat
2003/09/13 05:22:23 -0400 PIPEFROM_CMD
/export/home/root/tct-1.12/bin/md5 /bin/cp
2003/09/13 05:22:23 -0400 PIPEFROM_CMD
/export/home/root/tct-1.12/bin/md5 /bin/crontab
2003/09/13 05:22:23 -0400 PIPEFROM_CMD
/export/home/root/tct-1.12/bin/md5 /bin/date
```

Figure 5.2 shows a sample output that a grave-robber program generates after it analyzes files that may be crucial from a forensic perspective. The figure displays the programs on computers whose md5 signatures are generated by the grave-robber tool. These signatures can later be used to check the integrity of the programs.

```
swordfish.nss.udel.edu - PuTTY                                              _ | □ | x
bash-2.05# ./grave-robber -v |more
Determining OS (in determine_os())
command_to_list: /bin/uname -s
log_item: PIPEFROM_CMD /bin/uname #
command_to_list: /bin/uname -r
log_item: PIPEFROM_CMD /bin/uname -r
OS is: SUNOS5
Preparing the vault...
... in prepare_config_vault()

Starting preprocessing paths and filenames on swordfish...
        preprocessing /export/home/root/tct-1.12/conf/paths.pl
crunching dir   (in crunch)
command_to_list: /export/home/root/tct-1.12/bin/md5 /bin/acctcom
log_item: PIPEFROM_CMD /export/home/root/tct-1.12/bin/md5 /bin/acctcom
crunching dir   (in crunch)
command_to_list: /export/home/root/tct-1.12/bin/md5 /usr/sbin/arp
log_item: PIPEFROM_CMD /export/home/root/tct-1.12/bin/md5 /usr/sbin/arp
crunching dir   (in crunch)
command_to_list: /export/home/root/tct-1.12/bin/md5 /bin/at
log_item: PIPEFROM_CMD /export/home/root/tct-1.12/bin/md5 /bin/at
crunching dir   (in crunch)
command_to_list: /export/home/root/tct-1.12/bin/md5 /bin/cat
log_item: PIPEFROM_CMD /export/home/root/tct-1.12/bin/md5 /bin/cat
crunching dir   (in crunch)
command_to_list: /export/home/root/tct-1.12/bin/md5 /bin/cp
log_item: PIPEFROM_CMD /export/home/root/tct-1.12/bin/md5 /bin/cp
crunching dir   (in crunch)
command_to_list: /export/home/root/tct-1.12/bin/md5 /bin/crontab
log_item: PIPEFROM_CMD /export/home/root/tct-1.12/bin/md5 /bin/crontab
crunching dir   (in crunch)
command_to_list: /export/home/root/tct-1.12/bin/md5 /bin/date
log_item: PIPEFROM_CMD /export/home/root/tct-1.12/bin/md5 /bin/date
crunching dir   (in crunch)
--More--
```

Figure 5.2: Output of Grave-Robber

The -v option is used with the grave-robber program/tool to make the output more verbose, that is, with more detail. This option tells the grave-robber program to output everything line by line.

5.2.1.3 Mactime

After you run the grave-robber program, you can use the *mactime* program. MACtimes of files are an asset to any forensic investigation and at the same time are highly volatile since almost all file operations such as reading or writing will change them.

The mactime tool can directly obtain MACtimes. The syntax of mactime is:

> ./mactime <date>

In the syntax, the date argument specifies the display of only those files whose MACtimes have changed since the specified date.

Example 5.2

To use the mactime program to display a list of files modified since 9/11/2003, type the following command:

```
./mactime 9/11/2003
```

The output of this command is:

(date   time   size MAC perms owner group file)[....]

Apr 05 99 04:05:00 5506499 m.. -rw-rw-rw- root   mailman /var/log/syslog.7

Apr 10 99 04:05:00 6389017 m.. -rw-rw-rw- root   mailman /var/log/syslog.6

Apr 12 99 01:04:39 3978 .a. -rw------- root   mailman /var/log/arclog

Apr 12 99 14:10:15 3978 m.c -rw------- root   mailman /var/log/arclog

[....]

Mactime allows you to perform the following:

- Identify the files that have been touched/run/modified during a system boot
- Determine the file activity during the day or slice of time

Example 5.3

Figure 5.3 shows the list of files that have had their MACtimes changed since 9/12/2003.

Figure 5.3: Result of Mactime Tool

5.2.1.4 File Command

The file command identifies the type of a file using multiple tests. The syntax of the file command is:

file <filename>

In the syntax, filename specifies the file(s) that needs to be read.

Example 5.4

To assess the file type of /bin/wget, type the following command:

```
file /bin/wget
```

The following output is displayed:

```
/bin/wget: ELF 32-bit MSB executable SPARC Version 1,
dynamically linked, stripped
```

5.2.1.5 icat

The icat tool is similar to the UNIX cat command. The main purpose of this tool is to output the contents of a file. However, unlike the UNIX cat command, icat does not locate the file on the basis of its name, but provides output based on the inode number of the file. A device needs to be specified along with the inode number so that icat can search the device for a file with the specified inode.

The syntax of the icat command is:

./icat <storage device> <inode number>

This opens the named device and copies the files with the specified inode numbers to the standard output. The arguments that can be used with icat are:

- ▒ -f (fstype): Specifies the file-system type of the device. The default file-system type is system dependent. For example, in UNIX, the default type is ufs (Berkeley fast-file system), and in Linux, the default file-system type is ext2fs (second extended file system).

- ▒ -h: Skips over spaces in files so that the absolute-address information is lost. This option saves space when you are copying sparse files.

- ▒ -H (default): Copies spaces in files as blank blocks so that the absolute-address information is preserved. This option wastes disk space when you are copying files.

- ▒ -v: Enables the verbose mode for debugging purposes. It enables more specific data to be displayed about the current operation in progress.

#	Course	Section	Subsection
15.	Advanced Forensics	8.1. Kernel Module Forensics	8.1.2 Rootkits
16.	Advanced Forensics	8.1. Kernel Module Forensics	8.1.2 Rootkits
17.	Advanced Forensics	8.2 Malware Dissection and Analysis	N/A
18.	Advanced Forensics	8.2 Malware Dissection and Analysis	8.2.1 Process Wiretapping
19.	Advanced Forensics	8.2 Malware Dissection and Analysis	8.2.4 Filemon and Regmon
20.	Advanced Forensics	8.3 Analysis of /proc Directory	8.3.1 Structure of /proc Directory
21.	Linux System Forensics	5.3 The @Stack Sleuth Kit	5.3.2 Tools in TASK
22.	Linux System Forensics	3.1 Linux Forensics Essentials	3.1.1 Disk Imaging
23.	Linux System Forensics	5.2 The Coroners Toolkit	5.2.1 Tools in TCT
24.	Linux System Forensics	3.3 Investigation on Linux	3.3.2 Analyses of File System
25.	Linux System Forensics	5.2 The Coroners Toolkit	5.2.1 Tools in TCT
	Security Systems as Forensic Tools	7.2 Firewall as Evidence Collector	7.2.1 Role of Firewall in System Forensics
26.	Security Systems as Forensic Tools	7.3 Intrusion Detection as a Forensic Tool	7.3.1 Role of IDS in System Forensics
	Security Systems as Forensic Tools	7.1 Vulnerability Assessment Tool	7.1.1 Role of Vulnerability Assessment Tools in Investigation
	Security Systems as Forensic Tools		7.3.1 Role of IDS in System Forensics

Handwritten annotations (margin):
- Tool used to Boot/install or binaries to compute
- Tools Cmd Bar detecting installer boot test
- KSTAT - S
- Melingofware
- Cmd line tool — freeze or execute — kill cmd stop
- Regmon will do
- file
- pcat
- inode numb represent
- i/f On remove
- icat
- pcat
- reserve all after all packets
- Masa Reaction which ... root A B
- scan t... can fig use to Storage K
- Web we scan repr... thru sta... gei
- felscon-ty security — krotole
- NIDS example

47. Cover Check Rd... Sentant list of
48.

Response, 1/20/04

| Linux System Forensics | 3.1 Linux Forensics Essentials | 3.1.1 Disk Imaging |
| Linux System Forensics | 3.1 Linux Forensics | 3.1.1 Disk Imaging |

- Device: Disk special file or regular file containing a disk image. On UNIX systems, raw-mode disk access may give better performance than block-mode disk access. LINUX disk-device drivers support only block-mode disk access.

- inode: Concatenates the contents of all specified files as arguments.

Example 5.5

The following command copies the contents of a file with the inode number 383 to a standard output.

```
./icat /dev/dsk/c0t0d0s7 383
```

Figure 5.4 shows the output of this command.

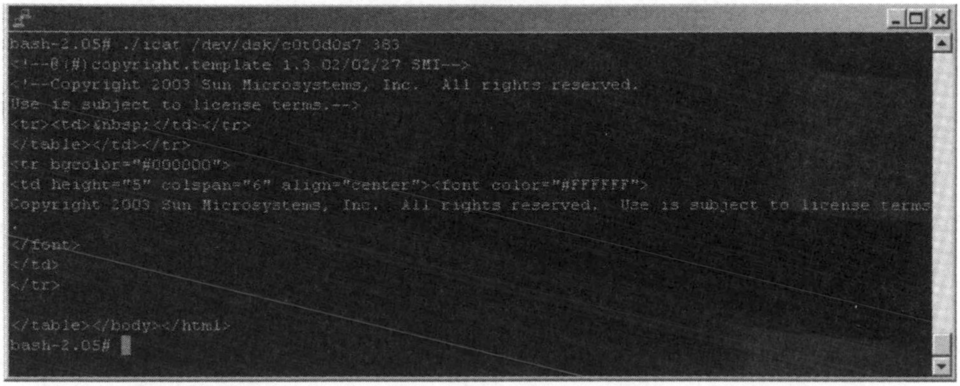

Figure 5.4: Result of icat Command

5.2.1.6 ils

This tool lists information about the inodes on a system. The syntax of the ils command is:

ils [-eorv] [-f fstype] device [start-stop ...]

ils [-aAlLvzZ] [-f fstype] device [start-stop ...]

The ils tool is similar in operation to the ls command, except that ils lists all the inodes in the directory. You need to specify a device from which ils can extract inodes. The arguments that can be used with ils are:

- -e: Lists every inode in the file system.

- -f fstype: Specifies the file-system type of the device. The default file-system type is system dependent. For example, in UNIX systems, the default type is ufs, and in Linux, the default file-system type is ext2fs.

- -o: Lists only inodes of the deleted files that are still open or are executable. This option is a shorthand notation for –aL. For more information on -aL, refer to the fine-controls section.

- -r: Lists only inodes of the deleted files. This option is a shorthand notation for -LZ.

- -v: Sets the verbose mode to on.

- Device: Disk special file or regular file containing a disk image. On UNIX systems, raw-mode disk access may give better performance than block-mode disk access. LINUX disk device drivers support only block-mode disk access.

- start-stop: Examines the specified inode number or number range. The start, the stop, or the -stop may be omitted.

Fine controls:

- -a: Lists only allocated inodes. Allocated nodes belong to files with at least one directory entry in the file system and to deleted files that are still open or executing.

- -A: Lists only unallocated inodes. These nodes belong to files that no longer exist.

- -l: Lists only inodes with at least one hard link. These nodes belong to files with at least one directory entry in the file system.

- -L: Lists only inodes without any hard links. These nodes belong to files that no longer exist and to removed files that are still open or executing.

- -z: Lists only inodes with zero status-change time. Presumably, these inodes were never used.

- -Z: Lists only inodes with non-zero status-change time. Presumably, these nodes belong to files that still exist or existed in the past.

The output begins with a two-line header that describes the data origin. This is followed by a one-line header that lists the names of the data attributes and then the actual attributes.

The fields in an inode entry for any file are:

- st_ino: Shows the inode number.

- st_alloc: Shows the allocation status, such as 'a' for an allocated inode and 'f' for a free inode.

- st_uid: Shows the owner user ID.

- st_gid: Shows the owner group ID.

- st_mtime: Shows the UNIX time (seconds) of last file modification.
- st_atime: Shows the UNIX time (seconds) of last file access.
- st_ctime: Shows the UNIX time (seconds) of last inode status change.
- st_dtime: Shows the UNIX time (seconds) of file deletion (LINUX only).
- st_mode: Shows the file type and permissions (octal).
- st_nlink: Shows the number of hard links.
- st_size: Shows the file size in bytes.
- st_block0, st_block1: Shows the first two entries in the direct block-address list.

Example 5.6

Figure 5.5 shows the output of the ils command. In the example, this command is used to list information about inode 7865.

Figure 5.5: Result of ils Command

Example 5.7

In this example, ls –i lists the files in a directory along with their inode numbers, as shown in Figure 5.6.

Figure 5.6: Result of ls-i Command

5.2.1.7 pcat

The pcat utility is another powerful tool in TCT. This utility copies process memory, that is, the RAM used by a program when it executes. This memory is very useful to an investigator because it contains information, such as passwords and file names.

The syntax of the pcat command is:

pcat [-hHv] [-m mapfile] process_id

The pcat tool is similar to the cat command in UNIX. However, in pcat, the file to be opened and displayed is not a typical file, but a process or program that is currently executing in memory. pcat extracts the program from RAM and not from the hard disk or the floppy disk. As memory is not continuous, there can be empty spaces in memory known as memory holes. pcat does not copy the holes, but extracts an exact image of the process. The pcat command requires the process ID (PID) of the process for copying.

The options available with pcat are:

- -h (default): Skips over holes in the process address space so that the absolute-location information is lost.

- -H: Keeps holes in the process address space so that the absolute-location information is unchanged. This option writes the holes to the output file.

- -m mapfile: Prints the process memory map to a map file, one entry per line. Each map entry consists of a region start address and the first address beyond that region.

Addresses are separated by a space and are printed as hexadecimal numbers (0xhhhh).

■ -v: Enables the verbose mode for debugging purposes.

5.2.1.8 Unrm and Lazarus Programs

unrm is a program that extracts all information from a UNIX file system that is not currently allocated. Therefore, if you have a system with a 10GB hard disk and only store 2GB of files on it, unrm will return 8GB of data to you.

unrm is run-as pre-processor to Lazarus, which is a data-recovery tool that recovers the deleted data from the data collected by unrm.

To run unrm, you first have to identify an appropriate system device from which to recover the unallocated disk space. Then, you need to identify a safe place to store the retrieved raw data. For example, the following command stores the raw data in the file allocated.dat.

```
./unrm /dev/hda1 > unallocated.dat
```

5.2.1.8.1 Lazarus

Lazarus works on a binary file and tries to break it down into smaller data blocks. While splitting the data into blocks, it tries to locate the type of data in the block. For example, it identifies whether the block contains HTML data or an image file. The size of the blocks is 1KB by default and can be changed by modification of the variable $BLOCK_SIZE in the TCT configuration file lazaraus.cf.

It is recommended that you first create separate directories to separate all the output data. The following options can be used with Lazarus:

■ -h: Creates an HTML-based view that can be used with any browser for easy access to individual blocks.

■ -D <dir>: Directs that all blocks be written to the given directory.

■ -H <dir>: Directs the main HTML files that provide the overall navigation to the specified directory.

■ -w <dir>: Directs that all other HTML output be written to the specified directory.

■ Binary file: Serves as input for Lazarus.

> Example 5.8
>
> In the following command, Lazarus operates on the disk image unrm-20010303.out and tries to extract meaningful files from it.
>
> ```
> . /lazarus -h -H . -D /spare/tct-data/blocks -w
> /spare/tct-data/html unrm-20010303.out
> ```
>
> Lazarus takes a considerable amount of time to split the input file into smaller blocks. The directory output for the same is:
>
> ```
> $ ls -la /spare/tct-data
> total 24
> drwxr-x---    4 kpk wheel 1024 Mar   3 22:36.
> drwxr-xr-x  23 kpk wheel 1024 Mar   3 22:25.
> drwx------    2 kpk wheel 2048 Mar   3 22:36 blocks
> drwx------    2 kpk wheel 5120 Mar   3 22:36 html
> -r--r-----    1 kpk wheel 545611359 Mar   3 22:16 unrm-
> 20010303.out
> -r--r-----    1 kpk wheel  233 Mar   3 22:35 unrm-
> 20010303.out.frame.html
> -r--r-----    1 kpk wheel   11359 Mar   3 22:36 unrm-
> 20010303.out.html
> -r--r-----    1 kpk wheel 1472 Mar   3 22:35 unrm-
> 20010303.out.menu.html
> ```
>
> This list shows the files that Lazarus has created in the /spare/tct-data directory.

The output files of the Lazarus command are stored on the disk according to a specific naming scheme. The first section of the name is based on numbers of the actual analyzed block. The second part is a single letter, as listed in Table 5.1, that specifies the file type. The two sections are separated by a period (.). All the files that contain text data are given the .txt extension, and the files that contain graphics are given a .gif or .jpg extensions.

Key letter	Explanation
A	archive
C	C code
E	ELF
f	sniffers
H	HTML
I	image/pix
L	logs
M	mail
O	null
P	programs
Q	mail
R	removed
S	lisp
T	text
U	uuencoded
W	password file
X	exe
Z	compressed
.	binary
!	sound

Table 5.1: Key Letter for File Type

The output an HTML page contains links to all the files arranged as a map. Access to specific files can be gained by clicking these links. The map uses the same approach to represent the type of each file as used to assign appropriate file names. The first block of a sequence of blocks is given an uppercase letter. The number of blocks represented within the map is encoded to save space. The first character represents one block or 0, the second 0 to 2 blocks, the third 0 to 4, and so on. If five characters are displayed for one type, this reflects 0 to 32 blocks of data.

Practice Questions

1. Write the syntax of icat?

2. What is the function of pcat?

3. List a few advantages of using grave-robber.

4. Write the command for viewing the files whose MACtimes have been modified since 9/9/2003.

5. What are the two logs generated by grave-robber?

5.3 The @Stack Sleuth Kit

TASK is a set of UNIX command-line programs that form a media-management tool for forensic and other types of file-system analysis. With built-in capabilities to handle file systems such as NTFS, FAT, FFS, EXT2, and EXT3, this tool can be used even on operating systems that do not have native support for these file systems. The TASK tools work in a non-intrusive manner and can extract any amount of data from file-system data blocks. These tools allow you to study the layout of disks and other media. Because the tools do not rely on the operating system to process the file systems, deleted and hidden content is also shown.

Support for popular and widely found partitions of different architectures such as DOS, BSD partitions (disk labels), MAC partitions, and Sun slices (Volume Table of Contents) are included in the Sleuth Kit. The tools can actually analyze data and detect and extract partitions and file systems for analysis.

5.3.1 Autopsy Forensic Browser

 Describe the functions of Autopsy Forensic browser.

It is very tedious to analyze an entire file system using command-line tools. The Autopsy Forensic browser is a graphical interface to the collection of tools that make up the Sleuth Kit. This GUI tool allows you to easily conduct an investigation and case management. Autopsy provides case management, image integrity, keyword searching, and other automated operations.

The Autopsy Forensics browser has the following features:

- Examines file system images generated by the dd command.
- Provides built-in support for the NTFS, FAT, FFS, EXT2FS, and EXT3FS file systems even when the host operating system does not have native support for it.
- Outputs both allocated and deleted file names.
- Outputs the details of file-system structures.
- Outputs the details and contents of all attributes for NTFS files, including all Alternate Data Streams.

- Creates timelines of file activity, import logs, and other time-based events. The timelines can be imported into a spreadsheet for creating graphs and reports.

- Provides time-based tools that take a time zone and time skew as arguments so that you can view times as they existed on the original host.

- Contains a hash lookup tool that creates an index of hash database files and performs quick lookups using a binary search algorithm. The tool supports the NIST NSRL, Hash Keeper, and custom databases that have been created with the md5sum or md5deep tools.

 More information on NIST NSRL and Hash Keeper can be accessed at http://www.nsrl.nist.gov and http://www.hashkeeper.org respectively.

- Allows you to view locally mounted file systems.

- Files structured according to file type. For example, all graphic images and executables can be easily located and examined. While they are sorted, hash databases can be consulted to ignore known files, such as system files that are trusted, and to alert when known rogue programs, such as known rootkits or inappropriate photographs are located. The extensions of files are also verified to identify hidden files. Pages of thumbnails can be made of graphic images for quick analysis by the forensic investigator.

- Allow tools to be run on a live UNIX system during incident response. These tools will show files that have been hidden by rootkits and will not modify the access time of files that are viewed.

- Allows partitions of different platforms to be extracted and analyzed using the media-management tools.

Autopsy has an HTML-based interface. You can connect to the Autopsy server from any operating system using any Web browser such as Netscape Communicator or Microsoft Internet explorer. It also provides a File Manager-like interface and displays information about deleted data and file-system structures. The Autopsy interface has the following sections:

- Case management: Investigations are grouped as cases that can contain one or more target computer systems. Each computer system can have its own time-zone setting and clock setting so that the times shown are the same as the original user would have seen. Each host can contain one or more file-system images for analysis.

■ File analysis: This analyzes the disk image with respect to the files and directories contained in them. This mode shows the file-system contents in the same way as normal users see them. Because the program itself is analyzing and interpreting disk-image information, you will be able to see files, such as removed files and hidden files and directories that you normally would not have seen.

Figure 5.7 shows Autopsy browser. The screen in Figure 5.7 consists of two distinct sections. The first section shows the files that Autopsy has found, including deleted files. The second section displays the contents of the currently selected file, including information such as the type of file.

FILE ANALYSIS	DATA UNIT	META DATA	IMAGE DETAILS	KEYWORD SEARCH	FILE TYPE	HELP	CLOSE

						?	X

Figure 5.7: Autopsy File Search

ALL DELETED FILES	r/r	lights.exe	1996.10.14 05:38:00 (GMT)	2002.06.13 21:08:40 (GMT)	2002.06.13 21:08:40 (GMT)	35600	48
✓	r/-	LMREPL.EXE	0000.00.00 00:00:00 (GMT)	0000.00.00 00:00:00 (GMT)	0000.00.00 00:00:00 (GMT)	0	0
EXPAND DIRECTORIES	r/r	LMREPL.EXE	1996.10.14 05:38:00 (GMT)	2002.06.13 21:08:40 (GMT)	2002.06.13 21:08:45 (GMT)	86800	48
✓	r/r	loadfix.com	1996.10.14 05:38:00 (GMT)	2002.06.13 21:08:40 (GMT)	2002.06.13 21:08:40 (GMT)	1131	48
	r/r	loadfix.com	1996.10.14 05:38:00 (GMT)	2002.06.13 21:08:40 (GMT)	2002.06.13 21:08:40 (GMT)	1131	48
✓	r/r	locale.nls	1996.10.14 05:38:00 (GMT)	2002.06.13 21:08:40 (GMT)	2002.06.13 21:08:40 (GMT)	145290	48
	r/r	locale.nls	1996.10.14 05:38:00 (GMT)	2002.06.13 21:08:40 (GMT)	2002.06.13 21:08:40 (GMT)	145290	48

ASCII (display - report) * Strings (display - report) * Export * Add Note
File Type: MS-DOS executable (EXE), OS/2 or MS Windows

```
String Contents Of File: C:/system32/krnl386.exe


<NEt
KERNSTUB: Error during boot
KERNEL
  GPV
/Microsoft Windows Kernel Interface Version 3.10
  ROMBIOS
 GLOBALUNLOCK
WOWCLOSECOMPORT
GLOBALDOSALLOC
GETPRIVATEPROFILEINT
```

Figure 5.7: Autopsy File Search

■ File-content analysis: The contents of files can be viewed as plain text or by extraction of the TEXT strings from binary files for basic executable analysis. Care is taken to ensure that the HTML browser does not process the file content. For example, an HTML file would be shown as raw text and not the formatted version. Figure 5.8 shows how file-context analysis is done in Autopsy. The screen in the figure consists of two columns. The left-most column has a field for entering the Master File Table (MFT) number of the file that needs to be viewed. The right column displays all the information about that file, including filename, file size, MACtimes, attributes, and file type.

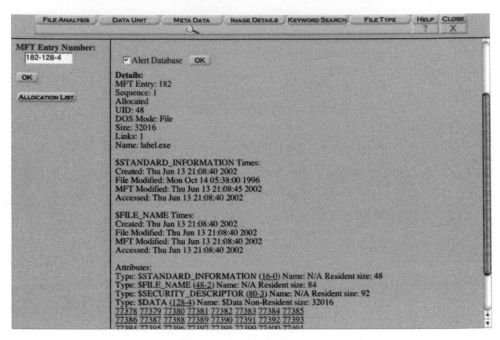

Figure 5.8: File Information

 The Master File Table in NTFS contains entries that describe all system files, user files, and directories.

- Hash databases: Examining a file system that potentially contains thousands and thousands of files can be a voluminous job. To make analysis of all files in the file system easier, the Sleuth kit matches file hash signatures with the files in popular hash databases such as NIST National Software Reference Library (NSRL) and other user-created databases. These databases categorize files as good and bad to help narrow down the search to exactly the correct rogue programs.

- Reports: The software can generate plain-text reports for data files and other file-system structures. This enables you to quickly make consistent data sheets during the investigation.

- Logging: Audit logs are created on an investigator level, case level, or host level so that previous operations by the investigator can be easily recalled. The commands and operations carried out by the investigator using the Sleuth Kit are also logged.

- Client/server model: Autopsy is HTML-based. Therefore, you do not have to be on the same system as the file-system images. This allows multiple investigators to use the same server and connect from their personal systems.

5.3.2 Tools in TASK

 Identify the functions of the TASK tools.

The tools available in TASK are:

- fstat: Displays file-system information and statistics, including layout, sizes, and labels.

- ffind: Finds the allocated and unallocated file names that point to a given meta-data structure. In addition, it finds the allocated and unallocated file names that point to a given inode data structure

- fls: Lists the allocated and deleted file names in a particular directory.

- icat: Extracts the data units of a file that is specified by its inode data address instead of the file name, as done with the cat command.

- ifind: Locates the inode information that has a given file name pointing to it or the inode information that points to a given data unit.

- ils: Displays the inode data structures and their contents in a pipe-delimited format.

- istat: Displays information and statistics about a given inode in an easy-to-read format.

- dcat: Extracts the contents of a given data unit.

- dls: Lists the details about data units and extracts the unallocated space of the file system.

- dstat: Displays the statistics about a given data unit in a format that is easy to read.

- dcalc: Calculates where the data in the unallocated space image (from dls) exists in the original image. This is used when evidence is found in unallocated space.

- mmls: Displays the layout of a storage device, including the unallocated spaces. The output identifies the type of partition and its length, which makes it easy to use the dd command to extract partitions. The output is sorted based on the starting sector, thus making it easy to identify gaps in the layout.

Practice Questions

1. List the file systems that can be assessed by TASK.

2. The graphical interface of TASK is known as _____.

3. List the different sections of Autopsy browser.

4. What is a MFT entry?

5. What is the role of file analysis in Autopsy?

Summary

- Some of the basic tools that forensic investigators must remember to carry for a system investigation are:
  - Storage devices
  - Screwdriver set
  - Boot disks for prominent operating systems such as Windows 95/98/2000/XP, Linux, Solaris, and Mac
  - Required software
- TCT is a collection of tools designed to help in the forensic analysis of a computer. It includes:
  - File
  - Grave-robber
  - icat
  - ils
  - Lastcomm
  - mactime
  - major_minor
  - md5
  - Pca
  - strip_tct_home
  - unrm
  - Lazarus
- TASK is a collection of UNIX-based command-line file systems and media-management forensic analysis tools.
- The Autopsy Forensic browser is a graphical interface to the tools in TASK. It enables you to conduct an investigation more easily.
- The Autopsy Forensic browser has sections for:
  - Case management
  - File analysis
  - File-content analysis

- Use of hash databases
- Generation of reports
- Information logging
- Client/server model

References

- www.snort.org
- http://www.fish.com/tct
- http://www.sleuthkit.org

Homework Exercises

1. Name and explain any three tools that are a part of TCT.

2. Explain how the Lazarus and unrm commands can be used to recover files.

3. Explain the three TASK tools.

4. Write a short explanation of the unallocated space in a storage device.

5. Write a brief description of the TCT and TASK toolkits, and explain why they are important.

6. Explain process memory, and identify the tool used to copy it.

7. Name the file systems that TASK supports. Specify how you can use TASK to mount a disk image with a file system NTFS.

8. Explain the output of the Lazarus command.

9. Who developed The Coroner's Toolkit? Describe some of the known bugs in TCT.

10. List and explain the steps involved in installing TCT.

11. Write the syntax for and describe the use of `ils`.

12. Write a short explanation of mactime tool.

13. Write a note on the unrm command, and explain its use.

14. What are hash databases?

Lab Exercises

Exercise 1

Objective

- Use the TCT and TASK toolkits to conduct a system forensic study.
- Install and compile TCT and TASK toolkits.
- Use the individual tools to analyze the file system of the computer.

Problem Statement

Consider yourself an investigator who has to analyze the hard disk of a suspect. First, it is important to devise a plan about how you will proceed in the investigation. You need to determine how TCT and TASK toolkits can be used in a forensic investigation. Further, you need to determine how the tools found in toolkits such as grave-robber and Autopsy can be used to scan the hard disk, generate reports, and collect data that can be submitted as evidence.

Use the tools in TCT and TASK to:

- Find the files modified in the last 24 hours
- Access application-log files (for example, Web-server and mail-server logs)
- Access system log files (user lists and generate-kernel logs)
- Retrieve deleted files and their contents

Lab Setup

- Computer running Linux 7.1
- The Coroner's Toolkit (TCT)
- TASK toolkit

Procedure

To install TCT, follow the steps given below:

1. Change the directory to /root/MyTools.

   ```
   cd /root/MyTools
   ```

2. Extract the TCT tar file.

```
tar -zxvf tct-1.12.tar.gz
```

3. Change the current directory to the TCT directory.

```
cd tct-1.12
```

4. Compile TCT.

```
make
```

TCT will be installed on the system.

To install TASK follow the steps given below:

1. Change the directory to /root/MyTools.

```
cd /root/MyTools
```

2. Extract the TASK tar file.

```
tar -zxvf Sleuthkit-1.65.tar.gz
```

3. Change the current directory to the TASK directory.

```
cd sleuthkit-1.65
```

4. Compile TASK.

```
make
```


To install Autopsy Forensic browser, follow the steps given below:

1. Change the directory to /root/MyTools.

```
cd /root/MyTools
```

2. Extract the Autopsy tar file.

```
tar -zxvf autopsy-1.74.tar.gz
```

3. Change the current directory to the Autopsy directory.

```
cd autopsy-1.74
```

4. Compile Autopsy.

```
make
```

5. Enter the path of Sleuth directory.

```
/root/MyTools/sleuthkit-1.65
```

6. Enter 'n' for NIST NSRL option.

7. Enter the path of the Evidence locker directory.

```
/root/MyTools/EL
```

8. Type the following command

```
./autopsy
```

The address as shown below is displayed:

```
http://localhost:9999/2561578881495220669/autopsy
```

9. Copy the address and open it in browser such as Mozilla. The screen as shown in Figure 5.9 is displayed.

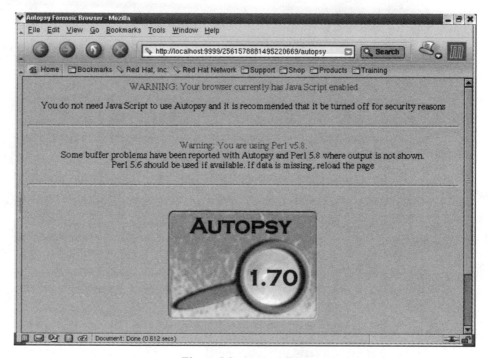

Figure 5.9: Autopsy Browser

You can now perform various tests and analysis through autopsy. You can create a new case for investigation as shown in Figure 5.10.

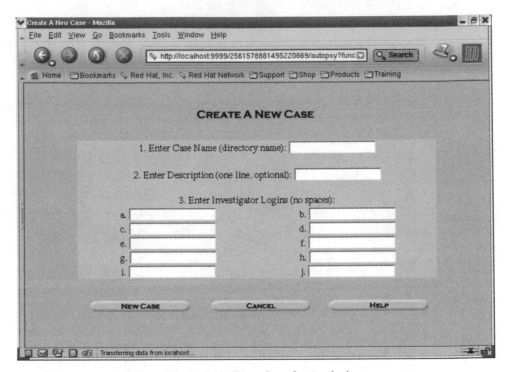

Figure 5.10: Enter Case for Analysis

Use grave-robber and Autopsy to gather information about your computer system.

Use the tools in TCT and TASK to:

- Find the files modified in the last 24 hours
- Access application-log files (for example, Web-server and mail-server logs)
- Access system log files (user lists and generate-kernel logs)
- Retrieve deleted files and their contents

You are free to experiment with the other programs found in the toolkit if you wish to further investigate any files.

Conclusion/Observation

You must have all the outputs of the tools in both the toolkits saved as evidence.

Lab Activity Checklist

S. No.	Tasks	Completed	
		Yes	No
1.	Downloaded and compiled TCT and TASK		
2.	Used all the tools including grave-robber		
3.	Gathered all the output generated by these tools		

Exercise 2

Objective

- Use Lazarus and Unrm to locate deleted files on the system.

Problem Statement

Locate the deleted file on the system.

For this exercise you will need to use a small disk such a floppy. Make sure the floppy is formatted with the ext2 file system. Now copy a few random files into this floppy and copy a file that you have created also into this floppy. Name this file myfile.in. Sync the file system and then delete the file from the floppy.

The above mentioned scenario has simulated a hacker destroying files on your computer. A floppy has been used as the recovery tools that you use would generate huge amounts of data if used on a hard disk. Consider that you are an investigator. Your task is to locate this deleted file.

Lab Setup

TCT (including lazarus and unrm utilities)

Procedure

1. For this exercise, first create a virtual floppy disk. This floppy is formatted with the ext2 file system. This virtual floppy functions exactly like a real floppy. Use the following commands to create the floppy:

   Create an image of a floppy.

   ```
   dd if=/dev/zero of=floppy.img bs=512 count=2880
   ```

   Let this image be formatted with the ext2 file system.

   ```
   mkfs -t ext2 floppy.img
   ```

   Mount this image to the file system.

   ```
   mount -o loop floppy.img /mnt/floppy
   ```

2. Copy a few random files into this floppy.

   ```
   cp  /root/MyTools/xyz   /mnt/floppy
   ```

3. Create a file named myfile.in and copy this file in the floppy.

```
cp myfile.in /mnt/floppy
```

4. Run "sync" on your system so that the file system flushes its read and write buffers.

```
sync
```

5. Delete the file myfile.in from the floppy.

6. Use Lazarus and Unrm to locate these files.

7. Provide the path to the instructor, where the deleted file is located.

Conclusion/Observation

The TCT utilities Lazarus and unrm are used to collect information on deleted files, which are usually located on the unallocated space on the computer.

Lab Activity Checklist

S. No.	Tasks	Completed	
		Yes	No
1.	Created and then deleted the file myfile.in		
2.	Used lazarus and urnm to locate the deleted file		

System-Forensics Legal Policies

6

In addition to the techniques of conducting examinations of systems and networks, investigators should be aware of the legal issues, policies, and laws pertaining to system crimes and presentation of digital evidence in court. This chapter provides insight into some of the important legal issues, policies, and laws that have a bearing on system forensics. At the end of the chapter, you will be able to:

- Examine the various legal provisions that are necessary for internal investigations.

- Explain the laws influencing real-time monitoring in the context of the electronic environment.

- Describe the liability of Internet Service Providers.

- Explain the legal issues that confront corporate and law-enforcement agencies in the course of system forensics.

6.1 Protecting the Network

System forensics has become an extremely important area of study from the legal viewpoint, as its primary aim is to assist the investigation of breaches of security or of certain criminal acts. It is extremely important that the processes and procedures followed in the course of system forensics can be legally tenable and hold up in a court of law.

The legal aspects related to system forensics are gradually assuming tremendous significance. At a time when the entire world is moving toward becoming an information society, information technology, computers, computer systems, and computer networks are assuming an important role in daily life. It is imperative that the investigator understand the various legal aspects and policies that impact system forensics. The United States has a robust framework in the context of system forensics.

This section deals with the various laws and policies pertaining to system forensics.

6.1.1 Legal Permissions Related to Internal Investigations

 Describe the different legal permissions related to internal investigation.

When a computer network is set up, its security is one of the major concerns. In the event of any breach of security, internal investigations of the network often must be performed.

The point for consideration is whether any legal permissions and restrictions are required in internal investigations. The relevant provision in this regard is the Fourth Amendment to the U.S. Constitution. The Fourth Amendment states:

"The right of the people to be secure in their persons, houses, papers, and effects, against unreasonable searches and seizures, shall not be violated, and no Warrants shall issue, but upon probable cause, supported by Oath or affirmation, and particularly describing the place to be searched, and the persons or things to be seized."

It is important to appreciate that the Fourth Amendment is not at all applicable to a search conducted by private parties who are not acting as agents of the government. Fourth Amendment is directed against the potential misuse by the Government and/or its agents. In a typical case, when a private individual, who is not a part of the state machinery or an instrument of the same, acts on his own accord and conducts a search and makes the results available to a law-enforcement agency, the Fourth Amendment of the U.S. Constitution does not deal with the facts and circumstances of such a case. So, in defining a network, an individual is entitled to conduct internal investigations for ensuring the network's security.

6.1.2 Legal Issues Related to Real-Time Monitoring

 Describe the legal issues relating to real-time monitoring of systems and networks.

In the context of electronic media consisting of computers, computer systems, and/or computer networks, the existing legal provisions provide a detailed framework. This regulatory framework is embodied in Electronic Communications Privacy Act, 1986. This law regulates the conditions impacting real-time monitoring.

 Title III of the Electronic Communication Privacy Act provides for prohibition of interception and disclosure of wire, oral, or electronic communications. This legislation defines electronic communications as:

"any transfer of signs, signals, writing, images, sounds, data, or intelligence of any nature transmitted in whole or in part by a wire, radio, electromagnetic, photo electronic or photo optical system that affects interstate or foreign commerce, but does not include:

(A) any wire or oral communication;

(B) any communication made through a tone-only paging device;

(C) any communication from a tracking device (as defined in section 3117 of this title); or

(D) electronic funds transfer information stored by a financial institution in a communications system used for the electronic storage and transfer of funds; "

It also defines the term "intercept" to mean: *the aural or other acquisition of the contents of any wire, electronic, or oral communication through the use of any electronic, mechanical, or other device.*

Section 2511 provides that, except as otherwise specifically provided in this chapter, any person who commits the stipulated acts will be punished or subject to suit. The stipulated conditions, which have been brought within the ambit of penalty by section 2511, include the following acts by any person who:

"(a) intentionally intercepts, endeavors to intercept or procures any other person to intercept or endeavor to intercept, any wire, oral, or electronic communication;

(b) intentionally uses, endeavors to use, or procures any other person to use or endeavor to use any electronic, mechanical, or other device to intercept any oral communication when –

> *(i) such device is affixed to, or otherwise transmits a signal through, a wire, cable, or other like connection used in wire communication; or*

> *(ii) such device transmits communications by radio, or interferes with the transmission of such communication; or*

> *(iii) such person knows, or has reason to know, that such device or any component thereof has been sent through the mail or transported in interstate or foreign commerce; or*

> *(iv) such use or endeavor to use*

>> *(A) takes place on the premises of any business or other commercial establishment the operations of which affect interstate or foreign commerce; or*

>> *(B) obtains or is for the purpose of obtaining information relating to the operations of any business or other commercial establishment the operations of which affect interstate or foreign commerce; or*

> *(v) such person acts in the District of Columbia, the Commonwealth of Puerto Rico, or any territory or possession of the United States;*

(c) intentionally discloses, or endeavors to disclose, to any other person the contents of any wire, oral, or electronic communication, knowing or having reason to know that the information was obtained through the interception of a wire, oral, or electronic communication in violation of this subsection;

(d) intentionally uses, or endeavors to use, the contents of any wire, oral, or electronic communication, knowing or having reason to know that the information was obtained through the interception of a wire, oral, or electronic communication in violation of this subsection; or

(e)   *(i) intentionally discloses, or endeavors to disclose, to any other person the contents of any wire, oral, or electronic communication, intercepted by means authorized by sections 2511(2)(a)(ii), 2511(2)(b)-(c), 2511(2)(e), 2516, and 2518 of this chapter,*

(ii) knowing or having reason to know that the information was obtained through the interception of such a communication in connection with a criminal investigation,

(iii) having obtained or received the information in connection with a criminal investigation, and

(iv) with intent to improperly obstruct, impede, or interfere with a duly authorized criminal investigation."

If a person commits any of the acts stated above, then that person will be fined or imprisoned for not more than five years or both. However, a person who engages in the commission of the various acts detailed above will further be subject to suit by the federal government in the court of competent jurisdiction.

Having so stated, the law makes a list of exceptions to the above-stated general principles. The law lays down some of the conditions in which real-time monitoring and/or interception is permitted.

The law makes it clear that it will not be unlawful for an operator of a switchboard, an officer, an employee, or an agent of a provider of wire or electronic communication services, whose facilities are used in the transmission of a wire or electronic communication. The services are used to intercept, disclose, or use communication in the normal course of employment while engaged in any activity, which is a necessary incident to the rendition of the service or to the protection of the rights or property of the provider of that service. However, a provider of wire communication service to the public shall not utilize service for observing or random monitoring, except for mechanical or service quality control checks.

The most important provision of law in Section 2511 states:

"Notwithstanding any other law, providers of wire or electronic communication service, their officers, employees, and agents, landlords, custodians, or other persons, are authorized to provide information, facilities, or technical assistance to persons authorized by law to intercept wire, oral, or electronic communications or to conduct electronic surveillance, as defined in section 101 of the Foreign Intelligence Surveillance Act of 1978, if such provider, its officers, employees, or agents, landlord, custodian, or other specified person, has been provided with -

(A) a court order directing such assistance signed by the authorizing judge, or

(B) a certification in writing by a person specified in section 2518(7) of this title or the Attorney General of the United States that no warrant or court order is required by law, that all statutory requirements have been met, and that the specified assistance is required . . ."

The court order and the certificate together must set forth the time period during which the provision of the information, facilities, or technical assistance is authorized and required.

However, the law clearly provides that no provider of wire or electronic communication service, officer, employee, or agent thereof, or landlord, custodian, or other specified person shall disclose the existence of any interception or surveillance or the device used to accomplish the interception or surveillance with respect to which the person has been furnished a court order or certification under this chapter, except as may otherwise be required by legal process and then only after prior notification to the Attorney General or to the principal prosecuting attorney of a State or any political subdivision of a State, as may be appropriate.

Any such disclosure shall render the person liable for civil damages. Under the Electronic Communications Privacy Act, it is not unlawful for an officer, employee, or agent of the Federal Communications Commission, in the normal course of his employment and in discharge of the monitoring responsibilities exercised by the Commission in the enforcement of Chapter 5 of Title 47 of the United States Code, to intercept a wire or electronic communication, or oral communication transmitted by radio, or to disclose or use the information thereby obtained.

The law also specifically provides that where a person, is a party to a wire, oral and electronic communications or if one of the parties of the said communications, has given prior consent of such interception, it shall not be unlawful for such a person, not acting under the color of law to intercept a wire, oral or electronic communication.

An officer, employee, or agent of the Untied States is permitted to conduct electronic surveillance as defined under the Foreign Intelligence Surveillance Act, 1978 in the normal course of his official duties as authorized by that Act. The law permits interception or access of electronic communications made through an electronic communications system that is configured so that such electronic communication is readily accessible to the general public.

Further, it has been declared that it shall not be unlawful for any person to intercept any radio communications, which is transmitted:

(I) by any station for the use of the general public, or that relates to ships, aircraft, vehicles, or people in distress;

(II) by any governmental, law enforcement, civil defense, private land mobile, or public safety communications system, including police and fire, readily accessible to the general public;

(III) by a station operating on an authorized frequency within the bands allocated to the amateur, citizens band, or general mobile radio services; or

(IV) by any marine or aeronautical communications system;

The applicable law makes it not unlawful for any person to engage in any conduct

(i) to intercept any wire or electronic communication the transmission of which is causing harmful interference to any lawfully operating station or consumer electronic equipment, to the extent necessary to identify the source of such interference; or

(ii) for other users of the same frequency to intercept any radio communication made through a system that utilizes frequencies monitored by individuals engaged in the provision or the use of such system, if such communication is not scrambled or encrypted. Further the law categorically states that it shall not be unlawful,

  (a) to use a pen register or a trap and trace device; or

  (b) for a provider of electronic communication service to record the fact that a wire or electronic communication was initiated or completed in order to protect such provider, another provider furnishing service toward the completion of the wire or electronic communication, or a user of that service, from fraudulent, unlawful or abusive use of such service.

Further, the law stipulates in the context of computer, computer system and computer networks that it shall not be unlawful under this chapter for a person acting under color of law to intercept the wire or electronic communications of a computer trespasser transmitted to, through, or from the protected computer, if:

(I) the owner or operator of the protected computer authorizes the interception of the computer trespasser's communications on the protected computer;

(II) the person acting under color of law is lawfully engaged in an investigation;

(III) the person acting under color of law has reasonable grounds to believe that the contents of the computer trespasser's communications will be relevant to the investigation; and

(IV) such interception does not acquire communications other than those transmitted to or from the computer trespasser.

Section 2512, categorically prohibits the manufacture, distribution, possession and advertising of wire, oral or electronic communication intercepting devices. Only in specific cases are the manufacture, distribution, possession and advertising of wire, oral or electronic communication interception devices permissible.

Section 2515 is extremely important in the context of real-time monitoring and System Forensics. Section 2515 states:

"Whenever any wire or oral communication has been intercepted, no part of the contents of such communication and no evidence derived therefrom may be received in evidence in any trial, hearing, or other proceeding in or before any court, grand jury, department, officer, agency, regulatory body, legislative committee, or other authority of the United States, a State, or a political subdivision thereof if the disclosure of that information would be in violation of this chapter"

Section 2516 provides the provisions for authorization of interception of wire, oral or electronic communication. The Attorney General, Deputy Attorney General, Associate Attorney General, or any Assistant Attorney General, any acting Assistant Attorney General, or any Deputy Assistant Attorney General or acting Deputy Assistant Attorney General in the Criminal Division specially designated by the Attorney General, may authorize an application to a Federal judge of competent jurisdiction.

This application is normally moved for, authorizing or approving the interception of wire, oral or electronic communication by the Federal Bureau of Investigations. This is done when such interception may provide or has provided evidence of the offences given in the detailed list of offences U/S 2516. These are offences, which are punishable with death or by imprisonment for more than one year and include offences, which involve murder, kidnapping, robbery, extortion, and also include offences, which are punishable under different provisions of law.

On hearing the application and after going through its contents, the judge may pass an exparte order, authorizing or approving interception of wire, oral, or electronic communications within the territorial jurisdiction of the court in which the judge is sitting (and outside that jurisdiction but within the United States in the case of a mobile interception device authorized by a Federal court within such jurisdiction), if the judge determines on the basis of the facts submitted by the applicant that:

(a) there is probable cause for belief that an individual is committing, has committed, or is about to commit a particular offense enumerated in section 2516;

(b) there is probable cause for belief that particular communications concerning that offense will be obtained through such interception;

(c) normal investigative procedures have been tried and have failed or reasonably appear to be unlikely to succeed if tried or to be too dangerous;

(d) there is probable cause for belief that the facilities from which, or the place where, the wire, oral, or electronic communications are to be intercepted are being used, or are about to be used, in connection with the commission of such offense, or are leased to, listed in the name of, or commonly used by such person.

Further, the Electronic Communication Privacy Act makes it clear that each order authorizing or approving the interception of any wire, oral, or electronic communication shall specify:

- the identity of the person, if known, whose communications are to be intercepted;
- the nature and location of the communications facilities as to which, or the place where, authority to intercept is granted;
- a particular description of the type of communication sought to be intercepted, and a statement of the particular offense to which it relates;
- the identity of the agency authorized to intercept the communications, and of the person authorizing the application; and
- the period of time during which such interception is authorized, including a statement as to whether or not the interception shall automatically terminate when the described communication has been first obtained.

The law has provided for a detailed procedure to be followed by the law enforcement agencies while doing interception. The contents of any wire, oral, or electronic communication intercepted by any means authorized by law shall, if possible, be recorded on tape or wire or other comparable device. The recording of the contents of any wire, oral, or electronic communication shall be done in such a way as will protect the recording from editing or other alterations.

Immediately upon the expiration of the period of the order, or extensions thereof, such recordings shall be made available to the judge issuing such order and sealed under his/her directions. Custody of the recordings shall be wherever the judge orders. They shall not be destroyed except upon an order of the issuing or denying judge and in any event shall be kept for ten years.

Practice Questions

1. Is the Fourth Amendment to the U.S. constitution applicable to private investigations by private entities?

2. Which law affects real-time monitoring in the context of the electronic medium in the United States?

3. Is interception of every electronic communication barred by the Electronic Communications Privacy Act, 1986?

6.2 Internet Service Provider Issues

Internet Services Providers (ISPs) are the service providers who provide Internet access to the general public, corporations, and other legal entities. Although ISPs are providers of access, they are not in a position to control the nature of the content of the Internet. Their position can be equated with that of pipeline services providers who provide connection to the main pipeline. What flows in the pipe is neither within their control, nor can it be controlled by them. That is why in all the courts of the world, ISPs are normally considered as mere access providers and are not liable for information flowing through the pipe. This is the legal position that exists in the United States as well. This section describes the legal issues pertaining to ISPs.

6.2.1 Working with ISPs

 Describe the legal issues related to downstream and upstream service providers.

When Internet service providers are informed about certain content that is obscene, obnoxious, defamatory or derogatory, the access providers are duty bound to remove the said offending content. If they fail to do so, they can be open to legal action. In the context of forensic policies and laws, these ISPs play an important role in terms of providing access to their logs to law-enforcement agencies. This is normally provided upon production of the appropriate court order. Under the provisions of the Electronic Communications Privacy Act, 1986, a person or entity providing an electronic communications service to the public shall not knowingly divulge to any person or entity the contents of a communication, while in electronic storage by that service.

Section 2703 of Title 18 specifies that the contents of communications are to be disclosed pursuant to an order of a court of competent jurisdiction.

6.2.2 International Legal Issues

 Describe the legal liability of ISPs.

The legal liability of ISPs remains the same worldwide, as it exists in the United States. However, in the International scenario, one does come across another viewpoint and perspective, which is the provision propagated by countries like India. India is one of the few countries in the world that actually makes ISPs liable for all third-party data and information made available by them on their services, barring two specific cases. Section 79 of the Indian Information Technology Act, 2000 states:

"79. Network service providers not to be liable in certain cases.

For the removal of doubts, it is hereby declared that no person providing any service as a network service provider shall be liable under this Act, rules or regulations made thereunder for any third party information or data made available by him if he proves that the offence or contravention was committed without his knowledge or that he had exercised all due diligence to prevent the commission of such offence or contravention.

Explanation.—For the purposes of this section, —

(a) 'network service provider' means an intermediary;

(b) 'third party information' means any information dealt with by a network service provider in his capacity as an intermediary ;"

Since ISPs are intermediaries, they fall within the category of network service providers.

In a global context, the importance of the fact that ISPs need to cooperate with law enforcement agencies in the investigations of offences can hardly be overstated. This is, of course, qualified by the argument that due processes of law must be followed in this regard.

Practice Questions

1. When an Internet Service Provider is notified of some obnoxious material on the service, what is the provider expected to do?

2. Can an Internet Service Provider disclose the contents of communications without any legal authorization?

3. What is the position of liability of Internet Service Providers in the U.S.?

6.3 Law Enforcement Agencies

Law-enforcement agencies have a direct relationship with system forensics because with each passing day, crimes relating to computer systems and computer networks are constantly increasing. Law-enforcement agencies are repeatedly called in to detect, investigate, and prosecute system crimes. These agencies are repeatedly called upon to regularly update their system forensics skills so as to meet the constant challenges presented by system criminals or cyber criminals.

6.3.1 Handling Law Enforcement

 Describe the role of law enforcement in system forensics.

Electronic communications, computer systems, and computer networks are devices of communication and recording. The communications and recordings that are a result of advanced technology are as much deserving of privacy as are ordinary posts or paper records. These are the property or the business of the people who are involved in them and must be given respect. U.S. laws protect citizens' privacy, and specifically the privacy of their computer systems and electronic mail is protected under the Fourth Amendment, as well as under several federal laws, namely the "Wire Tap Act," and provisions dealing with unlawful access to stored communication.

However, the law also provides exceptions through which the law can either intercept or alternatively procure already stored communications and other records of importance. In criminal investigations, the law-enforcement officers abreast of the technological advances and aware of the importance of system analysis are enabled to search and seize electronic equipment that may contain information that can be used as evidence in also in court and for investigation. The crime in question can be one inherently related to computers, for example, Internet child pornography or electronic embezzlement or fraud. Alternatively, the crime could be one in which the computer system or Internet is not actively used, but either the crime is planned through the Internet or records are kept on a computer system. In both these cases, it becomes very important for the system to be seized or procured or for it to be safe from any kind of tampering. The FBI uses the following statutes most frequently to investigate computer-related crimes:

- 18 U.S.C. 875 Interstate Communications: Including Threats, Kidnapping, Ransom, Extortion
- 18 U.S.C. 1029 Possession of Access Devices
- 18 U.S.C. 1030 Fraud and Related Activity in Connection with Computers
- 18 U.S.C. 1343 Fraud by Wire, Radio or Television
- 18 U.S.C. 1361 Injury to Government Property
- 18 U.S.C. 1362 Government Communication Systems
- 18 U.S.C. 1831 Economic Espionage Act
- 18 U.S.C. 1832 Trade Secrets Act

The relevant Federal statutes governing computer search and seizure and electronic evidence gathering include the following:

- 18 U.S.C. § 2510. Definitions
- 18 U.S.C. § 2511. Interception and Disclosure of Wire, Oral, or Electronic Communications Prohibited
- 18 U.S.C. § 2701. Unlawful Access to Stored Communications
- 18 U.S.C. § 2702. Disclosure of Contents
- 18 U.S.C. § 2703. Requirements for Governmental Access
- 18 U.S.C. § 2705. Delayed Notice
- 18 U.S.C. § 2711. Definitions
- 42 U.S.C. § 2000aa. Searches and Seizures by Government Officers and Employees in Connection with Investigation or Prosecution of Criminal Offenses

6.3.2 Pros and Cons of Law Enforcement

 Describe the pros and cons of law enforcement.

Whenever a crime occurs, it is always a tough decision whether to call in a law-enforcement agency or not. This is not an easy decision and normally depends on numerous factors that have a bearing upon the issue at hand.

Normally, it is a good step to call in the law-enforcement agency to investigate if the management of a company senses a crime. This is prudent as it not only assists the law-enforcement agency in detecting a crime, but also in investigations and prosecution of crimes involving computers, computer systems, and/or computer networks. Further, this is also seen as a manifestation of good corporate governance.

Actually, there is an increasingly large number of companies that are not willing to report a crime involving computers, computer systems, and/or computer networks. Companies today consider that the reporting of such crimes can negatively affect their image and reputation. It may also result in disclosure of information that may not be in the best interests of the company to disclose.

Reporting to the law-enforcement agency also entails an increase in expenditure because the concerned computers or computer systems become out of bounds for the company. The company then has to invest in extra computers. In addition, there are a number of other hidden expenses that a company will incur on reporting a matter to the law-enforcement agency. In many cases, the cost of actual damage may be less than the expenditures following the reporting of a crime to the law-enforcement agency, thereby making it economically unviable to report the matter.

A large number of companies are in the trust business, and they do not want to report such a crime involving systems because it may call into question their trustworthiness, credibility, and security. Many companies are also media shy and often do not report such matters for the fear of getting undesirable media coverage and publicity.

A number of factors ultimately go to affect a corporate decision about whether to report the matter to a law-enforcement agency. The management of a company weighs all the pros and cons before arriving at the decision that best suits their interests and businesses.

6.3.3 Information Disclosure

 Describe the legal issues related to information sharing, voluntary disclosure, and response to government requests.

Information on the Internet or on a computer system can be procured by law enforcement officers, thanks to voluntary disclosure by persons who hold or possess such information. The more popular way is to force or compel disclosures--not through the use of brute force, but through the use of legal means to compel disclosure.

6.3.3.1 Compelled Disclosure

Most information on the Internet is provided through Internet Service Providers (ISPs), and it is the best way to get information. There are five mechanisms, laid down by the Electronic Communications Privacy Act, by which a "government entity" can compel a provider to disclose certain kinds of information:

- Subpoena
- Subpoena with prior notice to the subscriber or customer
- Court order
- Court order with prior notice to the subscriber or customer
- Search warrants

There are some kind of information of which disclosure can be compelled by the use of a subpoena. This kind of information is merely basic subscriber information, that is, name, address, local and long distance telephone connection record or record of sessions times and durations, length of service (including the starting date) and types of service utilized, and telephone or instrument number or other subscriber number or identity, including any temporarily assigned network address, means, and source of payment for such service (including any credit card or bank account number).

The second kind of subpoena differs from the first only in that the enforcement officials are aware of the screen name under which the alleged criminal operates or is operating in order to carry out a computer crime. In such a case, most jurisdictions or local/state laws require special that permission be acquired from the court before an ISP is served with a request to obtain information that reveals a person's actual identity.

Crime investigation can also entail looking into e-mails received by clients of a provider. The law does not permit the unopened mails to be intruded upon by investigators; however, investigators can subpoena opened e-mails from a provider, but only if they comply with the notice provisions.

For obtaining the complete contents of any suspect account, investigators of a cyber-crime have to acquire a search warrant. Investigators can obtained a search warrant by showing probable clause as is done in any ordinary criminal investigation.

6.3.3.2 Voluntary Disclosure

Internet Service Providers provide two kinds of services:

- Services that are available to the public
- Services that are not available to the public

Providers who fall into the latter category may freely disclose both contents and other records related to stored communications. A provider of such services may reveal information to the government agencies, and if the provider does so willingly and voluntarily, there is no need for the law-enforcement officials to seek and obtain a legal order, subpoena, or warrant compelling such information. In the eyes of law, what is being provided freely needs no compulsion.

Providers whose services are open to the public are restricted from free disclosure of client information. The Electronic Communications Privacy Act prevents such providers from interfering in or voluntarily disclosing information about clients. However, the act also allows exceptions to the rule. The ECPA, in section 2702, lays down the situations in which a provider may voluntarily disclose information. Such a disclosure may be made when:

- The disclosure is necessarily incident to the rendition of the service or to the protection of the rights or property of the provider of the service.

- The disclosure is made to a law-enforcement agency, where the contents that have been disclosed were obtained inadvertently by the service provider service and such information appears to pertain to the commission of crime.

- The provider reasonably believes that an emergency involving immediate danger of death or serious physical injury to any person requires the disclosure of the information without any delay.

- Such disclosure is mandated by the Child Protection and Sexual Predator Punishment Act of 1998, Title 42, Section13032.

- The disclosure is made to the intended recipient of the communication, with the consent of the intended recipient or sender, to a forwarding address or pursuant to a court order or legal process.

Where the information in question is not the content of a communication to a client, but customer records, the service provider may, under the ECPA, voluntarily disclose such information to a government entity.

The response to a governmental request for information depends on the peculiar facts and circumstances of each case. If the request has been made following due process of law, then, as per the law, the concerned information would have to be handed over to the government.

6.3.4 Collecting Evidence for Trial

 Describe the different legal issues related to use of evidence in court trials.

System forensics and evidence are inter-connected and inter-related. System forensics helps in ensuring the authenticity of evidence related to computers, computer systems, or computer networks.

6.3.4.1 Reliable Evidence

The underlying principle of law related to system forensics is that the techniques, procedures, and methodologies adopted for forensic purposes must be legally followed and should withstand the test of law. This is possible when investigators follow the mandatory legal requirements. The law makes it imperative for the investigators to ensure the authenticity and veracity of the electronic document/computer hardware that they seize and investigate. This is essential not only to link an accused person to the actual crime, but also to ensure the creditability of the evidence. It can be done only when the requisite procedure of law is followed to the fullest possible extent. The inability to comply with the law casts doubt on the evidence collected, and it does not persuade either the court or the law-enforcement agency to rely on the evidence.

The time-honored principle in system forensics is that adequate safeguards and precautions must be kept and followed. These safeguards include adopting precautions at the time of seizing the computer or computer systems and establishing the chain of custody. This means that before entering a computer system, the investigator must make sure that all due processes of law have been followed.

The computer concerned must be seized in the presence of witnesses, and the hard disk must not be tampered with. On the contrary, a mirror copy of the said hard disk must be made, and the investigations should be carried out on such mirror copies. Numerous technologies are available in the public domain to facilitate the tasks of law-enforcement agencies and investigators in this regard.

Further, once the computer is seized, it must be properly sealed, and the chain of custody must be minutely monitored to prove that neither has the seal been broken nor has there been any tampering with the contents of the computers or computer systems, including its hard disk and all other removable disks. All these steps enable the preservation of the integrity of the evidence at issue.

6.3.4.2 Chain of Custody

Although there is a difference between physical evidence and electronic evidence, when it comes to the submission and recognition of evidence in the courtroom, many of the rules of handling remain the same. Collection, preservation, and tracking of electronic evidence are done in a manner to preserve the authenticity and admissibility of said evidence.

The chain of custody has to be appropriately established for upholding the integrity and authenticity of the information and data contained in the computer, computer systems, and computer networks. In common man's parlance, this actually means that the law-enforcement agencies and the investigators have to show that from the time they take the concerned computer or system or part thereof into custody until the time it is produced in a court of law, there is evidence that its contents have neither been tampered with nor their authenticity and veracity compromised.

This implies that from the time the computer system is seized to the time it is produced in the court, entire logs have been maintained specifying whose custody it was in, how it was transferred from one source to another, and what precautions were taken to ensure security and avoid the tampering with its contents. This is the most important factor in a court of law for upholding the veracity and integrity of all information resident in the seized computer or computer system. This explains why law-enforcement agencies place tremendous emphasis on the entire issue of chain of custody.

From the point of engagement between the client and the system forensic experts, all transactions must be well documented and detailed. The exchange of physical evidence or media is done using a recognized chain of custody documentation. All material received for analysis is logged and held in secure storage. All subsequent access to and handling of the system is logged, documented, and done in a forensically sound manner to meet the concerns of future authentication and submission.

Computer forensics software tools and procedures must be developed in accordance with U.S. Department of Justice Computer Evidence Processing Guidelines, to ensure the integrity of the evidence and a proper chain of custody over the evidence.

6.3.4.3 Admissibility of Evidence

Computer forensics has become a necessity in this age when most work is done through or by computer systems. An advocate has to ensure that system analysis is done in such a manner that important computer evidence may not be missed. Companies must ensure that their computer evidence is preserved, evidence comes in handy in civil suits launched by or against them. A majority of digital forensics involves the acquisition of hard disks and analysis of file systems.

In past cases, federal courts have evaluated the admissibility of computer records and focused on them as hearsay.

However, with the passage of time, it is expected that there will be changes in the perception of the courts relating to system forensics. Courts must necessarily move away from the one-size-fits-all approach, as they grow comfortable with the technicalities of computer forensics.

Computer-generated records that contain text can be categorized into two types:

- Computer-generated
- Computer-stored

Computer-stored records are those documents that contain the writing of some person or persons and happen to be in electronic form. These would include e-mails, word documents, Internet chat-room messages, etc. These documents must comply with the hearsay rule.

On the other hand, computer-generated records contain the output of computer programs, untouched by human hands. The issue in this case can hardly be whether a human's out-of-court statement was truthful and accurate (that is, a question of hearsay). Instead, the question is whether the computer program that generated the record was functioning properly (that is, a question of authenticity).

The rationale underlying the hearsay rule is that what is being conveyed is the statement(s) of another person, while such person is not under oath, and the truth of such hearsay cannot be tested by cross-examination. Being only human, the witness relaying such information may relay it inaccurately or misrepresent what had actually been said or perhaps distort some fact or occurrence. However, when the information is relayed not by a person but by a machine, there is no possibility of unconscious misrepresentation. Inaccuracy or discrepancy can arise only when such a machine is not functioning properly. The insight that computer-generated records cannot contain hearsay is important because courts that assume the existence of hearsay may wrongfully exclude computer-generated evidence if a hearsay exception does not apply.

Unlike computer-generated records, computer-stored records have to satisfy an exception to the hearsay rule, in case they are required to prove the truth of some matter asserted. The court will admit such computer-stored records only when satisfied that the statements contained therein were made under the circumstances that ensure their trustworthiness.

The most common hearsay exception applied in order to allow computer-stored records to be produced, as evidence is the business-record exception.

The exception to hearsay rules allows evidence that involves records of regularly conducted activity. According to the law, "*a memorandum, report, record, or data compilation, in any form, of acts, events, conditions, opinions, or diagnoses, made at or near the time by, or from information transmitted by, a person with knowledge, if kept in the course of a regularly conducted business activity, and if it was the regular practice of that business activity to make the memorandum, report, record, or data compilation, all as shown by the testimony of the custodian or other qualified witness, or by certification, that complies with Rule 902(11), Rule 902(12), or a statute permitting certification, unless the source of information or the method or circumstances of preparation indicate lack of trustworthiness. The term "business" as used in this paragraph includes business, institution, association, profession, occupation, and calling of every kind, whether or not conducted for profit.*"

There is, of course, a third category of computer records both computer generated and computer stored. For both, the issues will have to be countered – of hearsay and of authenticity. Parties seeking admission of such records should address both the hearsay issues implicated by the original input and the authenticity issues raised by the computer processing.

The judge, not the jury, determines in a pre-trial "Daubert Hearing" the reliability of scientific evidence, such as the output from a digital forensics tool. The Daubert process identifies four general categories that are used as guidelines for assessing whether the procedure followed is dependable:

- Testing: Can and has the procedure been tested?
- Error Rate: Is there a known error rate of the procedure?
- Publication: Has the procedure been published and subjected to peer review?
- Acceptance: Is the procedure generally accepted in the relevant scientific community?

Challenges to the authenticity of computer records often take on one of the following manifestations:

- Questioning whether the records were altered, manipulated, or damaged after they were created.
- Questioning the authenticity of computer-generated records by challenging the reliability of the computer program that generated the records.
- Questioning the identity of their author – the identity of the author can be established generally by circumstantial evidence.

The real challenge of system forensics is not in computer records stored in the ordinary fashion. The expertise or the skills of the system-evidence collector lies in finding the records that which are no longer actively present. For example, word documents are often updated or deleted. However, the remnants of the originals remain behind on the computer's hard-disk drive. An ordinary computer user is unable to reach these and, more often than not, does not even have any knowledge of it. As a result, this hidden data can become essential as documentary evidence when the user has been up to some kind of wrong doing. There are specialized tools and skills required for recovering and examining such data.

Although there are no formal rules for processing computer evidence, a computer forensics examination will generally include the following steps:

- Creating photo documentation of the computer in question--that is, photographing all angles and label wires to document the system's hardware components and the way they are connected.
- Mathematically authenticating data on all storage devices. This is done through the use of special software tools that calculate unique numerical signatures based on the contents of a drive. It is one way to ensure that the data on the storage device is the authentic mirror image of the original.
- Creating an evidence-grade mirror-image backup (exact copy, down to the last bit of data) of a hard-disk drive and other computer storage devices such as floppy disks and zip disks. This guarantee the preservation of the best evidence and is the basis for all the subsequent work.
- Storing evidence in a highly secure location. Maintaining a proper chain of custody is essential to any computer investigation. Depending on the discovery order for the case, the evidence may include the originals or just the mirror images.
- Creating a list of key search terms that, depending on the nature of the case, will "red flag" sites visited by the computer user in question: e-mail messages, Internet chat messages, word processing documents, and other files.

6.3.4.4 Other Evidential Issues

Some of the other issues that need to be addressed in relation to electronic evidence are:

- Best-evidence rule
- Cases in which electronic evidence can be used

6.3.4.4.1 Best-Evidence Rule

The best-evidence rule says that where the content of writing, recording, or photography is to be proved, the "original" writing, recording, or photograph is ordinarily required.

The question that is raised is whether printouts from a computer, that is, a copy of an electronically stored file, is an "original" for the purposes of the best-evidence rule. Computer language broken down is a collection of 0s and 1s. The print out, on the other hand, requires a lot of electronic and mechanical complexity. The question finds its answer in The Federal Rules of Evidence, which states:

"[i]f data are stored in a computer or similar device, any printout or other output readable by sight, shown to reflect the data accurately, is an "original"." [Fed. R. Evid. 1001(3)]

So, the best-evidence rule is satisfied if the printout is accurate.

6.3.4.4.2 Computer Printouts as "Summaries"

Parties can offer summaries of voluminous evidence in the form of "a chart, summary or collection" [Fed. R. Evid. 1006]. But this is subject to restrictions. Computer printouts are not necessarily summaries and thus do not always have to comply with the restrictions placed on summaries by the Federal Rules of Evidence 1006. However, where the computer printout in issue is merely a summary of other admissible evidence (say, the printout of a table made electronically on the computer system), Rule 1006 will apply to the printout in exactly the same way as it applies to other (non-electronic) summaries.

6.3.4.5 Cases in which Electronic Evidence Has Been or Can Be Used

Electronically collected evidence can apply in a variety of litigations, including cases of electronic embezzlement, violation of trade secrets, discrimination or harassment cases, and so on.

In a certain case, the ex-employee of Company X joined a rival company and was getting paid more than he was paid at Company X. The executives of Company X suspected that there had been some infringement of their intellectual property rights, and a motion for discovery was filed. Forensics specialists were called in. In cases of this sort, such computer forensic evidence would not be admitted unless forensics rules are strictly followed. The very first rule is that evidence must not be tampered with. So, the forensic specialists made a mirror image of Company X's engineering servers and the ex-employee's old computer, that is, captured the hard-drive contents without altering the original. Signs of copying to removable media were found in the engineer's computer.

Under a court order for discovery, the forensic specialists then searched the home computer of the engineer. This search indicated that the product-engineering drawings had been copied onto the home computer after the engineer had left the company (tool that was used revealed when the file was created, accessed, and modified). There was enough evidence then to investigate into the engineer's computer at his new employer. Similar drawings were found in the computer, but there were some differences. However, this difficulty became negligible when an e-mail passed between the engineer and his girlfriend was found. The e-mail detailed their mutual possession of the diagrams in question. The end result was that a court injunction was granted against the engineer and the rival company, an injunction restraining them from developing products based on Company X's intellectual property.

Consider an example to further understand how system forensics can be used for evidential purposes. Suppose a woman employee accuses her boss of sexually harassing her. She subsequently gets fired on the ground of inefficiency. She sues her ex-boss and former employer for sexual harassment. A forensics expert is hired who obtains the ex-boss's hard drive. Once a mirror-image backup is made, the expert recovers deleted e-mails that contain evidence that the ex-boss has a history of propositioning women juniors for "special favors." Thanks to this evidence, the ex-employer decides to settle, and, as part of the settlement, the woman is re-instated and the ex-boss fired.

6.3.4.6 Sarbanes-Oxley Act

The Sarbanes-Oxley Act was passed in 2000 in order to impose certain conditions on public companies and their accounting and auditing teams. Among other things, the act treats activities concerned with the retention and destruction of financial records.

Three new offences are added to the Federal Obstruction of Justice statute:

- Persons who knowingly alter, destroy, mutilate, conceal, or falsify any document or tangible object with the intent to impede, obstruct, or influence proceedings involving federal agencies or bankruptcy proceedings may be fined, imprisoned up to 20 years, or both.

- Accountants have to maintain certain corporate audit records or review work papers for a period of five years from the end of the fiscal period during which the audit or review was concluded. This section makes it unlawful to knowingly and willfully violate these new provisions (including any rules and regulations promulgated by the SEC) and imposes fines, a maximum term of 10 years imprisonment, or both.

- Acting or attempting to "corruptly" alter or destroy a record or other object "with the intent to impair the object's integrity or availability for use in an official proceeding" is punishable with fines and/or imprisonment of up to 20 years.

The Sarbanes-Oxley Act reinforces the idea that electronic data management should get top priority from corporate leadership, corporate counsel, and accounting/auditing personnel.

Practice Questions

1. What are the disadvantages of calling in a law-enforcement agency in a case relating to a systems crime?

2. How can an investigator ensure the integrity of evidence that he/she collects during the course of an investigation of a systems crime?

3. What does the best-evidence rule stipulate in the context of printouts?

Summary

- The requirements of the Fourth Amendment do not cover private searches by private entities.

- The Electronic Communications Privacy Act, 1986, is the relevant law relating to real-time monitoring.

- The interception of any wire, oral, or electronic communication is prohibited as a general rule, although the law has carved out numerous exceptions to this general rule.

- When notified of any offensive content, Internet Service Providers are duty bound to remove the offensive content; otherwise, they open themselves to legal action.

- Law-enforcement agencies have a direct relation with system forensics.

- Calling in a law-enforcement agency has its own advantages and disadvantages.

- There are numerous issues relating to information sharing and voluntary disclosure of information.

- Evidence collected by investigators must be authentic and of integrity.

- Great care must be taken to ensure that the evidence collected by system forensics is admissible as legal evidence in a court of law.

References

- http://www.usdoj.gov/criminal/cybercrime/
- http://www.usdoj.gov/criminal/cybercrime/searching.html

Homework Exercises

(handwritten: 6.3, 6.4, 6.7, 6.12, 6.2, 6.20, 6.22)

1. What legal provisions must be kept in mind during real-time monitoring in the electronic environment?

2. In what limited cases is interception of any electronic communication permitted by law?

3. What are the two prevailing schools of thought relating to liability of Internet Service Providers in the global context?

4. Why is it important to observe the chain of custody in system forensic evidence?

5. How can the authenticity and veracity of evidence collected by system-forensic methods be ensured?

6. What rules are applicable to the admissibility of electronic evidence collected with system-forensic methods?

Lab Exercises

Exercise 1

Objective

▓ Investigate a child pornography case.

Problem Statement

Consider the following situation. John, the system administrator of XYZ Corp., while updating antivirus software on the machines in his network, realized that one of the employees, Jack, might have been storing pornographic images of children (also known as kiddie porn). John reported this to management, and they notified law enforcement. Law enforcement carefully took disk images of Jack's NTFS c: drive, using dd command. They mounted this image on their machine for further investigation. They also took an md5sum of the drive image and compared it with the md5 hash of a fresh installation of the Windows system.

Assume that you are a part of law-enforcement team and are asked to take the investigation further. You are required to assess the drive image and submit your findings to the corporation.

Lab Setup

▓ Linux 7.1 machine.

▓ The location of the raw dd image will be provided by the instructor. The IMAGE NAME is Deadlyimage.img and its md5sum is stored in Deadlyimage.md5. The image is also mounted read-only on the file-system at /mnt/img as well. The forensic machine is on the network and can be reached at the IP address provided by the instructor through SSH. The image is around 2.5 GB.

Procedure

You can perform the investigation by using the following tools:

▓ dd

▓ Lsof

▓ String

- File
- FIND
- TCT And TASK

You can perform the following steps:

- Assess damage.
- Identify any malicious programs.
- Analyze the log files.
- Search for hidden and deleted files.
- Conduct keyword searches.
    - Prepare a forensic report. You can document information about the following:
        - Recovered deleted files
        - Recovered e-mails
        - Recovered e-mail attachments
        - The name of the image file found in the file system
        - Any important strings from slack or unallocated space

Conclusion/Observation

Write a report of the forensic analysis that you performed on the program. The report should essentially consist of:

- Objective
- Problem Statement
- Tools and Techniques Used
- Solution
- Conclusion

Lab Activity Checklist

S. No.	Tasks	Completed	
		Yes	No
1.	Analyzed programs and file		
2.	Implemented forensics tools and techniques		
3.	Prepared a report		

Security Systems as Forensic Tools

7

This chapter covers tools in three categories: Vulnerability Assessment Tools (VATs), firewalls, and Network Intrusion Detection Systems (NIDS). These tools are highly complex and enable you to protect a system from attacks. This chapter equips you to use these tools in the field of computer forensics. The chapter describes how to gather evidence using these security tools, which are usually found on all networked computers. At the end of the chapter, you will be able to:

- Describe the use of vulnerability-assessment tools.
- Describe the functions of Satan and Nessus, popular VAT tools.
- Explain the relevance of Nessus and Satan to an investigator.
- Explain the concepts and configurations of firewalls.
- Explain how firewalls can be used as evidence-collector tools.
- Describe the various Network Intrusion Detection System (NIDS) tools
- Describe Snort, a popular open-source NIDS tool.

PROXY

PACKET
FILTER
FILTER PACKETS

Firewall
- hard/software
- protects network
- organizes workstations
- rights + privileges
- filtering
- not sure setup properly

7.1 Vulnerability Assessment Tools

Vulnerability-assessment tools, also known as security scanners, enable security consultants to audit computer systems and networks. In the field of computer forensics, these tools enable you to narrow down the search for clues on a hacked computer. There are many available vulnerability-assessment tools.

This section describes the importance of vulnerability-assessment tools in system forensics. It also describes two widely used open-source tools, Nessus and Satan. Security Administrator's Tool for Analyzing Networks (Satan) was the original security auditing tool. It was the first program ever that could perform automated security auditing of computers. Dan Farmer, a renowned Internet-security expert, developed Satan.

A group of open-source developers developed Nessus, which has certain advantages over Satan. For example, it can scan for a larger number of security vulnerabilities than Satan.

7.1.1 Role of Vulnerability-Assessment Tools in Investigation

 Explain the role of vulnerability-assessment tools in forensics investigation.

Vulnerability tools are useful to the forensics investigator not only with respect to evidence gathering, but also from a general investigation perspective. The information gathered by the tools gives the forensic investigator valuable insight into the state of the target computer. When investigating a hacked computer, an investigator can lose a huge amount of valuable time in searching for clues about how the hacker might have entered the computer. Security scanners list security holes present on the computer and reduce the work because the investigator now has fewer leads to follow. Investigation based on the security report of the scanner reveals how the hacker entered the computer system. The investigator can search for clues in specific files related to the compromised software used to gain access to the system. For example, if an investigator runs a security scanner against a previously hacked computer, it generates a report that the IIS Web server running on the computer has a potentially hazardous security hole. After searching Web-server logs, the investigator realizes that there have been abnormal requests from a certain IP address to the Web server. After some more research, the investigator will realize that the requests were specially crafted to exploit the security hole in the Web server and gain access to the computer. Using a security scanner, the investigator can save huge amount of valuable investigation time by finding out the exact location from which the attacker compromised the system. Without this tool, the investigator would have had to look through hundred of logs before noticing something suspicious.

7.1.2 Security-Auditing Tools

- Describe the features of the Satan security-auditing tool.
- Describe the features of the Nessus security-auditing tool.

Nessus and Satan are fundamentally automated *hacking tools* that contain a database of security vulnerabilities, which can run into the thousands, as well as information about how each vulnerability can be exploited to gain unauthorized access to a computer. Using this knowledge about exploiting security holes, programs automatically attack the target computer and attempt to use the entire collection of security exploits against the target computer. During this operation, if any of the attacks is successful in gaining entry to the target computer system, then the attack is recorded, and finally a detailed report is generated. This report enables you to understand which computer system is vulnerable to what security hole. The reports also mention ways to fix the problem, thus minimizing your work. You need to update the database of these tools constantly to be able to deal with the most recent security holes. In addition to detecting active security holes, the scanners can also detect potential security holes and improve the overall level of security in the network.

7.1.2.1 Satan /saint

Satan enables you to find several network-related security problems. It is designed to test the target system or the target network for security problems, and if problems exist, it generates a useful informative report. Satan has a Web-based interface that can be accessed through a Web browser. At first, you need to select a target network or sub-net and click the Start button. Satan audits the target and then generates a report after completing its activity. Newer scanners search for hundreds of security holes, but Satan, being a slightly older software program, searches only for a few popular holes.

The vulnerabilities that Satan searches for are:

- NFS file systems exported to arbitrary hosts
- NFS file systems exported to unprivileged programs
- NFS file systems exported through the portmapper
- NIS password file access from arbitrary hosts
- Old sendmail mail server versions before 8.6.10, which are full of security holes
- REXD access from arbitrary hosts (remote -command execution)
- X server access control disabled (Unix GUI platform)
- Arbitrary files accessible through the Trivial File Transfer Protocol (TFTP)
- Remote-shell access from arbitrary hosts
- Writable anonymous FTP home directory

Satan now has many new versions, and the newest release of the Satan scanner is called *Saint*. It has more features than Satan, but is currently not as widely accepted as the Nessus scanner is.

Figure 7.1 shows a sample Satan-generated report.

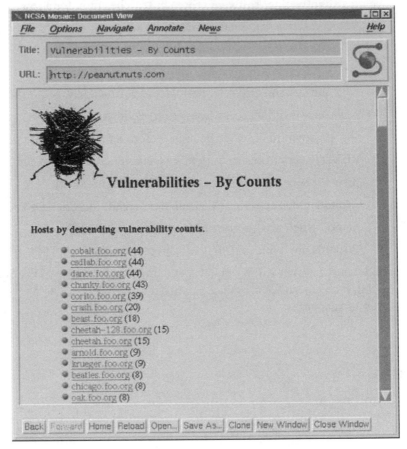

Figure 7.1: Satan-Generated Report

7.1.2.2 Nessus

Nessus is the next-generation security scanner. It has features such as modular design, internal scripting language, client-server model, encryption, and large vulnerability databases. Nessus groups its attacks into various categories. Before attacks are launched against the target, Nessus runs a series of information-gathering scans to learn more about the target computer. This gathered information is used by the various programs as they try to punch holes in the security system of the computer.

The reports generated by Nessus are advanced and contain more information than the reports generated by Satan or any other commercial software program.

To launch attacks against a target computer:

1. Log on to Nessus. Figure 7.2 shows the Nessus login interface. Logging is necessary to prevent unauthorized use of Nessus.

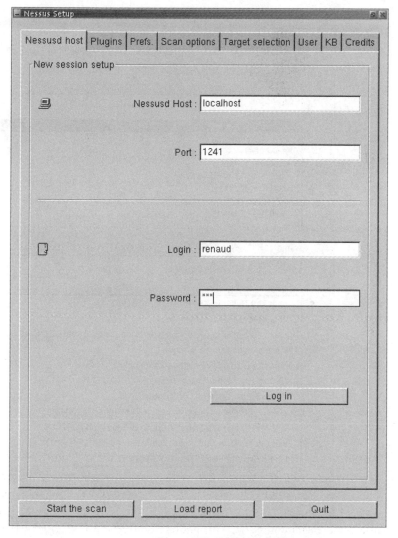

Figure 7.2: Login Interface

2. Select the attacks that must be run against the target computer, as shown in Figure 7.3. In the figure, the Plugin list allows you to select groups of attacks. The list below the Plugin list allows the user to select specific attacks. Most options are set by default and should not be changed, except for the username and password, which have to be same as the ones you set when you installed Nessus.

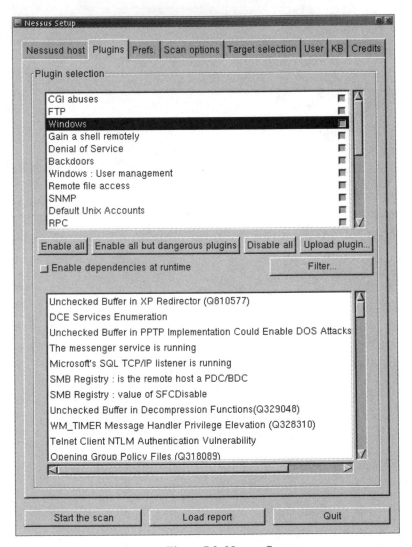

Figure 7.3: Nessus Set-up

By default, Nessus turns off highly dangerous attacks that could potentially crash the target computer. You can switch them on, provided you know the implication of the attack.

3. Select a single computer by its IP address, or a whole range of computers to scan, against which you need to launch the attack. This process of selecting the target computer is known as *target selection*. Figure 7.4 shows the target selection window.

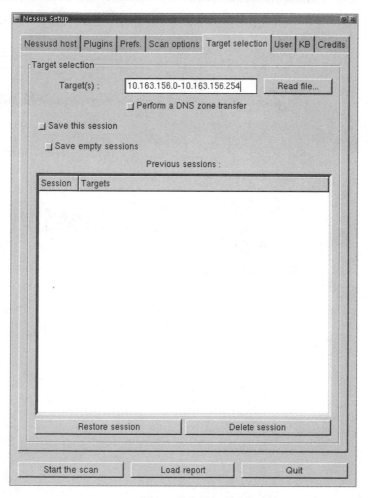

Figure 7.4: Target Selection

4. Click the **Start the scan** option. Nessus starts to scan multiple hosts simultaneously, as shown in Figure 7.5.

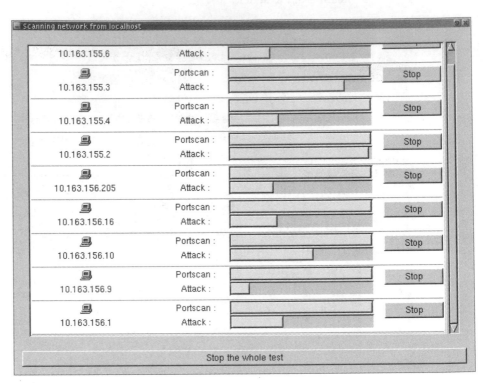

Figure 7.5: Scanning Process

After Nessus completes the scanning of the target computers, it generates a report of its activity. Figure 7.6 shows a sample report generated by Nessus.

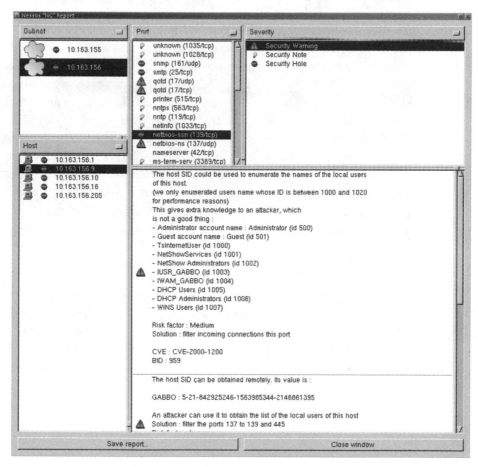

Figure 7.6: Scanning Report

The report is divided into three sections:

    a.   Security Warning: Contains only mild warnings concerning certain aspects of computer security, such as servers running on unusual port numbers or unnecessary server runnings.

    b.   Security Notes: Indicates possible places of future security risks.

    c.   Security Hole: Shows actual security vulnerabilities that exist on the target computer.

Case Study of Nessus

You are called to the scene of a hacked computer that was serving the domain www.timesofbombay.com. The system administrator, John, informs you that he found out about the hack from the defaced Web page of his Web site, which, instead of the original Web page, now has a page installed by the hacker to glorify himself. As an investigator, you need to gather evidence. As the first step, you generate disk images to have an unmodified copy of any evidence that you may later analyze. Then, you find out how the break-in occurred. The system administrator tells you that he had installed the latest version of the Web server software. Your start up your laptop with Nessus installed, connect it to his network, and get Nessus to run a security audit of the hacked Web-server computer. Soon, Nessus provides a neatly formatted report that shows:

- The Web-server software on the hacker machine was perfectly secure, but the ftp-server software being run by the administrator has a security hole.

- A time server is being run on the computer.

The information about the ftp-server software has now narrowed down your analysis to only the files related to the ftp server, such as ftp server logs and the ftp software binary. The other information about the time server is not of any direct use to you. But you inform the administrator about this so that he can turn it off and prevent any future attacks, if at any time the software turns up with a security hole.

Practice Questions

1. What is the role of vulnerability-scanning tools?

2. Name the first security-auditing tool?

3. List some of the vulnerabilities searched by Satan.

4. How is an attack on a target computer launched through Nessus?

5. What are the three sections of a Nessus-generated report?

7.2 Firewall as Evidence Collector

Firewalls are programs that decide whether to allow or block data from the network connection.

In a network, data travels in *packets*. A large file being transmitted over a network is broken down into small individual packets. Each of these packets has a destination address and a source address besides other header values. Firewalls scan the packet headers and make decisions about blocking or accepting the data packet. The rules fed to firewalls by users can be highly complex or simple rules that tell the firewall which source address to block packets from and which to allow from. Rules can be based on any of the information in the packet headers.

This section explains the importance of firewalls from a forensic investigator's perspective. It also describes how to configure and use firewalls.

7.2.1 Role of Firewall in System Forensics

 Describe the role of firewalls in system forensics.

Firewalls not only block or allow packets, but also record information about data flowing in and out of the computer because they look at every packet that enters or leaves the computer.

Suppose the forensic investigator is investigating a computer that has a data-logging firewall activated. Even if the attacker manages to bypass firewall blocks, the attacker's interaction with the computer over the network will be recorded in firewall logs.

The following example of a firewall focuses on the open-source IP-tables firewall for Linux. A user-level program can control IP tables that work as a Linux kernel module. The user-level program enables you to add, modify, and delete rules from the firewall.

Example 7.1

iptables is used from a forensic investigator's perspective for logging packets flowing to and fro from the target computer.

```
iptables  -A INPUT -p TCP  -j LOG --log-prefix
```

```
"Firewall log:"
```

The above command logs all TCP packets coming into the computer and into the system-log files with the prefix Firewall log. The prefix is used to grep firewall logs out of system-log files that contain logs of many other utilities.

There are many firewalls available to choose from, and all of them have extensive logging capabilities. The other popular firewalls are IOS (Cisco OS), IP Chains, IPTables, and SonicWall.

Example 7.2

The log file of the IOS firewall is:

```
Aug 19 04:02:34 1.example.com.nl 218963: Aug 19
04:02:32.977: \
    %LINEPROTO-5-UPDOWN: Line protocol on Interface
BRI0:1, changed \
    state to down
Aug 19 04:02:34 1.example.com.nl 218964: Aug 19
04:02:33.262: \
    %ISDN-6-DISCONNECT: Interface BRI0:1
disconnected from \
    172605440 teraar, call lasted 42 seconds
Aug 19 04:02:35 1.example.com.nl 218965: Aug 19
04:02:33.266: \
    %LINK-3-UPDOWN: Interface BRI0:1, changed state
to down
Aug 19 04:02:38 1.example.com.nl 218966: Aug 19
04:02:36.103: \
    %SEC-6-IPACCESSLOGP: list 102 denied tcp
10.0.0.1(4652) -> \
    10.0.0.2(80), 1 packet
Aug 19 04:02:45 1.example.com.nl 218967: Aug 19
04:02:43.543: \
    %ISDN-6-LAYER2DOWN: Layer 2 for Interface BR0,
TEI 86 changed to down
```

```
Aug 19 04:02:53 1.example.com.nl 218968: Aug 19
04:02:51.471: \
    %SEC-6-IPACCESSLOGP: list 102 denied tcp
10.0.0.3(2162) -> \
    10.0.0.4(80), 1 packet
```

Example 7.3

The log file of IP Chains is:

```
Oct 28 04:02:30 firewall kernel: Packet log: output
DENY eth0 PROTO=17 \
    10.0.0.1:137 10.0.0.2:137 L=78 S=0x00 I=36930
F=0x0000 T=64 (#7)
Oct 28 04:07:30 firewall kernel: Packet log: output
DENY eth0 PROTO=17 \
    10.0.0.1:137 10.0.0.2:137 L=78 S=0x00 I=37211
F=0x0000 T=64 (#7)
Oct 28 04:07:40 firewall kernel: Packet log: input
DENY eth1 PROTO=17 \
    10.0.0.3:138 10.0.0.4:138 L=256 S=0x00 I=37213
F=0x0000 T=64 (#7)
Oct 28 04:07:40 firewall kernel: Packet log: input
DENY eth1 PROTO=17 \
    10.0.0.3:138 10.0.0.4:138 L=236 S=0x00 I=37214
F=0x0000 T=64 (#7)
Oct 28 04:08:20 firewall kernel: Packet log: output
DENY lo PROTO=17 \
    10.0.0.5:138 10.0.0.2:138 L=256 S=0x00 I=37216
F=0x0000 T=64 (#7)
Oct 28 04:12:30 firewall kernel: Packet log: output
DENY eth0 PROTO=17 \
    10.0.0.1:137 10.0.0.2:137 L=78 S=0x00 I=37255
F=0x0000 T=64 (#7)
Oct 28 04:17:30 firewall kernel: Packet log: output
DENY eth0 PROTO=17 \
    10.0.0.1:137 10.0.0.2:137 L=78 S=0x00 I=37364
F=0x0000 T=64 (#7)
```

```
Oct 28 04:19:40 firewall kernel: Packet log: input
DENY eth1 PROTO=17 \
    10.0.0.3:138 10.0.0.4:138 L=256 S=0x00 I=37440
F=0x0000 T=64 (#7)
```

Example 7.4

The log file of iptables is:

```
Oct 30 07:42:29 firewall ipmon[16747]:
07:42:28.585962              ie0 @0:9 \
  b 192.168.48.1,45085 -> 192.168.48.2,22 PR tcp len
20 64 -S OUT
Oct 30 07:40:24 firewall ipmon[16747]:
07:40:23.631307              ep1 @0:6 \
  b 192.168.26.5,113 -> 192.168.26.1,3717 PR tcp len
20 40 -AR OUT
Oct 30 07:42:29 firewall ipmon[16747]:
07:42:28.585962              ie0 @0:9 \
  b 192.168.48.1,45085 -> 192.168.48.2,22 PR tcp len
20 64 -S OUT
Oct 30 07:44:11 firewall ipmon[16747]:
07:44:10.605416 2x           ep1 @0:15 \
  b 192.168.26.1,138 -> 192.168.26.255,138 PR udp len
20 257  IN
Oct 30 07:44:34 firewall ipmon[16747]:
07:44:33.891869              ie0 @0:10 \
  b 192.168.48.1,23406 -> 192.168.48.2,22 PR tcp len
20 64 -S OUT
```

Example 7.5

The log output of SonicWall is:

```
Jan   7 15:01:10 lire id=firewall sn=asdlFFFXSD \
     time="2002-01-06 22:42:13" fw=10.0.0.1 pri=6 c=1
m=30 \
     msg="Administrator login failed - incorrect
password" n=1 \
     src=10.0.0.2:LAN dst=10.0.0.1
Jan   7 15:01:16 lire id=firewall sn=asdlFFFXSD \
     time="2002-01-06 22:42:19" fw=10.0.0.1 pri=6 c=1
m=29 \
     msg="Successful administrator login" n=1
src=10.0.0.2:LAN dst=10.0.0.1
Jan   7 15:02:32 lire id=firewall sn=asdlFFFXSD \
     time="2002-01-06 22:43:34" fw=10.0.0.1 pri=5
c=128 m=37 \
     msg="UDP packet dropped" n=1 src=10.0.0.3:68
dst=10.0.0.4:67 dstname=DHCP
Jan   7 15:31:43 lire id=firewall time="2002-01-07
15:20:21" \
     fw=10.0.0.5 pri=6 proto=dns src=10.0.0.6
dst=10.0.0.8 rcvd=130 \
     sn=asdlFFFXSD 54 c=1024 m=98 n=31
```

The format of the above logs can change if a new version of the software is released. An investigator can gather the IP address, hostnames, the network interface from which the data can inform in case of multiple networks connected to one computer, the amount of data that was flowing down the connection, and other protocol-specific information such as the protocol number and the protocol name from the above logs.

Practice Questions

1. What are firewalls?

2. List a few popular firewalls.

3. What does the following entry do?

   iptables -A INPUT -p TCP -j LOG --log-prefix "Firewall log:"3

7.3 Intrusion Detection as a Forensic Tool

Intrusion detection is a new field that deals with real-time detection of attacks against a system by analysis of data flowing into the network. This cannot be done manually because data flows are voluminous, and it is not possible to analyze that much information quickly without the help of software. Network Intrusion Detection System (NIDS) is a program that match a predefined set of rules or attack signatures against all data flowing into a network or a computer. After detecting a match, NIDS signals the system administration that an intrusion has been attempted against the computer. There are many software packages designed to do this, including Snort, an open-source package. Snort is a complete NIDS package that can log alerts to everything from files to databases. This section describes the importance of log alerts in conducting a forensic study.

7.3.1 Role of IDS in System Forensics

Describe the role of an intrusion-detection system (IDS) in system forensics.

NIDS software such as Snort can provide evidence to a forensic investigator after an attack on a computer system. Snort logs show the investigator the IP address of the location from where the attack originated and the type of attack that was launched. Besides this, Snort can provide line-by-line information pertaining to the attack. Snort logs are more helpful to an investigator than firewall logs because firewalls logs are very large and not as easy to analyze as Snort logs.

Code 7.1 and Code 7.2 show entries from the log output of Snort after it detected an attack.

```
First log entry
[**] [1:1149:9] WEB-CGI count.cgi access [^^]
[Classification: access to a potentially vulnerable web
application] [Priority: 2]
04/22-15:08:19.956011 0:10:5A:27:A2: D -> 2:A0:24: BB: 7E: EB
type: 0x800 len: 0x245
192.168.0.213:3395 -> 66.216.127.26:80 TCP TTL: 128 TOS: 0x0 ID:
53462 IpLen: 20 DgmLen: 567 DF
***AP*** Seq: 0xE53734 Ack: 0x7EF7B6F8 Win: 0x2238 TcpLen: 20
[Xref => http://cgi.nessus.org/plugins/dump.php3?id=10049][Xref
=> http://cve.mitre.org/cgi-bin/cvename.cgi?name=CVE-1999-
0021][Xref => http://www.securityfocus.com/bid/128]
```

Code 7.1: NIDS Log Entry

The Classification field shows the access level the attack would have after compromising the security of the system. The Priority level shows the danger priority for this incident.

The priority level is on a scale of 1 to x, 1 being the highest priority and x being any number greater than 1 and the lowest priority.

```
04/22-15:08:19.956011 0:10:5A:27:A2: D -> 2:A0:24: BB: 7E: EB
type: 0x800 len: 0x245
```

The above line shows 0:10:5A:27:A2: D, the Mac address of the network interfaces. The Mac address is similar to the serial number of cards. It is unique to each network interface and can be used to link a computer with an attack.

```
192.168.0.213:3395 -> 66.216.127.26:80 TCP TTL: 128 TOS: 0x0 ID:
53462
```

The above line shows `192.168.0.213:3395 -> 66.216.127.26:80`, the source and destination IP addresses during the attack. The number after the colon at the end of the IP address is the port number.

```
[Xref => http://cgi.nessus.org/plugins/dump.php3?id=10049][Xref
=> http://cve.mitre.org/cgi-bin/cvename.cgi?name=CVE-1999-
0021][Xref => http://www.securityfocus.com/bid/128]
```

In the above line, Xref tag specifies links where investigators can find more information about this type of vulnerability. This information is very important to investigators. For example, the above Xref tag gives the investigator the url `http://cgi.nessus.org/plugins/dump.php3?id=10049` to an Internet site. If the site is opened with a Web browser, it will provide more information about the exploit.

Similar to the first entry, the log entry in Code 7.2 also describes the attack launched on the computer with the IP address `66.216.127.26`.

```
Second Entry
[**] [1:1149:9] WEB-CGI count.cgi access [**]
[Classification: access to a potentially vulnerable web
application] [Priority: 2]
04/22-18:28:18.158281 0:10:5A:27:A2: D -> 2:A0:24: BB: 7E: EB
type: 0x800 len: 0x245
192.168.0.213:4765 -> 66.216.127.26:80 TCP TTL: 128 TOS: 0x0 ID:
9812 IpLen: 20 DgmLen: 567 DF
***AP*** Seq: 0x19C523B  ACK: 0x7126B178  Win: 0x2238  TcpLen:
20
[Xref => http://cgi.nessus.org/plugins/dump.php3?id=10049][Xref
=> http://cve.mitre.org/cgi-bin/cvename.cgi?name=CVE-1999-
0021][Xref => http://www.securityfocus.com/bid/128]
. . .
```

Code 7.2: NIDS Log Entry

The summary of the Snort log entry in Code 7.2 is as follows:

- The MAC address of the location from which the attack originated: `0:10:5A:27:A2:D`
- The MAC address of the attacked computer: `2:A0:24: BB: 7E: EB:`
- The IP Address of the location from which the attack originated: `192.168.0.213:`
- The IP address of the attacked computer: `66.216.127.26:`
- Port attacked software was running on: 80, the Web-server port
- The name of the security exploit used: `WEB-CGI count.cgi access`
- Classification of the exploit: Priority 2
- Comment: Classification: Access to a potentially vulnerable Web application
- Date and time of attack: 04/22-18:28:18
- You can find more information about this exploit at: http://cgi.nessus.org/plugins/dump.php3?id=10049

The main page of the Snort management interface is called Snort Center. This page displays the general information about the computer that Snort is running on, as shown in Figure 7.7.

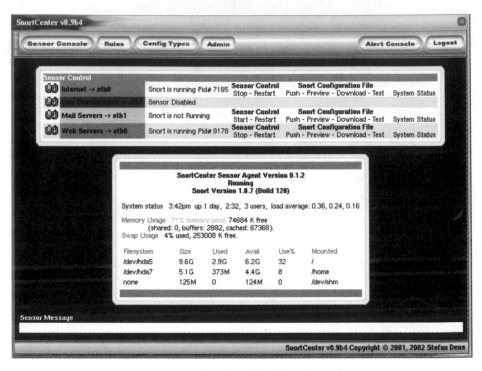

Figure 7.7: Snort Center

Figure 7.8 shows the attack signatures or rules that Snort uses to find attacks against the system. The rules with green check marks are the active rules.

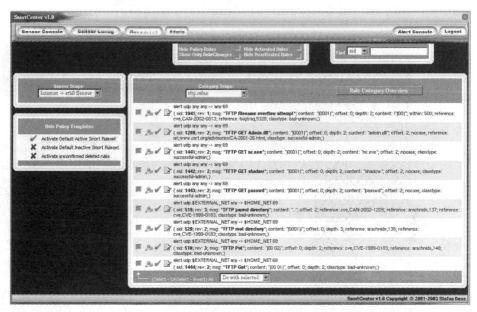

Figure 7.8: Signature and Rules for Finding Attacks

Figure 7.9 shows the groups that attacks are categorized into, based on the type of software on the server that is exploited into by Snort.

Figure 7.9: Groups of Attacks

Figure 7.10 shows the interface through which you can introduce new rules into the Snort rule set.

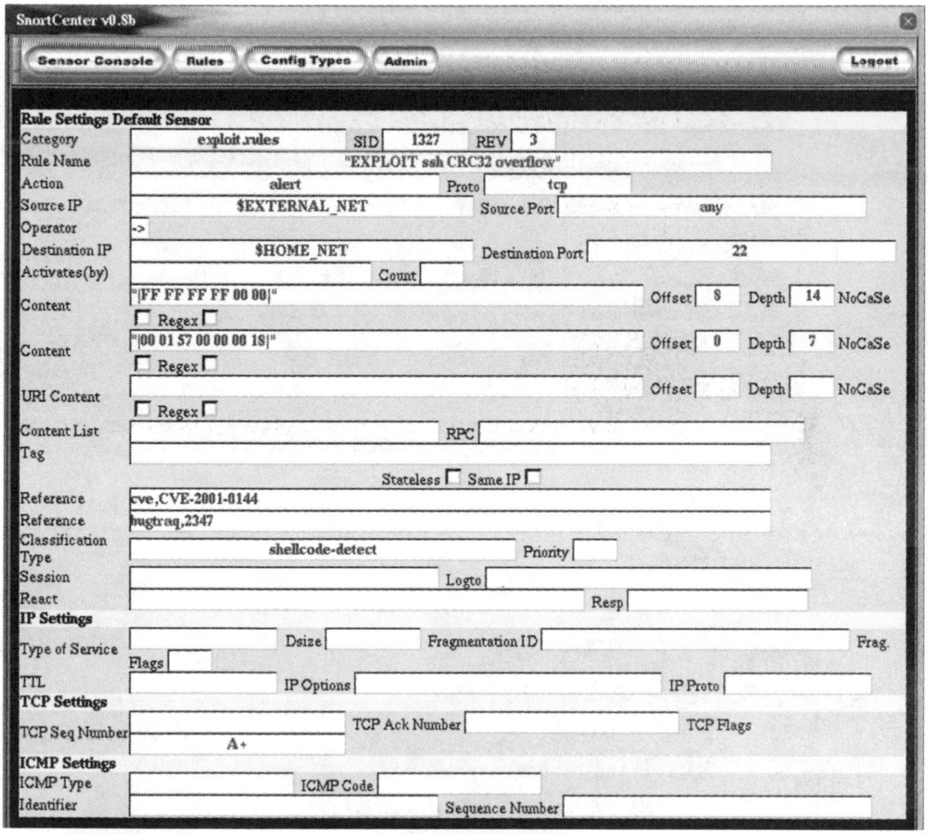

Figure 7.10: Defining Rules

Snort rules are stored in multiple files, and all of Snort's configuration data is stored in a file named snort.conf.

Code 7.3 is a Snort rule as defined in a Snort rule file.

```
Alert tcp $HOME_NET 23 -> $EXTERNAL_NET any (msg: "TELNET Bad
Login"; flags: A+; content: "Login failed"; nocase; classtype:
bad-unknown; Sid: 492; rev: 2; fwsam: dst, 1 day)
Alert: Snort rule will follow
Breakdown of the above snort rule
Tcp: Match rule against tcp traffic only
$HOME_NET, $EXTERNAL_NET - Variables for internal network and
external network
Msg: Message to log when this attack is detected
flags: A+ TCP flags A+ means with ACK set.
Content: String to be looked for in data packets in this case
"Login Failed".
```

Code 7.3: Snort Rule

Snort rule in Code 7.3 informs the user if it detects a failed login attempting to access the Telnet server.

Practice Questions

1. What is NIDS?
2. What is the function of Snort?
3. List the different fields of a Snort log entry.
4. What does the Xref tag in a Snort log entry specify?

Summary

- Vulnerability-assessment tools enable you to audit computer systems and networks for a wide range of security vulnerabilities.

- The information gathered by vulnerability-assessment tools can give a forensics investigator valuable insight into the state of the target computer.

- Nessus is one of the most popular hacking tools.

- Nessus has features such as modular design, internal scripting language, client-server model, encryption, and large vulnerability databases.

- Reports generated by Nessus have the following data:
    - Security warning
    - Security notes
    - Security holes

- Firewalls are programs that look at data coming in over the network connection and decide whether to allow or block the data.

- Investigators can gather the following information from firewall logs:
    - IP address
    - Hostnames
    - Network interface the data comes in on
    - Amount of data flowing down a connection
    - Other protocol-specific information

- NIDS is a program that matches a predefined set of rules or attack signatures against all data flowing into a network or a computer.

- Snort logs show an investigator the IP address of the origin of the attack and the type of attack that was launched.

References

- http://www.nessus.org
- http://www.snort.org
- http://www.netfilter.org

Homework Exercises

1. Explain Snort logs in detail.
2. Explain the use of a NIDS tool such as Snort in a forensics investigation.
3. Write a brief description of firewalls, and explain how you can use them as evidence gathering tools.
4. Write a brier description of NIDS tools and what are they used for.
5. What are MAC addresses, and how are they useful in forensics?
6. In 192.168.0.213:4765, which is the IP address and which is the port number?
7. What kind of information can you obtain from firewall logs?
8. Write brief explanation on iptables.
9. What are Snort rules?
10. What are firewall rules?

Lab Exercises

Exercise 1

Objective

- Use Snort to log network activity.
- Configure the iptables firewall to log network traffic.
- Use Nessus to audit your own computer for security holes.

Problem Statement

Consider yourself an investigator called in to investigate a hacked Web server.

Let your own machine be that Web server. Your job is to use Nessus to locate the security vulnerabilities of the computer, so that your analysis work in figuring out how the attacker entered the system is narrowed down to the logs related to the vulnerable server.

- Use iptables and Snort to set up a honey trap for the attacker in case of a return to use the hacked machine.
- The firewall should be configured to log activity to and from the ports Nessus has declared as security holes.
- Next, Snort should also be started so that it will detect any hacking activity on the server.
- Finally, Nessus should be again run on the computer, and this time Nessus is playing the part of a hacker. After Nessus has completed its activity, you should collect all the logs from the firewall and Snort that show an attacker (Nessus) attacking the system.

Lab Setup

Linux machine with the following installed:

- Snort
- iptables
- Nessus

Procedure

To install Nessus, follow the steps give below:

1. Login as root.

2. Change the directory to MyTools.

   cd /root/MyTools

3. Unzip the Nessus.zip file.

   ```
   Unzip -zxvf Nessus.zip
   ```

   The following four tar files will be extracted:

   - nessus-libraries-2.0.7.tar.gz
   - libnasl.-2.0.7tar.gz
   - nessus-core-2.0.7tar.gz
   - nessus-pluggins-2.0.7tar.gz.

4. Change to Nessus directory.

   ```
   cd Nessus
   ```

5. Extract the four files using the commands:

   ```
   tar -zxvf    nessus-libraries-2.0.7.tar.gz
   tar -zxvf    libnasl.-2.0.7tar.gz
   tar -zxvf    nessus-core-2.0.7.tar.gz
   tar -zxvf    nessus-pluggins-2.0.7.tar.gz
   ```

6. Install nessus libraries. Follow the sequence given below:

   ```
   cd nessus-libraries
   ./configure
   make
   make install
   ```

7. Install libnasl. Follow the sequence given below:

   ```
   cd libnasl
   ./configure
   make
   make install
   ```

8. Install nessus-core. Follow the sequence given below:

   ```
   cd nessus-core
   ./configure
   make
   ```

```
make install
```

9. Install nessus-plugins. Follow the sequence given below:

```
cd nessus-plugins
./configure
make
make install
```

10. Go to /usr/local/lib in /etc/ld.so.conf and type `ldconfig`.

11. Go back to Nessus directory.

```
cd   /root/MyTools/Nessus
```

12. Execute the following commands.

```
cd nessus-core; ./configure -disable; make && make install.
```

This will help you to install a strip down version of Nessus, incase you do not use GTK. The Nessus is now installed on the system.

GTK+ is a multi-platform toolkit for creating graphical user interfaces.

To create nessud account, follow the steps given below:

1. Add user to Nessus.

   nessus-adduser

2. Enter the username as user1.

3. Enter authentication (pass/cert) [pass] as pass.

4. Enter password.

5. Now enter the following rules for the user.

   For example,

```
Deny 10.163.156.1
Accept 10.163.156.0/24
Default deny
```

6. Press 'y' to confirm the entry.

To connect to nessusd as the new user, follow the steps:

1. Start nessud.

```
nessusd -D
```

The screen, as shown in Figure 7.11 appears.

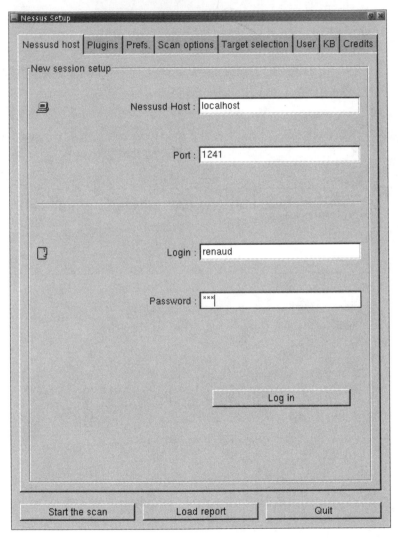

Figure 7.11: Log on to Nessus

Enter your login name and password and click **Log in** button. Select the attacks that must be run against the target computer, as shown in Figure 7.12.

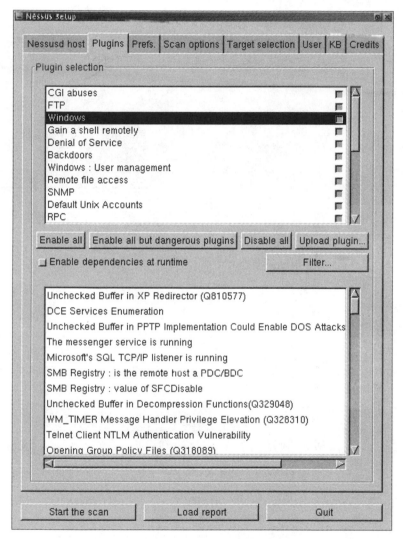

Figure 7.12: Launching Attacks

Select a single computer by its IP address, or a whole range of computers to scan, against which you need to launch the attack, as shown in Figure 7.13.

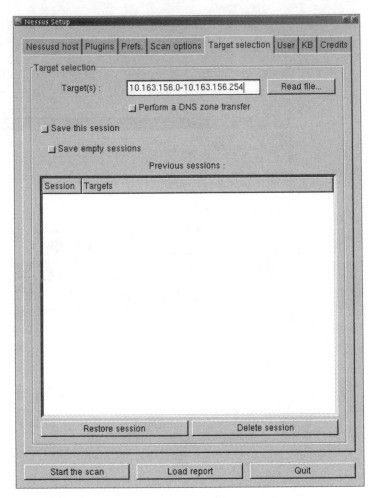

Figure 7.13: Target Selection

Click the **Start the scan** option. Nessus starts to scan the mentioned hosts, as shown in Figure 7.14.

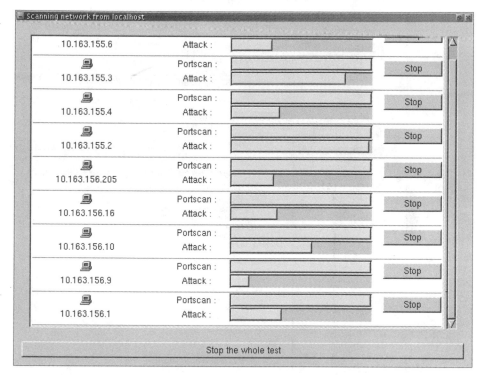

Figure 7.14: Scan on the Target Computer

A report similar to Figure 7.15 is generated after the scan.

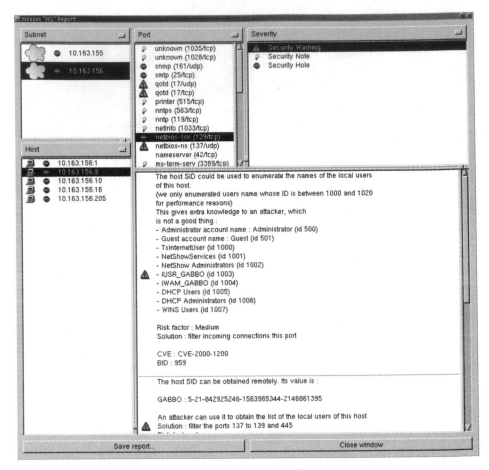

Figure 7.15: Nessus Report

Identify the security holes as reported by the Nessus scan. To create a honey trap you need now set Firewall and snort rules.

To install firewall rules to log data flowing in and out of insecure ports, as reported by Nessus, follow the steps given below:

1. Use the -j LOG command-line argument to the iptables tool. The firewall in this case should not be used to block any access to the computer.

2. Set the following rule in the firewall:

```
iptables  -A INPUT -p TCP  --dport 80 -j LOG --log-prefix
"LAB FIREWALL:"
```

This rule allows recording of any data flowing to and from the Web server.

 Web servers run on port 80; therefore, '—dport 80' has been used in the rule.

To install Snort and set rules, follow the steps given below:

1. Change to the directory MyTools

```
cd /root/MyTools
```

2. Extract the Snort tar file.

```
tar -zxvf snort-1.65.tar.gz
```

3. Change to the snort directory.

```
cd Snort
```

4. Compile and install Snort.

```
./configure
make
make install
```

Snort is installed on the system.

After defining rules for Snort and firewall, launch Nessus again on the system to simulate a hacker attacking the system. Collect all the logs generated by Nessus and the firewall as evidence.

Conclusion/Observation

In this exercise, you have learned to make use of the tools explained in the chapter in real-world situations.

Lab Activity Checklist

S. No.	Tasks	Completed	
		Yes	No
1.	Ran Nessus		
2.	Set up Firewall and Snort		
3.	Ran Nessus again to simulate an attack and collected all generated logs of Snort and firewall		

Advanced Forensics

8

To become a good investigator, you must understand complex operating system (OS) concepts and have a reasonable understanding of the kernel, in addition to studying forensic tools and techniques. This chapter deals with the advanced concepts of the operating system. At the end of the chapter, you will be able to:

- Explain the module architecture of the Linux kernel.

- Describe kernel-module rootkits and other advanced hacker programs.

- Identify systems with advanced hacker tools installed.

- Detail the /proc Linux kernel interface.

8.1 Kernel-Module Forensics

8.2 Malware Dissection and Analysis

8.3 Analysis of /proc Directory

8.1 Kernel-Module Forensics

The Linux kernel, which is the core of the operating system, allows users to extend its functionality using dynamically loaded modules that can be installed in the kernel. The kernel is designed to keep track of the modules and allow users to do almost anything using the loadable kernel modules (LKMs). Kernel modules are different from other programs because the modules run in kernel space and can easily crash the Linux system in the case of an error.

A kernel module is a small program that loads itself into the OS kernel in order to provide more features to the operating system. Rootkits are programs that work like kernel modules, but instead of adding useful features to the kernel, these programs add features that an attacker can use to take control of the computer. Almost eight percent of all successful break-ins result from a rootkit installed on the hacked computer. Kernel-module forensics deals with analysis and identification of rootkits.

8.1.1 Kernel Module Essentials

 Describe the various kernel modules and their functions.

A *kernel module* is an object file containing code and data to be loaded into a running kernel. When loaded, the module code resides in the kernel's address space and executes entirely within the context of the kernel. Technically, a module is a set of routines with two functions, init_module() and cleanup_module(), included. The init_module() function is executed after the module is loaded, and the cleanup_module() function is executed before the module is unloaded from the kernel.

LKMs are mainly used for:

■ Device drivers: Refer to programs designed to understand one specific hardware device. The OS uses them to talk to the hardware device. For example, there are device drivers to handle your mouse, keyboard, soundcard, and other devices. In this way, even if you attach a new hardware device to the computer, the OS need not know what it is. The drivers of the new hardware know about all the built-in features and allow the OS to use the device through the driver.

- File system drivers: Provide access to the various types of file systems available. Because an OS cannot be burdened with understanding all file systems, this functionality has been extended to modules. For example, if you need access to the NTFS file system, there is an LKM that can be inserted into the kernel. Whenever the kernel needs to mount or access a device that has the NTFS file system installed on it, it passes the calling routine to the module. Linux supports many file systems, a capability made possible by file-system modules. Currently, Linux supports NTFS, FAT32/16, EXT2, EXT3, UFS, RAMFS, REISERFS, JFS, and XFS.

- System calls: Instruct the kernel to perform various functions for the programs. System calls are the core elements of any operating system. Linux, which runs in the protected mode, does not allow user-level programs to directly access system hardware or the space of other programs because this can defeat security and stability of the operating system. For example, if Linux did not pass all hardware access through its kernel, a rouge program could easily crash the entire system. In Linux, if you need to write to the disk, read from memory, or print to the screen, you need to use system calls. You can add your own system calls to the kernel by using kernel modules.

- Network drivers: Handle the protocol stack such as TCP/IP or the IPX (Novell) protocol at the software level. If you want to change the working of TCP/IP on your Linux machine, you can write your own implementation of the protocol in a kernel module and upload it into the kernel. Network drivers do not control the network interface card (hardware) connected to your computer. That part is taken care of by the device driver for that hardware.

- Executable interpreters: Execute programs of several types. When you compile a program, the program gets converted into machine code, and special headers are added to the program. You need different kernel modules for interpreting and executing the various types of executable file formats. Most executable files in Linux use either the a.out or the elf executable format.

The Linux OS contains programs that enable you to manage these kernel modules. To use any of the utilities, you have to be the root or the super user.

The following programs enable you to use loadable kernel modules:

- Insmod: Loads the module. The syntax is:

  insmod <module filename>

  For example, the following command will add the firewall.o module in the kernel:

  ```
  insmod firewall.o
  ```

- Rmmod: Unloads the module. The syntax is:

  rmmod <module filename without extension>

  For example, the following command will remove the firewall.o module:

  rmmod firewall

- Depmod: Determines interdependencies between modules.

- Ksyms: Displays symbols that are exported by the kernel for use by new modules.

- Lsmod: Displays all the modules currently loaded in the kernel.

- Modinfo: Displays module information normally stored inside a module.

- Modprobe: Intelligently adds or removes a module or a set of modules. For example, if you must load module A before loading module B, Modprobe will automatically load module A when you tell it to load module B.

You can find most of the above utilities in the /sbin directory. Code 8.1 shows an example of a Linux kernel module.

```
*   hello.c - The simplest kernel module.
 */
#include <linux/module.h>   /* Needed by all modules */
#include <linux/kernel.h>   /* Needed for KERN_ALERT */


int init_module(void)
{
    printk("<1>Hello world 1.\n");

    // A non 0 return means init_module failed; module can't be
loaded.
    return 0;
}

void cleanup_module(void)
{
    printk(KERN_ALERT "Goodbye world 1.\n");
```

Code 8.1: Sample Kernel Module

Using the insmod command, the kernel module will print "Hello world" when it is loaded into the kernel. It will display "Goodbye world" when it is removed from the kernel by the rmmod command.

8.1.2 Rootkits

- Describe rootkits.
- Describe the methods of detecting kernel and non-kernel rootkits.

Rootkits are the most powerful weapons in the arsenal of a hacker. An attacker cannot use rootkits to gain access to a computer, but can use them only to maintain access to an already hacked computer because rootkits hide the activity of the hacker from system administrators. Rootkits come in many forms and set up a backdoor for the hacker to enter the computer at will. The simpler ones are versions of popular programs that have hidden backdoors allowing an attacker free access to the computer system. For example, after hacking into a computer, the attacker could change the executable of the shell, such as bash, with a similar shell executable, which has hidden features that allow the hacker full access using a certain key combination. The method in the above example would be used by a less skilled attacker. You can easily detect the shell manipulation and shut it down by replacing the hacked shell executable with the original one.

A relatively skilled attacker would use more craft and advanced rootkits known as kernel-module rootkits. Specially programmed kernel modules can manipulate the internal structures of the kernel, and attackers can have full control of the kernel. These rootkits employ stealth techniques using kernel features to hide from the user. Kernel-module rootkits do not show up if you try to see what modules are loaded. The attacker can insert backdoors into the computer and hide any program or the attacker's own presence on the system. Some kernel-level rootkits allow the attacker to capture all the data passing through the system, including keystrokes entered by the unauthorized user.

Rootkits are usually the first programs that the attacker downloads and installs after gaining control of a computer. As an investigator, you must understand rootkits and also rootkit detection. When analyzing systems, you must be sure that there is no installed rootkit that is preventing you from accessing important evidence. If you detect rootkits, you can easily remove the installed rootkits. As an investigator, you must not try to change the rootkit because this will change the configuration of the computer.

Some of the recent and most widely used rootkits are listed below. In addition to using these, exceptionally skilled attackers can easily create their own module rootkits.

- Knark: Hides files, directories, and sockets. The Knark rootkit comes as a kernel module named sysmod.o. This kernel module seizes control of systems calls such as read, execve, settimeofday, clone, kill, and fork. Knark also carries with it a group of security exploits that can be used to attack and seize control of other computers.

▨ RKIT: Takes control of the setuid system call to grant root access to any user. This is also a kernel-module rootkit, but it is by far the smallest in terms of functionality.

▨ Adore: Equals the Knark rootkit in complexity. It captures system calls such as fork, close, write, clone, kill, and mkdir. The rootkit comes with a user-space utility called ava, which controls and sends commands to the rootkit. The syntax of the ava command-like tool is:

./ava {h,u,r,R,i,v,U} [file, PID or dummy (for U)]

The following command-line arguments can be used with ava:

- h - hide file
- u - unhide file
- r - execute as root
- R - remove PID forever
- U - uninstall adore
- i - make PID invisible
- v - make PID visible

Example 8.1

Consider the following command:

`./ava i 6048`

This command makes the process whose ID is 6048 invisible to the user.

8.1.2.1 Methods of Detecting Rootkits

Rootkits remain hidden from the system administrator and perform tasks for the attacker, such as allowing the attacker to access the system at will. There are two types of rootkits, kernel and non-kernel. The methods of detecting the two types of rootkits are different.

8.1.2.1.1 Detecting Non-Kernel Rootkits

You can detect non-kernel-module rootkits using the tripwire tool, which signals whether any system executable has been modified in any way. Besides this, you can use the md5deep tool, which generates an md5 signature database of a newly installed system and matches it with an md5 signature database generated on the target computer. Differences in the md5 signatures of a file indicate that the file has been modified and raise doubts about the integrity and authenticity of the file.

For example, a comparison between the md5 hashes of the original and the compromised file could show disparities such as those illustrated in Code 8.2.

```
Generating a hash for the modified system:
md5sum /bin/bash (y|n|e|a)? yes
9db4112fdbd9bef96a54e722f7e07275   /bin/bash


md5 of unmodified bash:
3e5ae822ff407c0508a54fa821af5829
```

Code 8.2: Comparing MD5 Hashes

A visual match enables you to detect that the two md5 hashes don't match and that the bash program has been modified.

8.1.2.1.2 Detecting Kernel-Module Rootkits

To be able to detect kernel-module rootkits, you need to understand the concept of system calls in a Linux system. System calls act as gateways between the kernel and user programs. Because Linux is a protect-mode system, the kernel allows user programs to access critical parts of the computer only by using system calls. The kernel regulates system calls and prevents a single program from crashing the computer. In Linux, you need to do even small tasks--such as displaying a string on the screen, reading keys from the keyboard, or allocating some memory--using system calls such as read, write, and mmap.

The system calls mentioned above reside in the kernel and have specific addresses that tell user programs where they can be found. You can also find system-call addresses in a file called /boot/System.map. When a kernel-module rootkit captures system calls and redirects them through its own program, the addresses of the system calls change. This can give away even the most well hidden rootkit.

As an investigator, you need to match the addresses of system calls from the /boot/System.map file and from the kernel memory, which can be read from /dev/kmem. Any differences between the two indicate that a rootkit has been installed. You can also find out which rootkit has been installed by checking system calls that have been redirected.

You cannot interpret the /dev/kmem file on your own. Special utilities such as KSTAT enable you interpret the information in this file.

A program called KSTAT compares syscall locations between the /dev/kmem kernel memory and the /boot/System.map file. The syntax for KSTAT is:

kstat [-i iff] [-P] [-p pid] [-M] [-m addr] [-s]

In the above syntax:

- -i displays information about the requested interface. iff may be specified as "all" or as a name such as eth0.

- -P displays all processes.

- -p pid refers to the process ID of the queried task.

- -M displays the kernel's module list.

- -m addr refers to the hex address of the queried module.

- -s displays information about the system-calls table.

Normally, the best option to use is -s. The KSTAT -s command shows the kernels system-calls table.

Example 8.2

The `kstat -s` command displays the following sample kernels system-calsl table:

SysCall	Address
sys_exit	0xc0117ce4
sys_fork	0xc0108ebc
sys_read	0xc012604c
sys_write	0xc0126110
sys_open	0xc0125c10
sys_close	0xc0125d60
sys_waitpid	0xc0117ff8
sys_creat	0xc0125ca4
sys_link	0xc012de60
sys_unlink	0xc012dc90
sys_execve	0xc0108f18
sys_chdir	0xc01254a0
sys_time	0xc01184b4

---

sys_mknod	0xc012d77c
sys_chmod	0xc01256e4

The kstat -P command displays all the hidden processes in the system. It even displays processes that have been hidden by the rootkit. If you see a difference between the output of this command and the normal Linux ps command, then you can be sure that the rootkit is hiding a process. The hidden process is the difference between the two.

The following examples show how kstat enables you to detect the various types of rootkits.

▪ Detecting the Knark rootkit involves typing the kstat -s command to show the following output :

```
sys_fork        0xc284652c WARNING! Should be at 0xc0108c88
sys_read        0xc2846868 WARNING! Should be at 0xc012699c
sys_execve      0xc2846bb8 WARNING! Should be at 0xc0108ce4
sys_kill        0xc28465d4 WARNING! Should be at 0xc01106b4
sys_ioctl       0xc2846640 WARNING! Should be at 0xc012ff78
sys_settimeofday 0xc2846a8c WARNING! Should be at 0xc0118364
sys_clone       0xc2846580 WARNING! Should be at 0xc0108ca4
```

Code 8.3: Output of KSTAT for Knark

You can assess that Knark is running on the system from the system calls such as fork, read, execve, kill, and ioctl that have been altered.

■ Detecting the Adore rootkit involves typing the `kstat -s` command to show the following output:

```
sys_fork       0xc4051428 WARNING! Should be at 0xc0108c88
sys_write      0xc4051590 WARNING! Should be at 0xc0126b0
sys_close      0xc405163c WARNING! Should be at 0xc01264a4
sys_kill       0xc40514d0 WARNING! Should be at 0xc011060c
sys_mkdir      0xc405172c WARNING! Should be at 0xc012e540
sys_clone      0xc405147c WARNING! Should be at 0xc0108ca4
sys_getdents   0xc40512a4 WARNING! Should be at 0xc013022c
```

Code 8.4: `Output of kstat for Adore`

You can confirm the presence of the Adore rootkit by the modified system calls fork write, close, kill, mkdir, clone, and getdents.

Practice Questions

1. What is a kernel module?

2. What are the advantages of using kernel modules?

3. What is the function of the `insmod` command?

4. Differentiate between kernel and non-kernel rootkits.

5. Give few examples of kernel rootkits.

8.2 Malware Dissection and Analysis

Malware, short for malicious software, refers to the software designed to damage or disrupt a system using a virus, a rootkit, or a Trojan horse. As an investigator, you need to be familiar with the various code fragments and techniques used in malicious programs for attacking a system. This section covers methods of detecting and analyzing malicious programs.

8.2.1 Process Wiretapping

 Describe the methods for analyzing and detecting suspect programs.

Process wiretapping is the technique of analyzing programs while they are running on the system, without the programs' being aware of it.

When you detect a suspicious process executing on a computer, you need to analyze it without disturbing it. You perform this analysis on the target computer.

Case Study

For example, suppose that John, the system administrator of software company XYZ, Inc., runs `netstat` on his computer and detects a network connection. He runs `ps` to check what processes are running on the computer. He enters the `ps -aux` command and obtains the following output:

Figure 8.1: Result of ps Command

One of the processes in the listing shown in Figure 8.1 seems suspicious to him. As a preventive measure, he calls a system forensic investigator.

As an investigator, your first step during an analysis of a suspicious program should be to identify exactly what makes that process suspicious. You need to look for:

■ A process with start time matching that of the suspicious activity

■ A process with a misleading name to hide the real purpose or program

The next step is to view the files being used by this suspicious process. In the example, to view the files being used by the process with process ID 2793, you need to use the following command:

```
lsof -p 2793
```

The output is displayed in Figure 8.2.

Figure 8.2: Result of lsof Command

After viewing the listing, you can run the following command to find the executable for this program in the file system:

```
find /lib -inum 31013 -print
```

The above command will find any file in the file system whose inode number matches 31013, the number you obtained from the inodes being used by the program.

If the find returns with 0 files found, it means that the executable has already been deleted.

Investigating further, you detect the following suspicious activities pertaining to the process:

▨   The program is accepting connections on port 5120.

▨   No executable file is found.

After you confirm that the process is malicious, you need to immediately freeze the program from executing further so that no more damage can occur. Do not kill the process because you want to examine it, but freeze it in memory.

While performing the process analysis, you must keep in mind the following:

▨   Do not connect to the open port.

▨   Do not terminate or kill the process.

To freeze the process in memory, use the kill command with the STOP option. The syntax is:

kill –STOP <process id>

To freeze the process with process ID 31013, use the following command:

```
kill -STOP 31013
```

After freezing the command, you need to verify whether the process has actually been frozen by the KILL command. Use the following command to list all the processes on the computer that have been frozen:

```
ps -ax | grep T
```

The output of the command will be:

```
31013   ?      TW     0:0    <defunct>
```

The next step is to capture the process memory and the data. You can use the gcore command to force programs to copy their internal programs into a file. For example, the gcore 31013 command displays the following output:

```
gcore: core.12832 dumped
```

The internal programs of process 31013 are copied in the dumped file. You can view a listing of the file by using the following command:

```
ls -l core.31013
```

The output is:

```
-rw-r--r-- 1 root 8421808 Feb 24 09:29 core.12832
```

After you capture the suspect process data, you can:

- Examine the captured data with any standard debugger.
- Examine the captured data with simple tools such as strings or any binary editor.

Figure 8.3 shows a sample file as displayed by the binary editor Hexdump.

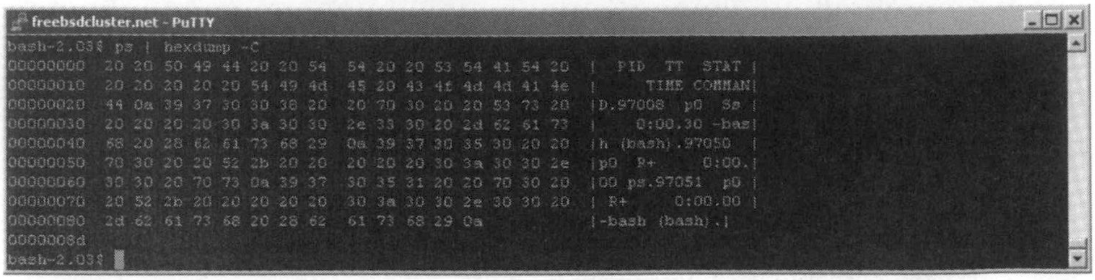

Figure 8.3: Hexdump Binary Editor

You can capture information about a process through the /proc directory. Files under /proc/<process id> give process information to the investigator. Table 8.1 shows a list of some process files in /proc.

File	Description
/proc/<pid>/mem	Process memory
/proc/<pid>/maps	Memory area, etc
/proc/<pid>/exe	The entire program

Table 8.1: Process Files in /proc

You need to analyze the process memory. The *process memory* is a combination of the program, which is the process, and the data generated or used by that program. You can capture the process memory using the pcat command, and you can examine it using the strings utility.

For example, to examine the process memory of the process with PID 31013, use the command:

```
strings core.31013 | more
```

Code 8.5 shows the output of the above command.

```
...more stuff...
..stuff...
Error: cant open file
kill
```

```
Error: can't open file
%s not found
bad port %s
Trying %s...
telcli: socket
:) %s port %d...
csh -bif
exec
pqrstuvwxyzPQRST
/dev/ptyXX
/dev/pty
/dev/ptyp
0123456789abcdef
/bin/csh
/dev/
/dev/tty
fork
/bin/csh
```

Code 8.5: Strings Command

In Code 8.5, the lines highlighted in black show that the process whose PID is 31013 has something to do with the /bin/csh program, which is a shell. But the process 31013 should have nothing to do with the physical location of a shell. This indicates that this process is a potential backdoor program trying to open a shell on the computer for a remote attacker.

A shell is a program that allows the attacker to enter and execute commands on a computer.

8.2.2 Fenris

 Describe the functions of the Fenris tool.

Fenris is a multipurpose tool that can be categorized as a multi-purpose tracer, graphical user-interface debugger, program-state analyzer, and partial code decompiler intended to make security audits and forensic analysis much easier for investigators. The Fenris tool can provide information about internal program structures, execution paths, and memory operations. You can use it to wiretap input and output operations performed by Fenris. Fenris is not a single tool but a toolkit, that is, a collection of very useful programs for process and program examination.

Before you learn how Fenris works and how it can be used in forensic investigation of executable binaries, you need to familiarize yourself with the workings of debuggers and executable files in the Linux file system.

- A debugger enables you to execute programs line by line so that the internal process can be examined. If you can set required breaks at certain locations, the program executes normally up to the break and then stops displaying all its memory and processor information.

- A decompiler does the opposite of what a compiler does. A compiler compiles source code into an executable program, whereas a decompiler changes the executable machine code back into the source program. Decompiling is a very complex task. Decompilers are not always accurate in output and are specific to the programming language.

Fenris has the following utilities that help in code analysis:

- Dress: Used as a stand-alone tool that reconstructs the internal pointers of the program.

- Aegir: An interactive debugger.

- nc-aegir: GUI for Aegir.

- Ragnarok: Program execution a path-examination tool.

Figure 8.4 shows Fenris decompiling an executable file.

```
eax 0x08053dd4   ebx 0x08053c88   ecx 0x401444c8   edx 0x08053bbc   esi 0x4001434c
edi 0xbffff4b4   ebp 0xbffff448   esp 0xbffff430   eip 0x0804fb23   flags odiSzapC
bffff470: f0 3d 01 40 01 00 00 00 c0 93 04 08 b4 f4 ff bf   | .=.@............
bffff480: 48 f9 03 40 dc 12 14 40 00 00 00 00 e1 93 04 08   | H..@...@........
bffff490: 50 95 04 08 01 00 00 00 b4 f4 ff bf 30 8f 04 08   | P...........0...
bffff4a0: 50 fb 04 08 f0 b0 00 40 ac f4 ff bf a4 43 01 40   | P......@.....C.@
0804fb23:        je        *0x804fb31
0804fb25:        movl      (%ebx),%eax
0804fb27:        addl      *0xfffffffc,%ebx
0804fb2a:        call      *%eax
0804fb2c:        cmpl      *0xffffffff,(%ebx)
0804fb2f:        jne       *0x804fb25
28869:00 <8049653> cndt: conditional block +5 skipped
28869:00 <8049664> cndt: on-match block +23 executed
28869:00 <804966d> cndt: on-match block +9 executed
28869:00 <8049676> cndt: conditional block +5 skipped
28869:00 <8049689> cndt: conditional block +69 skipped
28869:00 local fnct_7 (11600)
>> dynamic
At 0x4000943f, continuing to the main code...
>> Entered main code at 0x804fb23 [].
>> run
Resuming at 0x804fb23...
Processing, please wait...                                      [R]
```

Figure 8.4: Fenris

8.2.3 gdb Debugger

Explain the use of gdb.

gdb, the GNU Project debugger, allows you to see the inner workings of another program while that program executes. It allows you to observe what a program was doing at the moment it crashed.

gdb has the following features:

▪ Executes your program, specifying anything that may affect its behavior

▪ Stops your program on specific conditions

▪ Examines what happened when your program stops

gdb can debug any compiled program that can be executed by Linux.

You can download gdb from http://sources.redhat.com/gdb/.

8.2.4 Filemon and Regmon

■ Describe the use of the Filemon utility in forensics applications.

■ Describe the function of the Regmon application.

Filemon and Regmon are commercial applications. Filemon monitors all file activities such as read, write, open, and close. Regmon logs all reads and writes to and from the Windows registry. Both programs run only on the Windows operating system. The information that the programs provide is very useful because it enables you to understand the working of certain Windows programs. For example, suppose a program masquerading as a word processor begins to write and read into files or into areas of the registry that have no relation to it. You can conclude that this is a suspicious program.

You can also use Filemon and Regmon to detect spyware or malware installed on the computer. Programs such as spyware or malware usually try to write to make changes to the registry for gathering user information from the registry or file system. If you have Filemon and Regmon actively running, you can keep track of the file and the registry activity being performed by the program you are analyzing.

Figure 8.5 shows a sample screen of the Filemon program File Monitor. It shows the files opened by the process named PSP. The sixth column, named Result, shows SUCCESS for the files the program successfully opened, closed, or modified. The fourth column, named Request, shows the type of file operation being carried out, for example, write, read, open, close, and seek. The second column, Time, shows when the file activity was attempted.

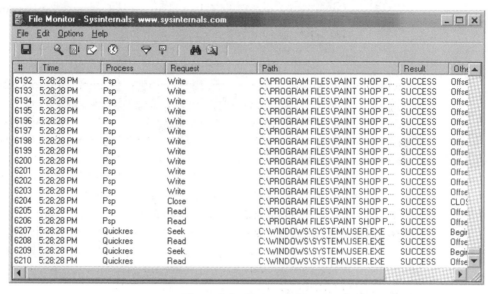

Figure 8.5: Filemon Utility

Figure 8.6 shows a sample screen of the Regmon Registry Monitor. It shows the registry activity being carried out by the program named PSP. All the columns are similar to the columns in the Filemon program, except for the fifth column, Path, which shows the registry path where the activity is being carried out. The seventh field, Other, shows the values being written to or read from the registry.

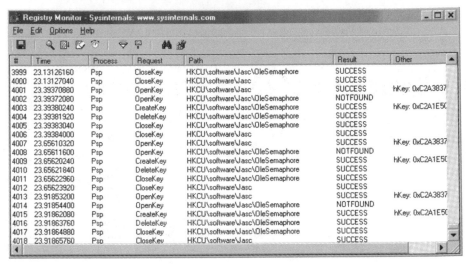

Figure 8.6: Regmon Utility

Practice Questions

1. What is process wiretapping?

2. What is the function of the `ps` command?

3. List the utilities of Fenris.

4. List the steps you would take to determine whether a program is malicious or not.

5. Differentiate between Filemon and Regmon.

8.3 Analysis of /proc Directory

The /proc directory is a virtual directory that works like an interface between user programs and the kernel. By setting and reading values from it, a user can change or see the state of the operating system. The /proc file system provides information about the status of the kernel and other information such as the type of hardware connected to the computer. This information is useful in collecting evidence.

8.3.1 Structure of /proc Directory

 Describe the structure of the /proc directory.

The /proc directory consists of a numerical sub-directory for each running process. Sub-directories are named by the process ID, and each sub-directory contains the following pseudo-files and directories. Table 8.2 lists the sub-directories.

Files	Description
cmdline	Contains process command-line arguments
environ	Contains environment variables
fd	Contains the directory that contains file descriptors
mem	Shows the amount of memory held by this process
stat	Shows the process status
status	Shows the process status in a readable form
cwd	Contains a link to the current working directory
exe	Contains a link to the executable program of this process
maps	Contains memory maps
root	Contains a link to the root directory of this

	process
statm	Shows process memory-status information
maps	Contains memory maps

Table 8.2: /proc Directory Structure

You can view the above information for a process by using the `cat` command. For viewing the status of a process, the syntax of the `cat` command is:

```
cat /proc/<process id>/status
```

Example 8.3

```
The following command displays information about the
process with the ID 1530.
Cat /proc/1530/status
Output:
Name:   java
State:  S (sleeping)
Tgid:   1530
Pid:    1530
PPid:   1515
TracerPid:      0
Uid:    4053    4053    4053    4053
Gid:    4053    4053    4053    4053
FDSize: 32
Groups: 4053 9402 53 51 9239 9238 5518 5265 83 40000
9257 9295 81
VmSize:    220504 kB
VmLck:          0 kB
VmRSS:      43436 kB
VmData:    178924 kB
VmStk:         40 kB
VmExe:         20 kB
VmLib:       4976 kB
SigPnd: 0000000000000000
SigBlk: 0000000000000004
```

```
SigIgn:  8000000000000000
SigCgt:  1000000380015ccf
CapInh:  0000000000000000
CapPrm:  0000000000000000
CapEff:  0000000000000000
```

The /proc file system also holds other information about the computer as listed in Table 8.3.

Files	Description
Apm	Advanced power management
cmdline	Kernel command line
cpuinfo	Information about the CPU
devices	Available devices (block and character)
Dma	Used DMS channels
File systems	Supported file systems
interrupts	Interrupt usage
ioports	I/O port usage
Kcore	Kernel-core image
Kmsg	Kernel messages
ksyms	Kernel-symbol table
loadavg	Load average
locks	Kernel locks
meminfo	Memory information
misc	Miscellaneous
modules	List of loaded kernel modules

Table 8.3: Process Files in /proc

The above files can be accessed by the method displayed in Example 8.4.

Example 8.4

> To view the names of the file systems that are compatible with your system's kernel, use the following command:
>
> ```
> cat /proc/file systems
> ```

The output is:

```
          ext3
    nodev    rootfs
    nodev    bdev
    nodev    proc
    nodev    sockfs
    nodev    tmpfs
    nodev    shm
    nodev    pipefs
    nodev    binfmt_misc
          ext2
    nodev    ramfs
          iso9660
    nodev    nfs
    nodev    autofs
    nodev    devpts
```

The above example shows the file systems that are compatible with this Linux kernel.

Reading the contents of these sub-directory files gives you a glimpse into the kernel tables and processes that manage overall system activities.

Example 8.5

You can check which and how many devices are currently configured in your system by using the following command:

`cat /proc/devices`

The output of the command is:

```
Character devices:
    1 mem
    2 pty
    3 ttyp
    4 ttyS
    5 cua
```

```
     7 vcs
    10 misc
128 ptm
136 pts
162 raw
254 aac
Block devices:
   2 fd
   3 ide0
   8 sd
  65 sd
  66 sd
```

Practice Questions

1. What is the importance of analyzing the /proc directory in system forensics?

2. List the sub-directories of /proc.

3. Write the syntax of cat command.

Summary

■ A kernel module is a small program that loads itself into the OSkernel to provide more features to the operating system.

  Kernel Modules can be used for:

  • Device drivers

  • File-system drivers

  • System calls

  • Executable interpreters

  • Network drivers

■ Rootkits are programs that work like kernel modules. Instead of adding useful features to the kernel, rootkits add features that an attacker can use to take control of the computer.

■ Examples of rootkits are:

  • Knark

  • RKIT

  • Adore

■ To detect kernel rootkits, you need to match the addresses of system calls from the /boot/System.map file and the kernel memory. The kernel memory can be read from /dev/kmem.

■ Special utilities such as KSTAT enable you to view the /dev/kmem file.

■ Process wiretapping is the technique of analyzing programs that are running on the system without letting them know that they are being analyzed.

■ You can capture the process memory by using the `pcat` command.

■ The `gcore` command forces programs to copy their internal programs into a file.

■ Process memory is a combination of the program, which is process, and the data generated by that program or used by that program.

■ Fenris is a combination of the following: multi-purpose tracer, graphical user-interface debugger, program-state analyzer, and partial-code decompiler. It is intended to make security audits and forensic analysis much easier for the investigators.

- Fenris provides the following the utilities:
  - Dress
  - Aegir:
  - nc-aegir
  - Ragnarok
- The GNU Project debugger (gdb) allows you to see the inner workings of another program while that program executes.
- Filemon monitors all file activities. Regmon logs all reads and writes to and from the Windows registry. Both programs run only on Windows operating systems.
- The /proc directory is a virtual directory that works as an interface between user programs and the kernel.
- Reading the contents of process sub-directory files in /proc gives you a glimpse into kernel tables and processes that manage the overall system activities.

References

- http://www.tldp.org/LDP/lkmpg/
- http://www.thehackerschoice.com/papers/LKM_HACKING.html
- http://www.linux.org/docs/ldp/howto/KernelAnalysis-HOWTO.html
- http://www.tldp.org/LDP/tlk/tlk.html
- http://rootprompt.org/article.php3?article=5426
- http://www.thc.org/papers/LKM_HACKING.html

Homework Exercises

1. Explain the /proc file system.

2. Write a brief description of the Fenris tool.

3. Explain the tools you would use to analyze a process running on a Linux machine.

4. Explain the steps involved in analyzing a running process.

5. What are the two fundamental types of rootkits?

6. Explain how you can tell what rootkit is installed.

7. Which tools are used to detect the two types of rootkits?

8. What is the function of `depmod` program?

9. Explain system calls.

10. What capabilities do rootkits have?

11. Explain kernel-module rootkits.

12. List the different types of kernel modules.

13. Write a note on gdb.

14. Write a brief note on Regmon and Filemon. Explain their role in system forensics.

15. Explain in detail the output of the `lsof` command.

Lab Exercises

Exercise 1

Objective

- Understand kernel rootkits by using them.
- Practice detecting kernel rootkits.

Theory

As an investigator, you need to understand how hackers work so that you will be better equipped to deal with the problems. In the first part of the lab exercise you play the role of a hacker by installing a rootkit on the computer and using it to learn first hand about how rootkits function. In the second part of this lab, you play the part of the investigator and prove that a rootkit has been installed on the given machine. You need to provide documentation that lists the steps you used to detect the rootkit.

- Download and install the Knark rootkit.
- Use what you have learned in this chapter to detect that the rootkit has been installed.

Problem Statement

- Install Knark on the machine.
- Install the KSTAT tool.
- Use the KSTAT tool to detect the Knark rootkit.

Lab Setup

- Machine with Linux 7.1 installed
- Knark rootkit installed on the system
- Tool to detect rootkit (KSTAT)

Procedure

To install the Knark rootkit on your machine:

1. Change the directory to root/Mytools.

   ```
   cd /root/MyTools
   ```

2. Unzip the Knark rootkit tar file.

   ```
   tar -zxvf knark-2[1].4.3.tar.gz
   ```

3. Change the directory to Knark.

   ```
   cd  Knark-2[1].4.3
   ```

4. Compile and install Knark.

After installing the Knark rootkit in the kernel, try to use its features to do things such as hiding files and processes.

To install the KSTAT tool on you machine:

1. Change the directory to root/Mytools.

   ```
   cd /root/MyTools
   ```

2. Unzip the KSTAT tar file.

   ```
   tar -zxvf kstat24.tgz
   ```

3. Change the directory to KSTAT/2.4.

   ```
   cd KSTAT/2.4
   ```

4. Compile and install KSTAT.

   ```
   ./install.sh.
   ```

Now, detect the Knark rootkit using the KSTAT utility. Document the report/log generated by KSTAT and present it to the instructor.

Conclusion/Observation

Here, you have learned about rootkits and how they are used. Moreover, you have learned how to detect installed rootkits on a computer.

Lab Activity Checklist

S. No.	Tasks	Completed	
		Yes	No
1.	Installed KSTAT		
2.	Installed Knark		
3.	Detected Knark's presence using KSTAT		
4.	Documented the report generated by KSTAT		

Exercise 2

Objective

- Recover deleted files.

Problem Statement

Consider that a hacker, Jack, has deleted log files and other files from a system to conceal his own intrusion. You as an investigator have to recover these files.

Lab Setup

TCT installed on the system.

Procedure

1. Use the tool 'ils' to generate a list of all deleted files on your hard disk.

   For example,

   ```
   ./ils -rf ext2fs /image/dev_hda1.img
   ```

   The above command will list out the inodes of all deleted files in the disk image dev_hda1.img.

2. Simulate the hacker's activity of file deletion by deleting the 'tcpdump' program from your computer after making a copy of it. Also records the inode number of the tcpdump program. For example,

   ```
   cp /usr/sbin/tcpdump /usr/sbin/tcpdump.bak
   ls -li /usr/sbin/tcpdump
   ```

   This command will give you the inode number of the tcpdump program.

3. Delete the tcpdump program.

   ```
   rm -rf /usr/sbin/tcpdump
   ```

4. Locate the deleted file with the help of icat utility with the inode number.

Conclusion/Observation

icat utility uses inode number to locate a particular file.

Lab Activity Checklist

S.No.	Tasks	Completed	
		Yes	No
1.	Made a copy of tcpdump program		
2.	Noted the inode number of tcpdump program		
3.	Deleted tcpdump		
4.	Used icat to locate the deleted file		

Network Forensics

9

This chapter explains the basic concepts of network forensics and provides you with an overview of OS fingerprinting and types of OS fingerprinting. The chapter also explains the concepts of encryption and tunneling, for example, wiretapping, network monitoring, and covert channels. In addition, this chapter describes the use of Ethereal and how to recover a rootkit from the data stream. At the end of the chapter, you will be able to:

- Explain the concept of OS fingerprinting.
- Explain encryption and tunneling in network forensics.

9.1 OS Fingerprinting

9.2 Encrypting and Tunneling

9.1 OS Fingerprinting

The greatest challenges in network security are identifying your enemy and protecting your network against threats from the enemy. Network forensics deals with the technology or methodology of analyzing a network and detecting the remote host responsible for hacking your network. *Fingerprinting* helps you learn about your enemy without the enemy's knowledge. OS fingerprinting involves determining the OS of the remote host by means of active and passive tools such as sniffer traces or analysis of OS response of the remote host by the sending of malformed data packets.

This section deals with OS fingerprinting. Using OS fingerprinting techniques, you can identify the OS used by the remote host and the characteristics of the remote host. The section also discusses the types of OS fingerprinting and the various fingerprinting techniques and tools used.

9.1.1 Overview of OS Fingerprinting

- Describe OS fingerprinting.
- Identify the fields of the IP and TCP headers.

OS fingerprinting is performed to identify the remote user who may be trying to access your resources such as some sensitive or confidential data that you need to send over a network to another system through Internet. The remote user can be identified by means of various active and passive tools. Each OS responds differently to different malformed packets. Malformed packets are those that have the same source and destination port as those of the normal packets, but are decoded differently. For example, in most operating systems, the maximum size of the data segment that can be transmitted between a sender and receiver is 4 bytes, which makes the minimum length of the TCP header 44 bytes. A data packet having a length of 40 bytes can easily be detected as a malformed or a crafted packet. To identify an OS, you need to create a database that stores the information about how different operating systems respond to different malformed packets. To identify the OS of the remote host, you send different malformed packets and compare its response with the data stored in the database to determine the OS.

Transmission Control Protocol/Internet Protocol (TCP/IP) is a network layer protocol. There are various TCP/IP signatures that help determine the OS used by the remote system. For understanding these signatures, a brief overview of the TCP/IP headers is essential. TCP/IP headers are used to communicate across a network over the Internet. TCP/IP is used to transmit datagrams from the source to the destination.

9.1.1.1 IP Header

Internet Protocol (IP) is the protocol used for communication on an interconnected network. An IP data packet consists of various field areas, as shown in Figure 9.1.

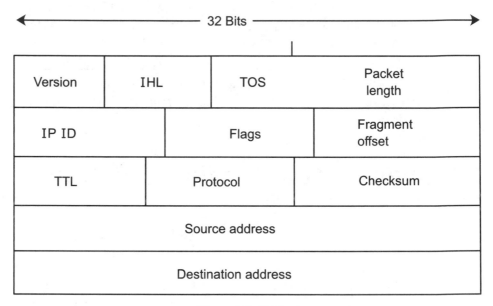

Figure 9.1: IP Header

The various fields in an IP data packet are:

- Version: Specifies the version of the IP being used.

- IP Header Length (IHL): Denotes the length of the header. This length is denoted in 32-bit words.

- Type of Service (TOS): Indicates the requirements of the data sent from the sender to the receiver. It specifies the type of service or the way in which a datagram needs to be handled. The default value of various operating systems is set to 00*00 (normal service). Some operating systems set the TOS value to 00*10 (minimize delay) for initializing telnet sessions. The TOS field has four fields that can be set for any of the values, such as 1000 (minimize delay), 0100 (maximize throughput),

0001 (minimize cost), 0010 (maximize reliability), and 0000 (normal service). TOS helps an analyst identify the OS used by a remote host.

- Total Length: Specifies the IP-packet length for an OS.
- IP ID: The identification field area that contains the integer value for identifying an OS.
- Flags: Consists of a field area of 3 bits. The two least significant bits of this field control the *fragmentation*, that is, the scattering of the same disk file over different areas of the disk. Fragmentation occurs when the files on the disk are deleted and new files are added to the disk. The low-order bit specifies whether the packet can be fragmented, and the middle bit specifies whether the packet is the last fragment in a series of fragmented packets. The most significant bit is left unused. The lower two bits help only in controlling the fragmentation.
- Fragment offset: Indicates the position of the current datagram in the current network traffic.
- Time To Live (TTL): Limits the packet lifetimes, which means that it indicates how long a packet can stay on the medium. The TTL contains a counter that is decremented every time a session is started when a connection is established, at which point the datagram is discarded. The maximum lifetime of 255 seconds is allowed for a datagram. The initial value of TTL refers to a lot of information about an OS such as which OS is being used and the time when a session was started.
- Header Checksum: Verifies the header. It detects any errors generated within a router due to bad memory.
- Source Address and Destination Address: Specify the sending and receiving nodes.
- Options: Allows IP to support various options such as security.

A *datagram* is one packet or unit of information. It provides the relevant delivery information, such as the destination address, sent through a packet-switching network.

9.1.1.2 TCP Header

TCP is the most widely used transport protocol in the Internet. When a TCP application sends data, it divides the data into a number of data units called TCP segments.

These segments consist of two parts. The first part contains the data to be transmitted, and the second part is the header that defines various parameters used in the TCP communication between the source and the destination. These TCP segments are then encapsulated within the data portion of an IP datagram and sent on to the destination.

Figure 9.2 shows the various field areas of a TCP header.

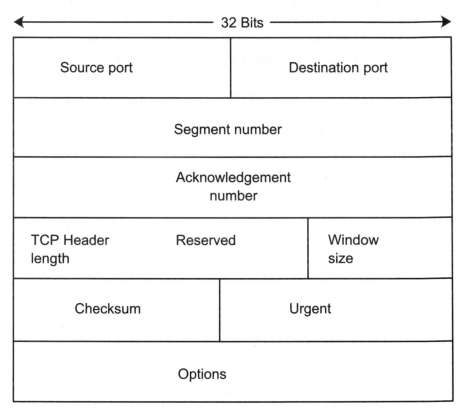

Figure 9.2: TCP Header

■ Source port and the Destination port: Specify the local end points of the connection. These fields tell you some details about an OS, such as the ports used by the OS of the sender and the receiver, but this information may not be sufficient for identifying an OS.

- TCP Header length: Specifies the length of the TCP header in 32-bit words.
- Window size: Specifies the size of the sender's receive window.

Window refers to the buffer space available for incoming data.

- Checksum: Provides reliability to the TCP. It indicates whether the header was damaged in the transmission.
- Urgent: Points to the first urgent data byte in the data packet. The urgent data packet may need to be transmitted first before the other data packets.
- Options: Specifies the various TCP options:
  - MSS (Maximum Segment Size): The datagrams are transmitted over the Internet in packets enclosed in transmission units and transmitted from the sender to the receiver. An MTU (Maximum Transmission Unit) is the maximum-sized transmission unit that a system can handle. MSS is the maximum size of the data segment that can be transmitted between a sender and a receiver.
  - Timestamp: Timestamp measures the time delays in sending and receiving data packets. The timestamp field has two sub-fields, timestamp value and timestamp echo reply that help measure the delays. The timestamp value specifies the time when a data packet is sent, while timestamp echo reply specifies the time when the response of the receipt is received from the receiver end.
  - Wscale (Window scale): wscale specifies the scale factor to be applied to the receive window. It shifts the window-size field's value up to a maximum value.
  - No operation (nop): nop is 1 byte in size and converts the TCP header length to a multiple of 4 bytes. It provides padding around other options. For example, if an option is of 3 bytes, nop is added to it to make it 4 bytes. Similarly, if an option is of 2 bytes, 2 nops are added.

- SackOK (Selective Acknowledgement): The sender uses SackOK to acknowledge the receipt of data sent. The sender has to retransmit a packet that has been left out or not received. If the data is sent without selective acknowledgment, the sender can acknowledge data packets up to the packet number before the missing packet. This means the sender has to resend the data after the packet missed out. For example, if a sender is sending 100 packets of data without using selective acknowledgement and the third packet is missing, the sender will receive the acknowledgment of first two packets only and will have to retransmit the remaining data packets.

The major TCP areas that determine the OS are:

- TTL
- Window size
- Type of service

You can analyze these factors to determine the OS. No single signature can reliably determine the OS used by the remote system. Combining the information of various signatures can increase the accuracy of the OS fingerprinting because two or more operating systems may share the same value of a particular field. The other areas or fields that can be helpful in identifying an OS are the sequence numbers, IP identification numbers, and various TCP/IP options.

9.1.2 Types of OS Fingerprinting

 Identify the various types of OS fingerprinting techniques.

You can classify the OS fingerprinting techniques into two types:

- Passive fingerprinting
- Active fingerprinting

9.1.2.1 Passive OS Fingerprinting

Passive OS fingerprinting involves analyzing a TCP packet trace from a remote host. The responses of different operating systems to a variety of malformed packets are analyzed, and the OS is identified. In passive OS fingerprinting, no special packets are sent to the remote host. This method is based on sniffer traces from the remote host. The packets sent from the remote host are analyzed, and on the basis of the sniffer traces of these packets, the OS of the remote system is determined.

You can compare the various operating systems according to the field values of the TCP/IP headers. Window size is an important and effective tool in determining an OS. The OS can be determined on the basis of the window size used and the frequency of change in the window size.

 Sniffer traces refer to the traces of the data packets that help in identifying the type of OS and other characteristics of an OS.

The field values for some of the operating systems are:

- Red Hat Linux 9.0

    - *Window size*: Red Hat Linux 9.0 sets its window size to 5,840 bytes by default. Linux maintains the same Window size throughout a session.

    - *Time to Live* (TTL): The TTL value for Linux 9.0 is set to 64 by default. In a Linux system, you can verify the TTL value by using the following command:

        ```
        More /proc/sys/net/ipv4/ip_defaut_ttl
        ```

    - *IP identification number*: In a Linux OS, the IP ID increments by 1 during each session once a connection is established.

    - *Packet Length*: The typical packet length of a Linux OS is 60 bytes. Therefore, if the trace value of packet length is 60 bytes, you can identify the OS as Linux.

    - *TCP options*: The TCP options for Linux operating systems are set to MSS, Timestamps wscale, sackOK, wscale, and 1 nop.

- Windows 2000

    - *Window size*: The window size is set to 16,384 bytes.

    - *TTL*: All Microsoft Windows operating systems use a TTL value of 128.

    - *IP identification number*: The IP ID is incremented by 1, as in Linux, during each session once a connection is established.

    - *Packet length*: The packet length for Windows 2000 is set to 48 bytes.

    - *TCP options*: The TCP options for Windows 2000 are MSS, 2 nops, and sackOK.

- OpenBSD
  - *Window Size*: Window size for openBSD is set to 16,384 bytes.
  - *TTL*: The TTL value for openBSD OS is 64, which is the same as for Linux operating systems.
  - *Packet length*: The packet length of openBSD OS is 64 bytes. This value is typical for this OS and is thus the key identifier.
  - *TCP options*: TCP options set for openBSD OS are MSS, timestamps, sackOK, and 5 nops.

You can see from the preceding data that by analyzing a combination of various field values, you can easily identify an OS. In fact, the greater the number of fields you compare, the better the results you can obtain in identifying the OS used by a remote host.

9.1.2.2 Active OS Fingerprinting

Active OS fingerprinting involves sending malformed packets to the remote host and comparing its response with a variety of malformed packets from the database. The database contains the information about the responses of different operating systems to different malformed packets. The tools used by the active OS fingerprinting technique for analyzing the responses of the remote host are nmap and Xprobe2. These tools form a fingerprint that can be queried against a signature database of various operating systems.

- *Stack querying*: A technique that determines the OS of the remote host. Packets are sent on the remote system to the network stack, and the analyst can analyze the response of the remote system. This is known as stack querying and aimed at a TCP stack. A TCP stack can be considered as a structure that stores information or data in a form such that the data entering last in the network goes out first. It involves sending standard and non-standard TCP packets to the remote host and analyzing the responses of different operating systems.

- *Initial Sequence Number* (ISN): A pattern that depicts how sequence numbers for subsequent packets are incremented. In addition, these numbers enable you to fingerprint an OS because they depict how data packets from an OS enter a network. The incrimination pattern of the ISN helps determine the OS.

- *ICMP-response analysis*: A method that verifies whether the remote OS is ICMP protocol. In ICMP response analysis, the ICMP messages are sent to the remote system, and its responses are analyzed.

- *Temporal-response analysis*: A method that uses TCP protocol and analyzes the retransmission timeout responses from a remote host.

 Internet Control Message Protocol (ICMP) is a protocol used to test for the connectivity and search for configuration errors on a network. ICMP tests whether a network is connected to another network, which means it tests for the inter-network connectivity. When a datagram cannot reach its destination or the gateway does not have the buffering capacity to forward a datagram, and when the gateway can direct the host to send traffic on a shorter route, ICMP messages are used.

The main difference between active and passive OS fingerprinting is that in active fingerprinting malformed packets are sent to the remote system. The following tools are used for detecting an OS:

- *Nmap*: Used to scan the ports on large networks. This tool can also be considered as a security scanner that scans the network. It determines which hosts are running and what services those hosts offer. You cannot scan for other protocols such as UDP, TCP, or ICMP with the help of one scanning mode. Nmap uses a scanning tool or technique known as NBTscan, a program that scans a network for NetBIOS name information. It does so by sending the NetBIOS status to each address and recording the received information such as the IP address, user-name logged in, Net BIOS computer name, and so on.

- *Xprobe*: Used to identify Microsoft-based operating systems. TCP is the protocol used for OS fingerprinting and is an alternative tool for the operating systems that are heavily dependent on TCP protocol for fingerprinting. The TCP implementation with Microsoft Windows 2000, Windows NT, and Windows XP are very close. With TCP protocol, you cannot differentiate between these operating systems. Therefore, Xprobe is used as an effective tool in *OS fingerprinting* specifically for Microsoft operating systems. Xprobe scans the network and produces a report in ASCII text format. This report contains the details of the OS obtained from the scan performed, is available to the client, and contains the complete information about the OS in Microsoft Word or PDF format.

Practice Questions

1. Name the different IP Header fields.
2. Illustrate a TCP Header diagrammatically.
3. Name the TCP areas that help in identifying an OS.
4. Differentiate between active and passive fingerprinting.

9.2 Encrypting and Tunneling

Encrypting is the process of converting an ordinary or plain text, which may contain sensitive data, into an unreadable form for intelligently hiding data from the intruders. The messages that are to be sent over a network are encrypted by the use of a function with the help of an encryption key. The encrypted data is known as cipher text. Even if the intruders accurately copy the complete cipher text, they do not know the decrypting key that only the intended receiver knows. *Tunneling* is a technique used for carrying a protocol across a different network. It is used when the source and the destination hosts are of the same type of network, but there exists a different network between them. In tunneling, the data is encrypted and encapsulated into a TCP data stream and is carried across the public Internet between two remote sites. Figure 9.3 illustrates tunneling.

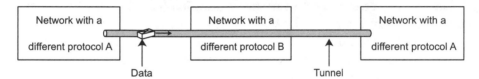

Figure 9.3: Tunneling

The protocol firewall allows the data to pass through without stopping when the data is sent through a protocol tunnel. In this technique of tunneling, two isolated networks are joined together. Protocols such as HTTP and SMTP satisfy the requirement that a protocol be allowed to pass through a firewall. This section explains the basic techniques of wiretapping and network monitoring for network investigators: using covert channels, using Ethereal to capture and analyze network traffic, and recovering a rootkit from the data streams.

9.2.1 Wiretapping and Network Monitoring

- Explain the concept of wiretapping.
- Describe the different methods used to monitor networks.

Monitoring a network is important for capturing data and analyzing it so that proper security measures can be taken to protect the network from malicious users. Monitoring of network traffic also helps in recording the data for future analysis. You can use tcpdump, Windump, and string commands to display the TCP packets and have an idea of what data is being transmitted over the entire network. The Snort tool allows you to define conditions that generate traps. Snort rules can be used to diagnose the network traffic and alert the investigator of suspicious network activity, so that the investigator can react in an appropriate manner. For example, if a network is not using a particular protocol, it can be configured with Snort alert rules so that it can trap all the data packets bound for the port of that particular protocol. In addition, monitoring the entire network traffic protects the highly confidential and sensitive data moving on the network. Using these rules reduces the chances of the data being disclosed illegally by any other user.

The tcpdump command is used to display the headers of packets on a network. The Windump dump command is the tcpdump command for Windows and is used to watch and diagnose network traffic for Windows OS.

In network forensics, the monitoring of the network is limited to the analysis of the traffic that passes over a network. You perform traffic analysis over a network by analyzing the TCP/IP headers of the data packets and inferring the addresses of the sender and the receiver from them. In addition, the flow of the data packets over some time depicts the time when a person is working on the network. TCP/IP headers also indicate the addresses of the systems communicating with one another. Network monitoring by forensic investigators also involves monitoring the network traffic for the Web sites visited by a remote host.

The complete analysis of the network traffic can be recorded and used to evaluate the intrusion on the network. Advanced Packet Vault (APV) is a technology used by forensic investigators to create a record of all the packets over the network. This technology encrypts data packets to maintain the integrity and security of the data by storing all the data over the network in an encrypted form.

In addition, it permits selected data traffic to be disclosed and the other data packets to be encrypted, thus having key values that are understood by the sender and the receiver only. For implementing the vault, network traffic is passed in an encrypted form. Vault implementation hides some traffic passing through the network by encryption of each data packet with a key dependent on the source and recipient's IP addresses. Operating systems such as Linux and FreeBSD have an open-source vault implementation.

The monitoring policy should specify that your company have the rights to monitor the network traffic. It should also specify the type of data that is stored on the company's systems. This data should be used internally by the company.

Wiretapping refers to tapping a network and retrieving information from the network traffic flowing from a source to destination. Wiretapping is illegal. In fact, a user must not hack back. Even if a company owns equipment that is capable of wiretapping a network, it should not wiretap a network. Monitoring network traffic involves detecting the attacks, which is a form of wiretapping. The network investigator must check any third person or a group of people that may be trying to intrude and get information out of a network. The network administrator creates logs that are useful in system investigation.

To hack back means to strike back at the computer that tries to hack your computer. Hacking back is a defensive strategy, but the U.S. government considers hacking back illegal because it too also hacking, and a crime committed to counter a crime can never be justified. It is also a form of cyber crime.

When an intruder wiretaps a network, the data on the network is being read by the intruder without the knowledge of the source and the destination. Wiretapping involves two main steps:

- Capturing: The intruder captures the information from the wire over the network.
- Selective filtering: The intruder then filters out the required information from the complete network traffic.

9.2.2 Covert Channels

 Explain the concept of the covert channels.

A *covert channel* is an indirect communication channel used by a sender to transfer data to the users who normally do not have access to this data. Such a communication channel can be exploited by a process, to transfer information in a manner that violates the system's security policy. Covert channels are also known as *subliminal channels*.

Transferring data using covert channels enables the user to transfer information through messages that appear harmless. The sender of the data communicating through covert channel does not encrypt any data, though it is understood by the receiver only. There is an agreement between the sender and the receiver before the data is sent. Covert channels are used in digital signatures.

An example of a covert channel is the prisoners' problem. Suppose there are 20 prisoners in a prison under the same warden. The warden puts each of the prisoners in a separate cell, and they are not allowed to communicate with one another. The warden takes each of the prisoners to a switch room where they are required to reverse the direction of a switch--that is, if the switch is in on position, the prisoner has to switch it off and vice versa. The warden calls one prisoner at a time and may call the same prisoner again and again and may skip some prisoners. The prisoners do not know which of them is being called, and they also cannot communicate with one another. When all the prisoners have visited the switch room at least once, the last prisoner has to say that all of them have visited the switch room, and if they don't indicate this to the warden, they will be punished. Now, the problem is how the prisoners tell one another whether they have visited the switch room or not. They make use of a covert channel. What prisoners do is that when they visit the switch room, they mark their name on the wall. Now, every prisoner visiting the room will come to know who has visited the room and can tell the warden when all of them have done so. The prisoners didn't do anything illegal. They were told not to communicate with each other, and that's what they did.

Similarly, the messages through covert channels are sent in a manner that an intruder cannot understand the message, because it is in some encoded form. The message is not encrypted. The digital signatures used by the sender and the receiver can authenticate the signature as well as extract the covert message.

In the case of TCP/IP, covert channels can be used to transfer data between a sender and a receiver in a surreptitious manner. The methods using covert channels for transferring data can be used in network sniffers and bypassing packet filters.

Covert channels are useful when you do not want to be associated with a node. Covert channels prevent association of the incoming and outgoing data. These channels are useful when encryption of data is restricted and outlawed. A covert-channel tunneling tool allows you to establish covert channels within a data stream. A data stream implies the network traffic flowing between interconnected networks.

Covert channels allow hackers to launch Distributed Denial of Service (DDoS) attacks. DDoS attacks are very complex and intelligent. A hacker gains access to a protected network and places some master and agent programs onto the systems. The malicious user contacts these master and agent programs with the help of covert channels such as ICMP and UDP protocols. Without using covert channels, malicious users or hackers cannot have access to these distributed agents.

You can effectively eliminate the threat of your system being hacked if such covert channels, which are the means of communication between the attacker and the agent, are eliminated. The analysis of covert channels by a network forensic investigator requires examination of the system for its size and complexity. The resources of the covert channel need to be identified, which can be done by the use of analysis of system representation. A tool known as Shared Resource Matrix (SRM) is an analytical tool for searching the covert channels.

9.2.3 Collecting Evidence from Network Traffic

 Explain the methods of collecting evidence from the network traffic.

When the data transferred on a network is attacked, you need to track the network traffic. However, the process of collecting forensic evidence for the purpose of investigation is a difficult process. Electronic evidence is not permanent and is very difficult to understand because there are many obstacles involved in collecting evidence.

Following are few of the obstacles in collecting evidence about the network traffic:

- Difficult to investigate: The tracking process of the data is performed after the transmission of the data is complete.

- Vulnerable electronic data: When data is transferred on the network, it is vulnerable to changes when it passes through different types of networks.

9.2.3.1 Need for Collecting Evidence

You need to collect evidence from network traffic for the following reasons:

- Prevention: It is necessary to collect evidence from network traffic when your network has been attacked because if you can track the source from where your network was attacked, you can take preventive measures in the future to counter such attacks.

- Responsibility: When your network is attacked, there are two responsible parties, the attacking party and the victim. The attacker is responsible for damaging the data, and the victim is responsible for preventing further attacks.

The various types of evidence that you can use to collect information from the network traffic are:

- Real: In real evidence, the administrators monitoring the network traffic can actually see the sequence of attack being made on the network. This may include log files, which keep a record on all the activities of your network, used for auditing the network traffic.

- Testimonial: A witness to prove the authenticity of the evidence always supports this kind of evidence. This evidence can be trusted only when the supporting witness is reliable.

- Hearsay: This is indirect evidence that is presented by a witness. This evidence might not be legally proved for their correctness. Therefore, this kind of evidence must be avoided, for example, a document provided by a witness without the knowledge about the correctness.

When you collect evidence to obtain information from the network traffic for tracking any intrusion into the network, you need to check for the following features to consider the evidence useful:

- Authentic: The evidence should be such that it can be proved as related to the event for which you were using the evidence. That means that the evidence is not unrelated to the attack. For example, if you are using a log file as evidence to prove a specific user's login time, the log file must contain the user ID of that particular user.

- Can be proved legally: The evidence should be such that it can be proved in court or in a place where you can get compensated for the damage to your network. Evidence that can be proved in a court is technically correct. For example, if an intruder has manipulated the data on a network, you should present in the court the original data that you had sent and the data that was actually transferred.

- Complete in all respects: The evidence that you are collecting must not be incomplete in any respect. For example, you may show evidence to prove that an attacker logged in at a particular time and information about all the other users who had logged in at the same time. You can prove that others who had logged in at that time, all except the attacker, had no intentions of destroying data.

- Reliable: The evidence you are collecting must be correct. For example, if you want to prove a specific user's login time, you should have a log file that is automatically generated by the system and not written manually.

- Easy to prove: The evidence should be clear and easy to understand. The evidence should be such that it can be easily understood by anyone who does not have any technical knowledge. For example, a log entry might be difficult for a non-technical person to interpret. However, if the entry is explained in simple terms, it is easily understood.

For collecting evidence on a network, you need to perform the following steps:

- Identifying: Decide whether all the data flowing on a network needs to be monitored or whether only some particular data needs to be captured. It is essential that you distinguish between evidence and the data that is not useful. The following questions can help you decide whether the identified evidence is useful:

  - What data needs to be collected?
  - Where can it be collected from?
  - Where and how is it stored?

This will make the retrieval of the data easy.

- Preserving: Once you have collected the evidence, you need to preserve it as closely as possible to its original state. The data that flows on the network should be captured on hard disks or magnetic tapes so that it can be used for later reference. If changes are made to the evidence, you should be able to justify them.

- Analyzing: After you store the evidence, you need to analyze it. Only a qualified person should perform the analysis process. In this step, you need to use various tools such as tcpdump and snore to monitor the network traffic.

- Presenting the evidence: You should present the evidence in a manner that is understandable to even a non-technical person. The data that you collect using the tools must be presented in an easy-to-understand format.

9.2.4 Ethereal

 Use Ethereal to examine a compromise in promise.

tcpdump and Ethereal are software tools used to capture data packets on a network. Ethereal is a GUI-based packet sniffer that is easier to use than tcpdump because it is available in a user-friendly format. Ethereal uses almost the same commands and filters as tcpdump, and both use the pcap library for capturing data packets. Ethereal is a free network-protocol analyzer for UNIX and Windows operating systems that allows you to capture data packets from a network and interactively browse the contents of the network frames. It allows you to examine data from a live network or from a captured file on disk. A captured file is a file created by the Network Monitor to store the captured files.

You can interactively browse the captured data and view the data in the packet. Using Ethereal software, you can capture data from a live network connection. The data may also be read from a capture file using tcpdump, Sniffer Pro, Novell's LANalyzer, and ISDN4BSD tools. Ethereal decompresses the files, which can be compressed with gzip. You can edit or modify the captured files programmatically by using a command-line switch. Ethereal captures packets and helps the administrator study the information from those packets. The captured network packets can be saved on the disk. Ethereal provides a systematic view of each data packet.

A security analyst or an administrator uses the Ethereal software to perform forensic tasks for security of a network. The advantage of using Ethereal tools is that with the help of Network Forensics Analysis Tool (NFAT), the Ethereal tools can capture data and analyze the data on the network. NFAT helps the network investigator monitor the network for network traffic and perform forensic analysis to analyze the network for any suspicious data and also for malicious users.

The system administrators can analyze the data on the network for security needs of the data and prevent the data from being damaged. Ethereal is a flexible tool because it allows the user to read the captured data packets from other programs such as tcpdump and snoop.

The Ethereal tool has the following features:

- Captures the data into capture files
- Reads the data captured by the tcpdump command
- Browses the captured data in a GUI mode
- Saves or prints the output
- Selectively views the information

A *network monitor* is a tool that can be used in a Windows 2000 Server to capture and display information received from a LAN. Network administrators use this tool to troubleshoot and detect networking problems.

9.2.5 Rootkit

Recover a rootkit from the data stream.

A hacker usually gains access to a system by hacking the user password on the network. Information about the user IDs on the network and their respective passwords are collected by the rootkit, which is a set of tools used by hackers for gaining administrative access to a system.

A *rootkit* is a collection of programs used by hackers to crack or break into a network. A rootkit is installed on a system to give the intruder root access to a system by either exploiting the known vulnerability or cracking a user password. The intruder uses the rootkit to mask intrusion, obtain administrator rights, and gain access to a computer or computer network. It also provides the IDs and passwords of other systems on the network to the intruder. The rootkit also contains utilities that monitor traffic or data streams and modify the system tools existing on the network. The data stream is the network traffic that flows in an interconnected network.

One way to recover a rootkit is to delete all files that have been corrupted by the rootkit and install them anew. The drawback of this method of rootkit recovery is that you have to delete all the data saved in the files. Therefore, a better method of rootkit recovery is to follow the steps of the rootkit installation and recover the deleted or modified files.

The following steps allow you to recover a security lapse causing a rootkit attack on a system on the network:

- Remove the rootkit from the system.

- Employ a better firewall that detects the system threats on the network and secures the system from rootkit attacks.

- Back up the system database to combat security-related threats.

The various steps of recovering a rootkit from a data stream are:

- Monitor intrusion of the system by checking the system files. A change in the system files settings indicates a rootkit installation on the system.

- Execute the chkrootkit from the Internet location www.chkrootkit.org.

- Compare the file size of the system with the original system files on Red Hat Linux.

- Check whether netstat has been changed from the original version.

- Obtain the list of deleted files by using the ils command.

A security precaution for rootkit recovery is to remove the computer from the network before you proceed with the rootkit recovery. Use CDs and floppies for the construction process instead of copying any files over the network.

For more information on rootkit recovery, refer to the Internet link http://www.porcupine.org/forensics/tct.html.

The chkroot command sets the root-drive letter mapped to the user's home directory, which is used for mapping applications.

The chkrootkit command in Linux allows you to investigate your system for modified system files. You can execute the chkrootkit command in the expert mode of a Linux OS to detect strings in binary programs that had caused rootkit installation on your system by hackers. Run the chkroot command in expert mode, that is, using the –x option. You can examine suspicious Trojaned system processes and scripts in the binary programs. You can see data with the following command:

```
#./chkrootkit -x | more
```

The script for the chkroot command includes the following options:

- netstat
- egrep
- find
- echo
- cut
- id
- strings
- ls

These commands are used with chkroot. For example, the egrep command specifies the path names inside the system commands. The netstat command is used to display the protocol statistics and current TCP/IP network connections.

9.2.6 Forensic Challenges

Discuss the various network forensic challenges.

Today, cyber crime or e-crime has become a major challenge for network system administrators and forensic experts all over the world. It has become a global plague that has to be combated by law enforcement. The laws of different governments have failed to effectively deal with cyber crimes. With the constant increase in the use of computer technology, the extent of cyber crimes has also increased.

Electronic crime involves crimes or offences in which a computer is used as a tool to commit these crimes or as the target of an offence.

Hackers use various tools for hacking networks:

- Anonymous re-mailers: Used by hackers to hide their identity.
- Sniffers: Used by intruders to intercept network traffic.

- Password crackers: Used by intruders to crack the encrypted password of any file.

- Steganography: Used by hackers to encrypt data in the form of graphics or audiotapes and to extract information from the network traffic.

Network forensics is important and required in cases of cyber crimes. The use of the Internet has expanded to a wide variety of fields such as e-commerce, online banking, education, and conducting the business of department stores, hospitals and drug stores. With increased use of Internet, the vulnerability of the systems connected on a network has also increased, as well as the challenges for forensics and investigation departments. With consistent increase in the use of the Internet all over the world, the number of hackers worldwide has greatly increased. According to statistics, there are around 17 million hackers in the U.S. alone. These hackers differ in their knowledge, skills, resources, and, most important, their motives.

With the increase in crime in the networking field, network forensics also suffers from shortcomings. One of the greatest challenges the network forensics is facing is that of the network bandwidth. Increasing the bandwidth of the communication channel will help improve the storage capacity and higher transfer rate, forensic investigation and responses have to employ methodologies and the technologies to successfully and effectively detect and protect the network systems from e-crimes such as hacking.

To summarize, network forensics faces the following major challenges:

- Collecting evidence from network traffic: It is difficult to find evidence of e-crime or malicious data from enormous amount of network traffic and requires a great amount of technical skill and knowledge.

- Tracing the anonymous hacker: It is quite difficult to trace the source and destination of a communication over the Internet because there are multiple Internet providers (ISPs), and each of them provides information for tracing the source and destination of an Internet communication.

- Training: Technical training and knowledge must be provided to investigators who have to be able to investigate and analyze a network system effectively to ensure system security.

- Jurisdictional issues: Traditional jurisdictional issues do not deal with the cross-border e-crimes. Differences in the laws of different nations for dealing with cyber crimes poses difficulties for forensic investigators. In addition, there is no centralized authority or group that has jurisdictional rights to deal with e-crimes. The jurisdictional conflicts have given rise to a major fallback on resolving the crimes related to computer networks.

- Other technologies: Technologies such as WAP (Wireless Application Protocol) and Bluetooth have increased the complexity of network forensics because these technologies allow accessing the Internet by the use of mobile phones and wireless communication. As a result, it has become difficult for analysts and investigators to analyze the systems and detect any intrusion.

Bluetooth is a wireless communication technology that allows you to connect to at least eight devices, such as mobile phones, through the Internet and form a personal area network.

Case Study

John is a network administrator at SafeData, Inc. He recently received complaints from the system administrator, Bill, that data on the network is being continuously lost or modified by an intruder on a remote system. Bill was unable to identify the OS of the remote host. So, Bill wants John to help him identify the OS used by the intruder. John plans to use passive OS fingerprinting techniques to identify the OS used by the remote host and determine the field area values of the TCP packets used by the remote host. By analyzing the TCP/IP headers, John can determine the OS used by the intruder's remote system because the combination of field values of TCP packets varies in different operating systems. The different field values that John will be analyzing include the TTL value, the packet length, the Window size, and the IP ID number. In passive fingerprinting, the sniffer traces from the remote host are analyzed. Using this method, John will analyze the packets sent from the remote host and determine the OS of the remote system.

Practice Questions

1. What is tunneling?

2. What is meant by APV?

3. What are the obstacles in collecting evidence from network traffic?

4. Name few tools used by hackers to hack a network?

Summary

■ Using OS fingerprinting techniques, you can identify the OS used by the remote host and the characteristics of the remote host.

■ The major TCP areas that determine the OS are:

- TTL
- Window size
- Type of service

■ You can classify the OS fingerprinting techniques into two types:

- Passive fingerprinting
- Active fingerprinting

■ Encryption is the process of converting an ordinary or plain text, which may contain sensitive data, into unreadable form to intelligently hide data from intruders.

■ Tunneling is a technique used to carry a protocol across a different network.

■ Monitoring a network is important for capturing data and analyzing it so that proper security measures can be taken to protect the network from malicious users.

■ Monitoring of network traffic also helps record the data for future analysis.

■ APV (Advanced Packet Vault) is a technology used for creating a record that stores all the packets over the network. This technology uses encryption for the data packets to maintain the integrity and security of the data.

■ A covert channel is an indirect communication channel used by a sender to transfer data that is sent to the users who normally do not have access to the information.

■ To track the information on the data being transferred on a network, you need to track the network traffic.

■ To collect evidence from network traffic, perform the following steps:

- Identification
- Preservation
- Analysis
- Presentation

■ Ethereal uses almost the same commands and filters as tcpdump because both use the pcap library to capture data packets. Ethereal is a free network-protocol analyzer for UNIX and Windows operating systems that allows you to capture data packets from a network and interactively browse the contents of the network frames.

- Information about the user IDs on the network and their respective passwords is collected by the rootkit, which is a set of tools used by hackers for gaining administrative access to your system.

References

- http://www.fcw.com/fcw/articles/2003/0707/tec-review-07-07-03.asp
- http://www.omicron.ch/images/silentrunner/SR_Information_Security.pdf
- http://www.systemexperts.com/tutors/IDS_SecSymp01.pdf
- http://www.mynetsec.com/html/encryption.html
- http://www.incidents.org/papers/OSfingerprinting.php
- http://www.library.itt-tech.edu: Look under the Net Resources link for more information

Homework Exercises

1. What is the goal of conducting network investigations?

2. Explain the various TCP options.

3. What is passive fingerprinting?

4. Discuss in brief the administration's policy on encryption.

5. What is meant by stack querying?

6. Prepare a report on detection and prevention tools such as anti-viral products, password policies, and firewalls.

7. Explain the nmap technique used in active OS fingerprinting.

8. Why do you need to collect evidence from network traffic?

9. What are some of the challenges faced by network forensics?

10. Differentiate between the different field values of the TCP packets of Linux and OpenBSD operating systems, and specify the typical field areas for each OS.

11. Which tool of active OS fingerprinting is used specifically for Windows OS and why?

Lab Exercises

Exercise 1

Objective

■ Display the different field values for TCP packets in Red Hat Linux 7.1.

Problem Statement

■ View the different field areas of TCP packets for the Red Hat Linux 7.1 OS.

■ Run the http://www.library.itt-tech.edu in the Mozilla Web browser, and view the TCP packets for the same.

■ Discuss the importance of different field-area values.

Lab Setup

■ Red Hat Linux 7.1

■ CPU with Pentium III processor

■ 128-MB RAM

■ 8 GB or more of the hard-disk space

■ Internet Connection

Procedure

1. Log in as the root user in Red Hat Linux 7.1 OS.

2. From the main menu, click **System Settings** -> **Terminal**.

3. Run the yahoo.com site in Mozilla Web browser.

4. At the command prompt, type the command tcpdump to view the tcp packets, as
   shown in Figure 9.4.

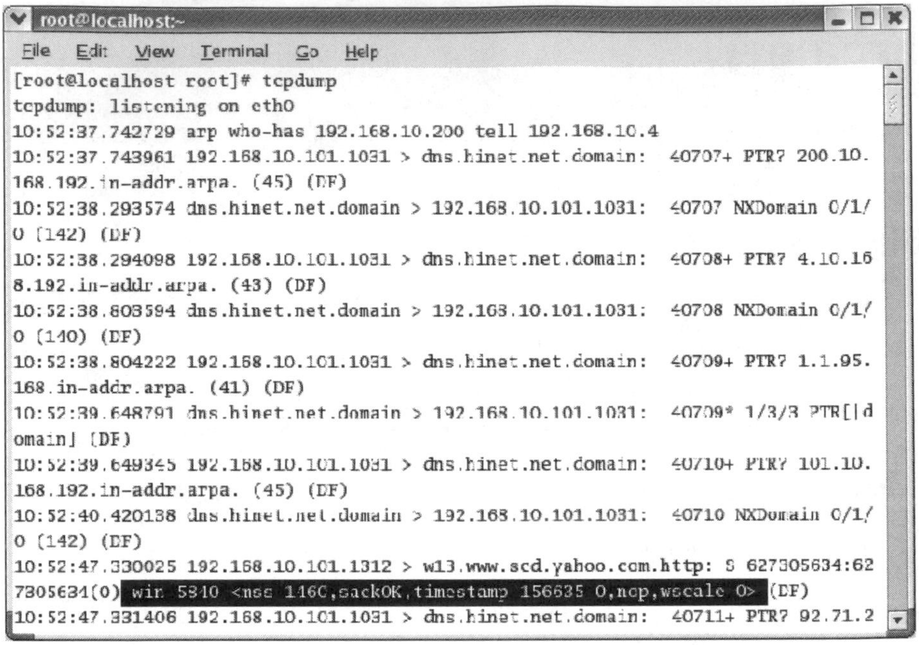

Figure 9.4: tcpdump Command

As can be seen in the above window, from the highlighted region, the fields are:

- Window size: 5,840 bytes
- Mss: 1,460
- Timestamp: 156,635
- Nop = 1

By default, Linux 7.1 sets the following TCP options:

- Mss
- Timestamp
- Nop
- Wscale
- sackOk

5. To view the Time to Live (TTL) value of the Linux 7.0 OS tcp packets, give the command more /proc/sys/net/ipv4/ip_default_ttl. The following window shown in Figure 9.5 appears.

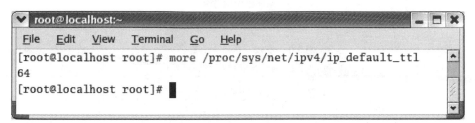

Figure 9.5: View the TTL Value

As seen in the above figure, the TTL value for Red Hat Linux 7.0 is 64.

The importance of different field values is discussed below:

- Window size: Specifies the size of the sender's window.

- TTL: It indicates the lifetime for a packet, that is, how long a packet can stay on the wire in the network?

- MSS: The maximum size of the data segment that can be transmitted between a sender and receiver.

- Timestamp: Measures the time delays in sending and receiving data packets.

- Wscale (Window scale): Specifies the scale factor to be applied to the receive window. It shifts the window-size field's value up to a maximum value.

- NOP (No operation): 1 byte in size. It converts the TCP header length to a multiple of 4 bytes and provides padding around other options.

- SackOK (Selective Acknowledgement): Use by the sender to acknowledge receipt of the data sent. The sender has to retransmit the packet that has been left out or not received.

Conclusion/Observation

You should be able to use the tcpdump command successfully.

Lab Activity Checklist

S. No.	Tasks	Completed	
		Yes	No
1.	Gave tcpdump command		
2.	Viewed the different field values of the tcp packets		
3	Discussed the importance of different fields		

Exercise 2

Objective

■ Capture a file using the Ethereal software tool.

Problem Statement

Jason is the network administrator at Networking Solutions, Inc. He wishes to use a GUI tool on Windows 2000 platform to monitor a file named Authored Chapter present in the D:\ drive of his system.

■ Use the Ethereal tool to capture the TCP packets of the file.

■ View the summary of the TCP packets.

■ Break down the details of the protocols used.

Lab Setup

■ Windows 2000 OS

■ Ethereal 3.0 Version

■ Winpcap library

Procedure

1. Open the Ethereal window from the **Start** menu, as shown in Figure 9.6.

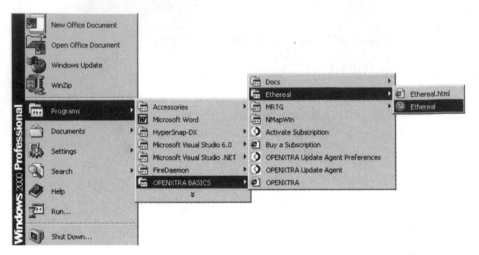

Figure 9.6: Open Ethereal

2. Click **Ethereal** in the above window. The following window appears, as shown in Figure 9.7.

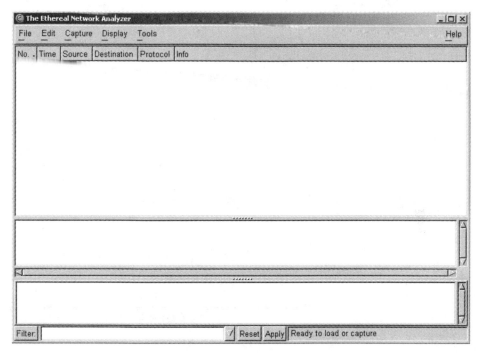

Figure 9.7: Ethereal Network Analyzer

3. Click **Capture** -> **Start**, as shown in Figure 9.8.

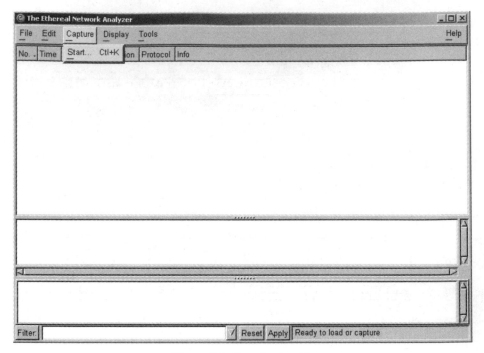

Figure 9.8: Start Packet Capture

4. When you click the **Start** option, the following window appears, as shown in Figure 9.9.

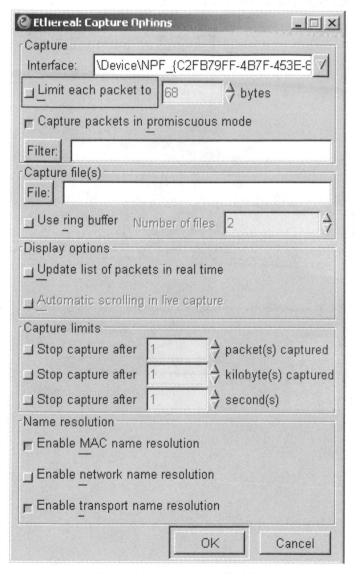

Figure 9.9: Ethereal: Capture Options

5. Click the **File** button, and browse the file you need to capture. Click the options you require, and click **OK**.

6. When you click OK, the following window appears, as shown in Figure 9.10.

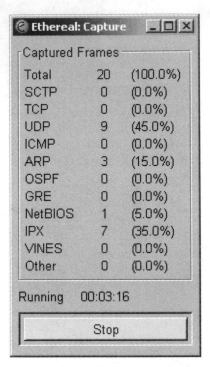

Figure 9.10: Ethereal: Capture

7. Press the **Stop** button after some time if you have not mentioned any capture limit value.

8. The following window appears, as shown in Figure 9.11.

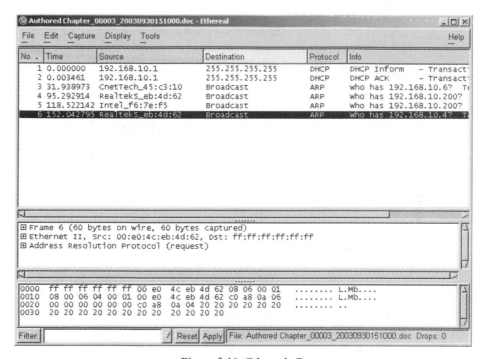

Figure 9.11: Ethereal: Capture

9. Three windowpanes open. The upper one shows the packets with their source and destination addresses, protocols, and summary information. The middle pane shows the detailed information about the packet you have selected. The lower pane shows the ASCII data in the packet.

10. To open a file, click **File** -> **Open**. Browse, and select the file you need to view, as shown in Figure 9.12.

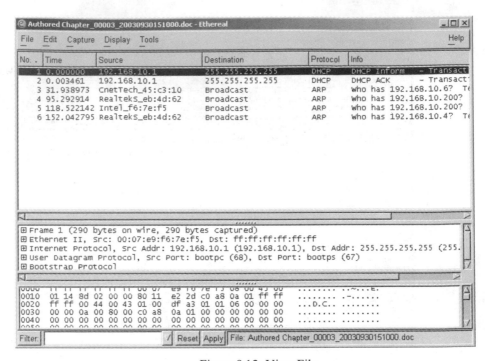

Figure 9.12: View File

11. To display the details of the TCP packets, expand the Internet protocol in the middle window, as shown in Figure 9.13.

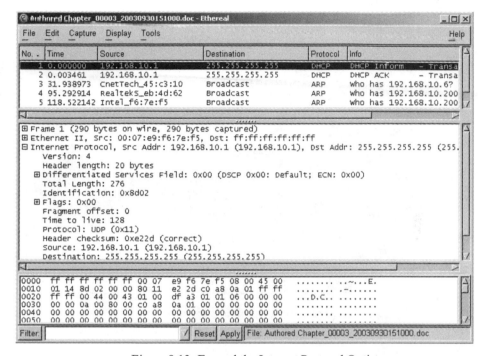

Figure 9.13: Expand the Internet Protocol Option

12. Figure 9.13 shows the details of all the field values of the TCP packet.

13. To display the summary of all the details of the TCP packets captured, click
Tools -> **Summary**. The following window appears, as shown in Figure 9.14.

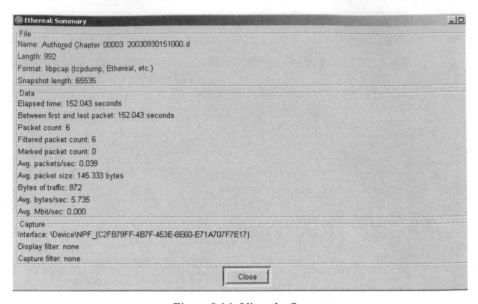

Figure 9.14: View the Summary

14. Also, you can view the breakdown of all the protocols used by the TCP packets. Click **Tools** -> **Ethereal**: Protocol Hierarchy Statistics, as shown in Figure 9.15.

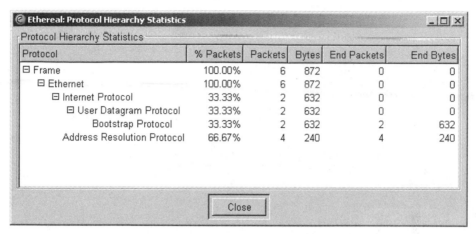

Figure 9.15: Ethereal: Protocol Hierarchy Statistics

Conclusion/Observation

You are able to use the Ethereal tool to capture files successfully.

Lab Activity Checklist

S. No.	Tasks	Completed	
		Yes	No
1.	Opened the Ethereal tool		
2.	Captured the file		
3	Viewed the summary of the TCP packets		
4	Broke down the protocols used		

Glossary

A

Application Error Record: Records an error or loggable event in an application

Autopsy Forensic browser: Is a graphical interface to the collection of tools that make up the Sleuth Kit

B

Backdoor: An undocumented way of gaining access to a program, Internet service, or an entire computer system

Bash shell: A shell, or command language interpreter, that appears in the GNU operating system

binary file: A file stored in a binary format. It can easily be interpreted by computers, but not humans

Boot disk: A diskette from which you can boot your computer

C

Cache: A special high-speed storage mechanism. It is usually a reserved section of main memory or an independent storage device

Client/Server model: A network architecture in which each computer or process on the network is either a client or a server. Servers are powerful computers or processes dedicated to managing different services. Clients are workstations on which users run applications. Clients rely on servers for resources and services

Covert Channels: Is an indirect communication channel that is used by a sender to transfer data to the users who normally don't have access to that data. Such a communication channel can be exploited by a process to transfer information in a manner that violates the systems security policy.

D

Data analysis: An investigation phase in which the data identified and collected in the identification and collection phases are analyzed. This phase provides information on the sequence of events that may have occurred in the process of committing a crime.

Data blocks: A group of records on a storage device. Blocks are operated as units

Data collection: An investigation phase, in which all possible sources of information are studied, and then the relevant information is collected in a forensically sterile environment.

Data identification: An investigation phase, that involves defining the information that is required and depends on the type of crime committed.

Data presentation: The final stage of forensics investigation, in which all the findings are documented and the forensics report is made. The report may be used within the organization to punish an employee or in a court of law for legal prosecution of an attacker.

dd: A utility used to copy data from the specified input device to the specified output device. The input and output devices can be files or streams.

Debugfs: A file system debugger used to perform maintenance operation on the file system

Debugger: A special program used to find errors (bugs) in other programs

Degausser: A device used to remove magnetism from a device.

Depmod: A tool to create a "Makefile", based on the symbols it finds in the set of modules mentioned on the command line

Device driver: A program that controls a device.

Digital evidence: It includes deleted files or emails, computer logs, spreadsheets, and accounting information

Disk editor: Application that look at the byte information on the storage device regardless of the file system

Disk imaging: The term used to create an exact, bit for bit copy of the contents of any storage device connected to a computer

dls: A command that lists the details about data units and extracts the unallocated space of the file system

Dstat: A command that displays the statistics about a given data unit in a format that is easy to read

Dual boot: An operating system configuration that allows the user to boot the computer system from one of two different operating systems, installed on the same hard drive

Dumpel: A utility that converts log information into text files

E

EnCase: A complete forensic package popularly used for disk imaging and disk-image analysis in computer forensics community.

Encryption: A process of converting an ordinary or plain text into unreadable form so as to hide data from the intruders

Evidence: A piece of information that provides an idea or clue that may lead to the source of an event or to another piece of information, which may finally lead to the source of the event

EXT2: The Second Extended File system is an extensible and powerful file system for Linux

EXT3: The ext3 file system is an enhanced version of ext2 file system

Evidence-chain model: A model that illustrates the discrete sets of actions carried out by an insider attempting to inflict malicious damage in an intranet environment

F

Ffind: A tool that finds the allocated and unallocated file names that point to a given meta-data structure.

FILE command: The command that analyzes the data inside any file and displays the file type

file command: The command that identifies the type of a file using multiple tests

File recovery: The art of getting back files that have already been deleted

File system: The system that an operating system or program uses to organize and keep track of files

FIND tool: A complex and powerful tool in used to search for files stored on the file system

Fingerprinting: A method to help you learn about your enemy without the enemy's knowledge.

Firewall: A program that decides whether to allow or block data from the network connection

fls: A tool that lists the allocated and deleted file names in a particular directory

fstat: A tool that displays file-system information and statistics, including layout, sizes, and labels

G

Galleta: A tool that analyzes cookies from Web sites that have been stored on the computer. It can extract valuable information from the cookies and output it in a field-delimited manner.

Ghost imaging: A method of converting the contents of a hard drive into an image, and then storing the image on a storage device. Ghosting software is used for this purpose.

Grave-robber: A data-capturing tool that understands the structure of a Linux system. After performing automated analysis of the system, this tool proceeds to save only those files that contain important system information from the forensic point of view.

H

Hacker: A person who gains unauthorized access to computer systems for the purpose of stealing or corrupting data

Hash: A number generated from a string of text, with the help of a formula

Hash Keeper: A tool that creates hash sets and compares them with a hash database.

Hashing: The process of generating hash values for accessing data or for security

Hex Editor: A program used to edit nontext files, such as program files, or to view these files. It displays the data of the file in hexadecimal notation

History file: A type of log file which holds information on user activity like commands the users entered at the command prompt and pages the users surfed on their browsers

Honeypot: Trap designed to mimic systems that an intruder would like to break into but limit the intruder from having access to an entire network

I

icat tool: A tool used to output the contents of a file. icat does not locates the file on the basis of its inode number

IDS: (Intrusion Detection System) The tool that inspects all network activities and identifies suspicious patterns that may indicate an intrusion into a network system

Ifind: A command that locates the inode information that has a given file name pointing to it or the inode information that points to a given data unit

IH: The field that denotes the length of the header. This length is denoted in 32-bit words

ils: The tool that lists information about the inodes on a system

Image Master: A storage device that can be directly connected to the target computer to create the disk images

inode numbers: Data structures that contain

Insmod: The command to load a module into the kernel, and resolves all symbols from the exported kernel symbols, with version information, if available. The module will get its name by removing the '.o' extension from the basename of the object file.

Investigation process: The process of tracking, in order to find information

Investigation: The process of collecting, analyzing, and recovering evidence, and presenting a report detailing a crime

IP tables: The tool that inserts and deletes rules from the kernel's packet filtering table

IP: Abbreviation of Internet Protocol. IP specifies the format of packets and the addressing scheme.

IPX (Novell) protocol: Short for Internetwork Packet Exchange, a networking protocol used by the Novell NetWare operating systems.

K

Kernel: The central module of an operating system. It is the part of the operating system that loads first, and it remains in main memory machine and software which perform the role of the trusted arbitrator in the Kerberos protocol.

Ksyms: ksyms shows the exported kernel symbols.

L

L0pht crack: A program used for breaking Windows password files.

Lastcomm: The command that gives information on previously executed commands

Lazarus: A utility that works on a binary file and tries to break it down into smaller data blocks. While splitting the data into blocks, it tries to locate the type of data in the block

LiSt Open Files (LSOF): A diagnostic tool that displays information about the files opened by processes. The file can be a normal file, a directory, a special file, a stream, a library, or a network file, which could be an NFS file or a BSD socket.

loadable kernel modules (LKM): Loadable Kernel Modules used by the Linux kernel to expand his functionality

Log files: A file that lists actions that have occurred. For example, Web servers maintain log files listing every request made to the server.

Logical investigation: Investigation process that takes a look at the log files and tries to locate information that can be used as evidence of who committed a crime

Lsmod: The command that shows the loaded modules

M

MAC_DADDY: A tool that can be used for MACtimes forensic analysis. It is written entirely in Perl and requires the perl interpreter to be loaded on the investigator's system.

Mactime tool: Tool that can directly obtain MACtimes.

Malware: Short for malicious software, it refers to software designed specifically to damage or disrupt a system, such as a virus or a Trojan horse

MD5: An algorithm, created by Professor Ronald Rivest, used to create digital signatures. MD5 is a one-way hash function, meaning that it takes a message and converts it into a fixed string of digits, also called a message digest

md5deep: A cross-platform program to compute MD5 message digests on an arbitrary number of files

md5sum: A program that uses the md5 algorithm to generate 128-bit hash of the data fed to the md5sum program.

Mmls: The command used to display the layout of a storage device, including the unallocated spaces

Modified, Access, Created (MAC) Time: In Linux and other UNIX variants, file times and dates are stored as three separate fields which are: creation time, last access time, and last write/modification time. This information is stored in the inode of the file. These three fields are used to detect changes on a target system which is suspected of being possibly compromised.

Modinfo: The command used to display information about loaded kernel modules

Modprobe: The command that allows high level handling of loadable modules

Mounting: Process of making a mass storage device available

MOUNT utility: The utility used on the investigator's computer to allow the OS to access a storage device, which in this case is usually the device that contains the disk image of the target computer

N

Nessus: Tool with a modular design, internal scripting language, client-server model, encryption, and large vulnerability databases

Network Forensics: Deals with the technology or a methodology of analyzing a network and detecting the remote host responsible for hacking your network.

Network Intrusion Detectors (NIDs): Applications that allows the individual packets flowing through a network to be analyzed. The NIDS can detect malicious packets that are designed to be overlooked by a firewall's simplistic filtering rules.

NFS file systems: Abbreviation of Network File System, a client/server application designed by Sun Microsystems that allows all network users to access shared files stored on

Nmap: A tool for scanning the ports in large networks. It determines which hosts are up and what services those hosts offer.

Non-kernel rootkits: Trojan horse programs which are usually versions of common programs found on the server modified so that they have a hidden feature which can be used by the attacker to gain unauthorized access.

NTFS file system: Stands for NT file system, and is the native file system of Windows.

O

One-way encryption (asymmetric encryption): Encryption method which uses one key to encrypt a message and another to decrypt a message

One-way hashing: An algorithm that turns messages or text into a fixed string of digits, usually for security or data management purposes. Messages encrypted through one way hashing are difficult to decipher.

OS Fingerprinting: A process that involves determining the operating system of the remote host using active and passive tools such as using sniffer traces or analyzing the response of the OS of the remote host by sending it malformed data packets.

P

Pasco: A tool that parses the information in an index.dat found in Microsoft Internet Explorer's cache directory and outputs the results in a field-delimited manner so that the evidence can be imported into a spreadsheet program for analysis

Password: A secret series of characters that enables a user to access a file, computer, or program

Pcat: A powerful tool in TCT that copies process memory, that is, the RAM used by a program when it executes

Perl: Short for Practical Extraction and Report Language, is a programming language usually used for writing CGI scripts

Physical investigation: Investigation process that include identifying or locating physical evidence, such as the removal of computer hardware

Physical memory: Memory referring to the actual RAM chips installed in a computer

Portmapper: A server that converts TCP/IP protocol port numbers into RPC program numbers

Process logs: Logs that contain logs for Web server access log and mail server logs

Password shadowing: A technique used where the password field of the file is stored elsewhere in a file, which is protected from all users except the root or Superuser

R

Rmmod: A command used to unload loadable modules from the kernel

Rootkit: Programs installed by hackers on attacked systems to help hide their own presence

Retina: Light sensitive nerve tissue in the eye that converts images from the eye's optical system into electrical impulses that are sent along the optic nerve to the brain.

Role-based authentication: The concept of basing access privileges on a person's role in the organization, rather than their user name.

S

Security Administrator's Tool for Analyzing Networks (Satan): A VAT that enable you to find several network-related security problems. It is designed to test the target system or the target network for security problems, and if problems exist, it generates a useful informative report.

Security Identifiers (SID): A unique value of variable length used to identify a trustee (the user account or group account)

Security policy: A set of objectives, rules of behavior for users and administrators, and requirements for system configuration and management that collectively are designed to ensure Security of computer systems in an organization.

Shell: A shell is the command processor interface. The command processor is the program that executes operating system commands.

Slack space: The unused space in a disk cluster

SMART: Acronym for Self-Monitoring, Analysis and Reporting Technology, an open standard for developing disk drives and software systems that automatically monitors and reports problems in a disk drive

Snort: A complete NIDS package that can log alerts to everything from files to databases

STRINGS utility: A utility used to extract all the readable text strings from the executable file

SUID/GUID Files: Two bits on the array of security attribute bits associated with each file on a Linux file system

Swap Space: A process used to replace pages or segments of data in memory. The operating system copies as much data as possible into main memory, and leaves the rest on the disk. When the operating system needs data from the disk, it exchanges a portion of data (page or segment) in main memory with a portion of data on the disk.

System Audit Records: Records security events such as a wrong password event

System calls: Functions build into the kernel of an OS, which are used for every operation on that system.

System Error Records: Records general and critical system errors such as errors at the kernel level

System forensics: The application of computer investigation and analysis techniques in the interests of determining potential legal evidence.

System logs: Logs that log all system messages and system initialization information

Saint: The new version of Satan

T

Target computer: In context of system forensics, is the system on which the criminal launches an attack.

TCP (Transmission Control Protocol) protocol: One of the main protocols in TCP/IP networks. TCP enables two hosts to establish a connection and exchange streams of data.

The @Stack Sleuth Kit (TASK): A set of UNIX command-line programs that form a media-management tool for forensic and other types of file-system analysis

The Coroner's Toolkit (TCT): A small collection of tools designed to help in the forensic analysis of a computer

Timestamp: A parameter that measures the time delays in sending and receiving data packets

Trojan horse: A destructive program that masquerades as a benign application

Trust relationships: Network relationships that allow single-domain models to be interconnected, which means that they can now share user accounts and other resources across domains

TTL: A counter, which limits the packet lifetimes, that is, it indicates how long a packet can stay on the wire/medium

Tunneling: A technique, which is used to carry a protocol across a different network

U

Unallocated space: Memory area that refers to currently unused, but possibly the repository of previous data that is relevant evidence

UNMOUNT: A command used to detach the media on which the disk image was stored from the investigator's computer

Unrm: A program that extracts all information from a UNIX file system that is not currently allocated

V

Virtual memory: An imaginary memory area supported by some operating systems

Vulnerability Assessment Tools (VATs): The automated process of proactively identifying vulnerabilities of computing systems in a network in order to determine if and where a

system can be exploited and/or threatened

W

Web caches: Web caches are Web pages saved by the browser software to the local hard disk so that any future access to these pages can be faster

Window scale: The field that specifies the scale factor to be applied to the receive window. It shifts the window size field's value up to a maximum value

Windows operating system: The family of operating systems for personal computers

Windows Registry: A database system in the Windows operating system having a tree-like structure, which stores information about the hardware and the software on the OS

X

Xprobe: A tool used to identify Microsoft-based OS. TCP is the protocol that is used for OS fingerprinting. Xprobe is an alternative to the tools, for the operating systems which are heavily dependent on TCP protocol for fingerprinting.

Bibliography

- Marcella Jr, Albert J. and Greenfield Robert S. 2002. *Cyber Forensics: A Field Manual for Collecting, Examining, and Preserving Evidence of Computer Crimes.* Book only edition (January 23,). Auerbach Pub

- Casey, Eoghan. 2001. *Handbook of Computer Crime Investigation: Forensic Tools & Technology.* Academic Press; 1st edition

- Kruse II, Warren G, and Heiser, Jay G. 2001. *Computer Forensics: Incident Response Essentials.* Addison-Wesley Pub Co.

- Hosmer, C. 1998. *Time-Lining Computer Evidence. Information Technology, Conference,* IEEE.

- McLean, Ian. 2000. *Windows 2000 Security – Little Black Book.* The Coriolis Group.

- Caswell Brian, Beale Jay, Foster c.James, Faircloth Jeremy.2003.*Snort 2.0 Intrusion Detection.* Book and CD-ROM edition. Syngress

- Northcutt Stephen.1999. *Network Intrusion Detection: An Analysts' Handbook.*1st Edition. Que

Index

A

Application Error Records,4.22

APV, 9.14, 9.26, 9.27

B

backdoor, 8.6, 8.17, 4.10,4.25

binary file, 5.17, 5.23

boot disk, 5.5, 4.16, 5.4, 5.27

C

cache,4.31

Checksum, 9.5, 9.7

Covert Channels, 9.16

D

data analysis, 1.17, 1.18, 1.23

data collection, 1.11, 1.14, 1.23

data identification, 1.13, 1.23

data presentation, 1.19, 1.23

dd utility, 3.4, 3.31

debugfs, 3.27, 3.28, 3.34

debugger, 3.27, 8.15, 8.18, 8.19, 8.28, 8.29

degausser, 1.15

depmod, 8.5, 8.31

device driver, 5.13, 5.14, 8.3, 8.4, 8.28

digital evidence, 2.1, 2.9, 6.1, 4.31, 2.5, 4.1

disk editor, 3.4, 4.14,4.15,4.21,4.34, 5.5

disk imaging, 3.3, 3.31, 5.4, 5.5, 4.1, 4.5, 4.14, 4.21,

dls, 5.25, 5.26

dstat, 5.25

dumpel,4.22, 4.23, 4.34, 4.52

E

Encryption, 9.27

Evidence, 1.6, 1.20, 1.24, 2.3, 2.5, 2.17, 2.29, 2.3, 1, 3.1, 3.13, 4.26, 4.31, 5.32, 6.20, 6.22, 6.25, 6.26, 6.28, 7.1, 7.14, 9.17, 9.18, 9.19

EnCase, 3.7, 4.5, 4.6, 4.51

EXT2, 3.4, 3.22, 5.21, 8.4

EXT3, 3.4, 3.22, 5.21, 8.4

Evidence-chain mode, 2.17

F

file command, 3.11, 5.12

file recovery, 3.34, 3.26, 3.32

file system, 3.4, 3.8, 3.9, 3.10, 3.22, 3.23, 3.25, 3.26, 3.27, 3.34, 3.36, 5.6, 5.12, 5.13, 5.14, 5.17, 5.21, 5.22, 5.24, 5.25, 5.26, 5.27, 5.30, 5.31, 5.36, 5.37, 6.22, 6.32, 8.4, 8.14, 8.18, 8.20, 8.23, 8.25, 8.31, 4.4, 4.9, 4.11, 4.14, 4.15, 4.16, 4.17, 4.19, 4.48, 4.50, 4.51

FIND tool, 3.4, 3.31

Fingerprinting, 9.1, 9.3, 9.8, 9.10, 9.11, 9.12, 9.25, 9.27, 9.30

Firewall, 1.8, 2.29, 7.14, 7.15, 7.16, 7.17, 7.18, 7.20, 7.29, 7.31, 7.32, 7.39, 7.40, 7.41, 8.4, 8.5, 9.13, 9.22

fls, 5.25, 4.50

Fragmentation, 9.5

fstat, 5.25

G

Galleta, 4.4, 4.51

Grave-robber, 5.8, 5.9, 5.10, 5.20, 5.31, 5.34, 5.35

H

Hacker, 1.4, 1.8, 1.19, 3.1, 3.3, 3.12, 3.21, 3.29, 3.35, 5.36, 7.3, 7.12, 7.32, 7.40, 8.1, 8.6, 8.33, 8.36, 9.17, 9.21, 9.24, 4.9, 4.37

Hash Keeper, 5.22

Hashing, 3.13

History files, 3.16, 3.17, 3.31

I

icat, 3.23, 3.32, 5.6, 5.12, 5.13, 5.20, 5.25, 5.27, 8.36, 8.37

IDS, 2.18, 2.29, 7.20, 9.29

ifind, 5.25

IHL, 9.4

ils, 3.23, 3.32, 5.6, 5.13, 5.15, 5.25, 5.27, 5.30, 8.36, 9.22

Image Master, 5.3

inode number, 3.8, 3.9, 3.23, 5.6, 5.12, 5.13, 5.14, 5.16, 8.14, 8.36, 8.37

insmod, 8.4

investigation process, 1.18, 2.1, 2.3, 2.8, 2.10, 2.12, 2.28, 3.19

investigation, 1.6, 1.7, 1.8, 1.10, 1.11, 1.12, 1.13, 1.14, 1.15, 1.17, 1.18, 1.19, 1.20, 1.22, 1.23, 1.25, 2.1, 2.3, 2.4, 2.5, 2.6, 2.7, 2.8, 2.10, 2.11, 2.12, 2.13, 2.14, 2.15, 2.16, 2.17, 2.18, 2.19, 2.23, 2.24, 2.25, 2.26, 2.28, 2.29, 2.30, 2.33, 3.1, 3.3, 3.5, 3.19, 3.20, 3.21, 3.25, 3.31, 3.34, 5.1, 5.3, 5.5, 5.10, 5.21, 5.25, 5.27, 5.31, 5.34, 6.3, 6.6, 6.8, 6.15, 6.19, 6.24, 6.27, 6.31, 7.3, 7.31, 8.18, 9.15, 9.17, 9.24, 4.1, 4.3, 4.6, 4.9, 4.10, 4.18, 4.22, 4.25, 4.26, 4.34, 4.41, 4.51, 4.54

IP Header, 9.4, 9.12

IP ID, 9.5, 9.9, 9.25

IP protocol, 1.19, 3.15, 3.18, 3.29, 3.30, 6.31, 7.4, 7.9, 7.14, 7.15, 7.16, 7.18, 7.20, 7.22, 7.23, 7.29, 7.31, 7.37, 8.4, 9.3, 9.4, 9.5, 9.6, 9.8, 9.9, 9.11, 9.12, 9.14, 9.15, 9.25, 4.9, 4.17, 4.30

iptables, 7.14

IPX (Novell) protocol, 8.4

K

kernel, 8.1, 8.3, 8.5, 8.6, 8.7, 8.8, 8.25, 8.28

Ksyms, 8.5

L

Lastcomm, 5.6, 5.27

Lazarus, 5.17, 5.18, 5.27, 5.30, 5.36, 5.37

LiSt Open Files (LSOF), 3.5

log files, 1.14, 3.15, 4.51

Logical investigation, 2.13, 2.14, 2.29

M

MAC_DADDY, 3.25, 3.32

mactime tool, 5.10, 5.30

MACtimes, 3.23, 3.25, 3.30, 3.32, 3.34, 5.10, 5.11, 5.20, 5.24

malware, 8.1, 8.12

MD5, 3.4, 3.13, 3.19, 3.21, 3.22, 3.31, 3.36, 5.6, 5.8, 5.9, 5.27, 6.31, 8.8, 4.3, 4.4, 4.10, 4.11, 4.19, 4.20

md5deep, 5.22, 8.8, 4.4,4.10,4.13,4.51

md5sum, 3.21, 3.22, 3.31, 3.36, 3.37, 5.22, 6.31, 8.8, 4.19

mmls, 5.26

Modified, 3.Access, 3.Created (MAC) Time, 3.23

MOUNT utility, 3.4, 3.10, 3.31

mounting, 3.4, 3.19, 3.21, 3.25, 3.30, 4.48

MSS, 9.7, 9.9, 9.10, 9.33

N

Nessus, 7.1, 7.3, 7.4, 7.5, 7.6, 7.7, 7.8, 7.9, 7.10, 7.11, 7.12, 7.13, 7.29, 7.32, 7.33, 7.34, 7.35, 7.38, 7.39, 7.40, 7.41

network forensics, 1.6, 9.1, 9.14, 9.24, 9.30

Network Monitoring, 9.14

NFS file systems, 7.5

NFS, 3.5, 7.5

Nmap, 3.29, 9.10, 9.11, 9.30

non-kernel rootkits, 8.6, 8.11

Nop, 9.32

NTFS file system, 8.4, 4.48,4.49,4.52

O

one-way encryption, 3.13

OS Fingerprinting, 9.1, 9.3, 9.8, 9.10

P

packets, 2.28, 7.14, 7.28, 9.3, 9.5, 9.7, 9.8, 9.9, 9.10, 9.11, 9.14, 9.15, 9.20, 9.25, 9.27, 9.30, 9.31, 9.32, 9.33, 9.34, 9.35, 9.41, 9.43, 9.44, 9.45

Pasco,4.5

password, 1.27, 1.28, 2.20, 2.21, 3.13, 3.14, 3.31, 9.24, 4.31,4.32,4.51

pcat, 5.16, 5.20, 8.16, 8.28

Perl, 3.25

physical investigation, 2.13, 2.29

physical memory, 1.16

R

Recycle Bin,4.9,4.31,4.32,4.51

rmmod, 8.5

rootkit, 3.29, 8.3, 8.6, 8.7, 8.8, 8.10, 8.11, 8.12, 8.31, 8.33, 8.34, 9.1, 9.13, 9.21, 9.22, 9.28, 4.11

S

SackOK, 9.8, 9.33

Saint, 7.5

Satan, 7.1, 7.3, 7.4, 7.5, 7.6, 7.7, 7.13

slack space, 1.21, 4.51

SMART,4.6

snort, 3.29, 7.1, 7.20, 7.21, 7.23, 7.24, 7.25, 7.26, 7.27, 7.28, 7.29, 7.31, 7.32, 7.40, 7.41, 9.14

STRINGS utility, 3.5, 3.12, 3.31

SUID/GUID Files, 3.23

System Audit Records,4.22

system calls, 8.4, 8.7, 8.8, 8.11, 8.28, 8.31

System Error Records,4.22

system forensics, 1.1, 1.3, 1.4, 1.5, 1.7, 1.9, 1.10, 1.12, 1.13, 1.14, 1.23, 1.25, 1.27, 2.3, 6.1, 6.3, 6.15, 6.20, 6.22, 6.24, 6.26, 6.28, 7.3, 7.14, 7.20, 8.31

System logs, 3.15

T

target computer, 2.5, 2.10, 3.3, 3.10, 3.19, 3.20, 3.21, 3.25, 3.27, 5.3, 5.4, 5.22, 7.3, 7.4, 7.6, 7.7, 7.8, 7.9, 7.11, 7.13, 7.14, 7.29, 7.36, 8.8,4.12, 4.10, 4.14, 4.16, 4.17, 4.18, 4.35, 4.39, 4.52

TCP Header, 9.6, 9.7, 9.12

TCP protocol, 9.11

TCP/IP, 8.4, 9.3, 9.8, 9.9, 9.14, 9.17, 9.23, 9.25

The @Stack Sleuth Kit (TASK), 5.1

The Coroner's Toolkit (TCT), 5.1, 5.6, 5.31

Timestamp, 2.27, 9.7, 9.32, 9.33

Trojan horse, 3.5, 3.12, 3.21, 8.12 ,4.10,4.11, 4.26, 4.41

trust relationships,4.44, 4.52

TTL, 7.21, 7.22, 9.5, 9.8, 9.9, 9.10, 9.25, 9.27, 9.33

tunneling, 9.1, 9.13, 9.17, 9.26

U

unallocated space, 1.21, 2.20, 2.21 , 3.26, 3.28, 5.25, 5.26, 5.30, 5.37, 6.32, 4.15

UNMOUNT, 3.19

Unrm, 5.17, 5.36, 5.37

V

virtual memory, 1.15, 1.16

Vulnerability Assessment Tools (VATs), 7.1

W

Web caches,4.31,4.51

Window scale, 9.7, 9.33

Windows operating system, 8.20, 8.29, 9.9, 9.20, 9.28, 4.9, 4.14, 4.35, 4.48

Wiretapping, 8.12, 8.22, 8.28, 9.1, 9.13, 9.14, 9.15

Wscale, 9.7, 9.32, 9.33

X

Xprobe, 9.11